FURTHER VOICES IN V

Further Voices
in Vergil's *Aeneid*

R. O. A. M. LYNE

CLARENDON PRESS · OXFORD

Oxford University Press, Walton Street, Oxford OX2 6DP
Oxford New York Toronto
Delhi Bombay Calcutta Madras Karachi
Kuala Lumpur Singapore Hong Kong Tokyo
Nairobi Dar es Salaam Cape Town
Melbourne Auckland Madrid
and associated companies in
Berlin Ibadan

Oxford is a trade mark of Oxford University Press

Published in the United States
by Oxford University Press Inc., New York

© R. O. A. M. Lyne 1987
First published 1987
First published in paperback 1992

All rights reserved. No part of this publication may be reproduced,
stored in a retrieval system, or transmitted, in any form or by any means,
without the prior permission of Oxford University Press.
Within the UK, exceptions are allowed in respect of any fair dealing for the
purpose of research or private study, or criticism or review, as permitted
under the Copyright, Designs and Patents Act, 1988, or in the case of
reprographic reproduction in accordance with the terms of the licences
issued by the Copyright Licensing Agency. Enquiries concerning
reproduction outside these terms and in other countries should be
sent to the Rights Department, Oxford University Press,
at the address above

This book is sold subject to the condition that it shall not, by way
of trade or otherwise, be lent, re-sold, hired out or otherwise circulated
without the publisher's prior consent in any form of binding or cover
other than that in which it is published and without a similar condition
including this condition being imposed on the subsequent purchaser

British Library Cataloguing in Publication Data
Data available

Library of Congress Cataloging in Publication Data
Lyne, R. O. A. M.
Further voices in Vergil's Aeneid.
Bibliography: p.
Includes index.
1. Virgil. Aeneis. 2. Virgil—Style.
I. Title.
[PA6825.L96 1986]   873'.01   86-16404
ISBN 0-19-814092-4 (Pbk.)

Printed in Great Britain
on acid-free paper by
Bookcraft (Bath) Ltd.
Midsomer Norton, Avon

TO THE MEMORY
OF
ANDREW NEIL CROMPTON
1964–1985

Acknowledgements

My sincere thanks are due to Peter Brown, Don Fowler, Peta Fowler, and Jasper Griffin, who have once more read great batches of typescript for me. These generous scholars have supplied me with acute criticisms, positive suggestions, and facts. I hope they will find these pages sufficiently changed. The mistakes that remain are of course due to my own negligence or stubbornness. Linda, Raphael, and Rosy Lyne also helped me in various vital ways, and in other circumstances this book would have been dedicated to them.

I think most Oxford dons owe debts of gratitude to their students. But during the years in which I have been writing this book, I have been lucky enough to come into contact with some particularly brilliant young minds. Five Balliol undergraduates have helped me so much that it would be ungrateful not to mention them by name: Jane Ayling, Andrew Crompton, Rupert Holderness, Helen Quinn, and Matthew Taylor.

Andrew Crompton was killed in an accident on Mont Blanc, on 13 July 1985, aged 21. We who grieve must avoid facile hyperbole; but I record with no exaggeration that, as an interpreter of Vergil, Andrew Crompton had no equal. To the memory of this extraordinarily gifted young scholar I dedicate this book, in gratitude and humility.

R.O.A.M.L.

Preface to the Paperback Edition

Since first writing this book I have not significantly changed my interpretation of any of the individual passages discussed; my view of the poem as a whole is, likewise, substantially intact. I am aware that some scholars may find my way of expressing myself (basically, arguing for the existence of 'Further Voices') a little old-fashioned. This, however, has the virtue of swift comprehensibility. Nevertheless, if I were rewriting the book, I should take more account of the approaches and terminology of modern narratology. Already in my second book on the *Aeneid*,[1] titles which *Further Voices* had eschewed featured in the bibliography and had an effect on the writing: G. Genette, *Narrative Discourse*, translated by J. E. Lewin (Oxford, Blackwell, 1980), and S. Rimmon–Kenan, *Narrative Fiction: Contemporary Poetics* (London and New York, 1983). And I might now be particularly coloured in my expression and approach by Don Fowler's stimulating article 'Deviant focalisation in Virgil's *Aeneid*', *PCPhs* NS 36 (1990), 42–63. So I confess that the critical discourse of *Further Voices* is a little behind the times—a fact that I regret, but not agonizingly. 'My book is designed to stand or fall . . . by the practical exegetical value of the examples.'

Bibliographically—besides Fowler's article and the other works mentioned above—I would stress the usefulness of the following items that have appeared since *Further Voices*, or too late for *Further Voices* to take proper notice of them: D. C. Feeney, *The Gods in Epic: Poets and Critics of the Classical Tradition* (Oxford, 1991); S. J. Harrison, *Oxford Readings in Vergil's Aeneid* (Oxford, 1990): this contains many of the articles listed in the *Further Voices* bibliography, besides a fine introduction by Harrison himself ('Some Views of the *Aeneid* in the Twentieth Century'), and other useful material; James J. O'Hara, *Death and the Optimistic Prophecy in Vergil's Aeneid* (Princeton, NJ, 1990); Irene J. F. De Jong, *Narrators and*

---

[1] *Words and the Poet: Characteristic Techniques of Style in Vergil's Aeneid* (Oxford, 1989).

Focalizers: The Presentation of the Story in the Iliad (Amsterdam, 1987);[2] P. R. Hardie, *Virgil's Aeneid: Cosmos and Imperium* (Oxford, 1986); and G. B. Conte *The Rhetoric of Imitation: Genre and Poetic Memory in Virgil and Other Latin Poets*, translated from the Italian and edited with a foreword by C. Segal (Ithaca, NY and London, 1986).[3] I should also explain why, since it has caused some annoyance, I referred to and used the third German edition of V. Pöschl's epoch-making *Die Dichtkunst Virgils: Bild und Symbol in der Äneis* (Berlin and New York, 1977) in both *Further Voices* and *Words and the Poet*. I did this because it is an enlarged and improved version of the original; I might have added, however, that an English translation of the original edition (1950) does exist, V. Pöschl, *The Art of Vergil: Image and Symbol in the Aeneid* (Ann Arbor, Mich., 1962). Finally, a book which is forthcoming and which we should all look out for is Richard Tarrant's *A Commentary on Virgil Aeneid XII*, to be published in the Cambridge Greek and Latin Classics Series (General Editors: E. J. Kenney and P. E. Easterling). It may (for one thing) take us beyond the—by now—tired labels of 'optimists' and 'pessimists'.

[2] This perceptive book encourages a radical rereading of Homer—and, had it been available to me, I should have modified some of my comments on Homeric narrative technique in Ch. 6. It also has a great deal to teach the interpreter of the *Aeneid*.

[3] I announced the imminence of this translation in the hardback edition of *Further Voices*, but was myself obliged to use the Italian originals.

Contents

Introduction	1
1. *In Medias Res:* Examples Various	4
Appendices	56
1. Analysis of Poetic Diction in *Aeneid* 7.291ff.	
2. Some Unpoetical Diction in *Aeneid* 7.291ff.	
2. Gods and Men	61
3. Allusion	100
4. The Hero and His Son	145
5. Dramatic Irony	207
6. Further Voices	217
Select Bibliography	239
Index	

Introduction

The *Aeneid* is an unusually complex and rich poem. Its dense texture conveys a multiplicity of meanings. More particularly, I would say, it conveys a multiplicity of opinions; it offers a variety of ways of interpreting the events enacted. It is as if one heard different voices speaking to one in and behind the action. And 'voices' is the term I find most useful in trying to explain how this complex poem works; I use it not wholly metaphorically. I shall now proceed to outline with all brevity what I mean by the 'further voices' of the *Aeneid*. I would not wish to dignify my approach with the title of 'theory'. It is simply one way of looking at the communicative methods of Vergil's poetry. After my outline account I shall turn straight to examples, the core of the book. At the end I shall return to expound my approach, my way of viewing the *Aeneid*, more fully. But I should like to stress at the beginning that my book is designed to stand or fall not by the impressive way in which I choose to phrase my approach, but by the practical exegetical value of the examples.

Vergil supplies an action which can have an impact on us very much like Homer's. We may find an epic story delivered in a language substantially traditional and epic by an epic poet who defers, admittedly with some equivocation, to a Muse. More particularly, we may gain the impression of an unfolding drama, as we do in the *Iliad* or *Odyssey*: the anonymous narrator removes himself from the stage, permitting himself no evident authorial interference with the shape, sequence, or texture of the narrative and little or no scope for his own subjective reactions to the actions presented. The action and characters achieve their own momentum and independence—as in a drama. To find this sort of *Aeneid* is, I say, possible. Vergil makes it possible, by policy: it is to this end that he launches the poem in the language of the epic poet, substantially maintains such traditional language, and adheres to much of Homer's narrative technique in the ways indicated. And when he does this, to the extent that he does this, he is using what I would call an 'epic voice'. If we hearken to this voice, and to it alone, we find our conventional epic: 'objective', credible, univocal. And our univocal epic is unshocking in tone and substance, indeed (and more particularly) patriotic and inspiring. Of course, the story of the *Aeneid* will at times cause any moderately sensitive reader some sadness. But those who seek a fundamentally sound, imperial poem need not be disappointed or disturbed: the epic voice is there to speak to those with such positive expectations.

But there are 'further voices'. In various unobvious ways Vergil takes liberties with the texture of his narrative, and its shape. Devices are exploited to insinuate ramifying meanings and messages for those prepared to listen. Further voices intrude other material and opinions, and these may be disturbing, even shocking. Further voices add to, comment upon, question, and occasionally subvert the implications of the epic voice.

A further voice is characterized by *discretion*: a reader inclined to hearken to the epic voice is not irritatingly diverted; and yet also by *persistence*: such voices are irremovably there. To effect their communication they exploit (*a*) 'invention' and 'arrangement' (I use the handy if schematic rhetorical terms: in Latin, 'inuentio', 'dispositio');[1] and they exploit (*b*) style. They operate (*a*) by the provoking inclusion of unexpected, and in terms of the epic plot unnecessary, material; and by juxtaposing material in tendentious ways. They may (*b*) lean on suggestive devices of style such as imagery, ambiguity, allusion.

Among epic voice and further voices, which is Vergil's own? Which is Vergil's among the variety of opinions? The inadmissible question is intriguing. At any one time: one? both? all? At any one time we shall come to our own conclusions, if we think the question admissible or interesting. In describing the operation of Vergil's text and its voices, I have often failed to suppress my own opinions about Vergil's opinions. I am

---

[1] For a brief definition of rhetorical 'inuentio' and 'dispositio' see Cic. *Inv*. 1.9. In judicial oratory one seeks to 'invent' and 'arrange' facts or arguments in such a way as to produce the most *persuasive* text. In dramatic poetry one seeks to 'invent' and 'arrange' facts etc. in such a way as to produce the most interesting, striking, significant text.

Introduction 3

also aware that I have in general used the term 'Vergil' in ways which may seem to some inexact or old-fashioned. For example, I refer to the man who creates and controls all voices in the *Aeneid* and to the man who may personally identify himself with one of these voices by the same title: Vergil. I do not think that it is realistic to seek more exactness when referring to the complex individual who invents, makes, and utters a poem, and thinks his thoughts. And I think that not to refer to him produces unnecessarily lifeless criticism—and is in a sense ungrateful. But, as I have said, the value of this book is supposed to reside in the practical exegetical value of its examples; and if I have phrased myself in exceptionable ways I hope this will not completely obscure the discoveries I have made.

I now turn to examples. Chapter 1 heads boldly into the poem, commenting on a variety of topics and formal devices. The ensuing chapters then pick up and develop the more salient of the subjects mentioned. In the process, assumptions that this first wide-ranging chapter necessarily makes are justified, and terms that may seem to merit more elucidation are given further attention.

1
In Medias Res: Examples Various

1. An intervention; imagery and allusion: Aeneas and Ajax

In Book 12 Trojan victory is imminent. At the beginning of the book a truce is arranged and a duel between Turnus and Aeneas organized. Aeneas views the prospect of this duel in what we could call a truly Augustan manner.[1] His attitude to the business of combat is clement and relatively dispassionate, and he sees the purpose of it as the establishment of peace (note especially lines 176ff.): it is as if he has the civilized, imperial instructions of Anchises ringing in his ears (6.851–3):[2]

>   tu regere imperio populos, Romane, memento
>   (hae tibi erunt artes), pacique imponere morem,
>   parcere subiectis et debellare superbos.

Do you, Roman, remember to rule the nations with your power—these will be the arts for you—and to impose civilization upon peace, to spare the subject, and to war down the proud.

When the truce is treacherously broken, the same high-mindedness is maintained: he tries to stem the violent, irrational tide (313ff., 'quo ruitis . . . o cohibete iras' ['Where are you rushing to . . . Oh, restrain your anger']). Then he is wounded; and the galling frustration of his inactivity—during which time Turnus rampages freely—produces a grimmer, less dispassionate Aeneas. When his wound is cured, he arms

---

[1] My article 'Vergil and the Politics of War', esp. 196ff., amplifies and justifies this and the other remarks on the context in Book 12.
[2] On Anchises' instructions see below, n. 62 and Ch. 4 p. 187. I take the phrase 'to impose civilization upon peace' to be Vergil's compressed and poetical way of saying 'to impose peace *and* civilization, upon the world'. In Anchises' view war, together with judicious clemency, should be a means to a great end: peace, civilization, empire. Similarly Aeneas, but with even more idealism—at this stage.

In Medias Res: Examples Various

'auidus pugnae' ['hungry for battle'] (430), and returns to the fray (441 ff.). At this stage his view of the purpose of the conflict (peace) is unchanged; but his attitude towards the conduct of it is now emphatically passionate. And the reader now pays, or should pay, rapt attention—for he has frequently seen that passion can obstruct the hero's sense of duty and responsibility.[3]

As Aeneas charges back on to the plain, sweeping his columns along with him, Turnus sees him, the other Italians and Juturna see him, and they fear. And Vergil supplies an illustrative simile, tied in particular to Aeneas, here termed the 'Rhoetean general' (450 ff.):

> ille uolat campoque atrum rapit agmen aperto.
> qualis ubi ad terras abrupto sidere nimbus
> it mare per medium (miseris, heu, praescia longe
> horrescunt corda agricolis: dabit ille ruinas
> arboribus stragemque satis, ruet omnia late),
> ante uolant sonitumque ferunt ad litora uenti:
> talis in aduersos ductor Rhoeteius hostis
> agmen agit . . .

Aeneas flies on, sweeping his dark column over the open plain. As when a storm cloud sweeps towards the land cutting off the sun's light (alas! the hearts of pitiable farmers know it from afar and shudder: destruction and ruin will it bring to trees and crops, it will overthrow all far and wide); before it fly the winds bringing their uproar to the shore: even so did the Rhoetean general lead his column against the enemy ranged against him . . .

What does the simile tell us? On an obvious level it is graphic, illustrating the fearsomeness of Aeneas' advance and the fearful expectancy of the Italian enemy. That, we could say, is the message of the epic voice. But do we detect anything else? Is there any further voice, discreetly commenting?

Clearly, I think, yes. The first point to notice is that in terms of the simile, the Italians are the 'agricolae', the farmers; and within the simile we find an exclamation expressing sympathy for these farmers: 'miseris heu'. Whose voice is this? Now interventions into the narrative are not in principle, as we shall see, alien to the epic voice (p. 233). But here an unexpected and

---
[3] See, e.g., Ch. 4 pp. 182–8.

perhaps discordant note is intruded, and a further voice is, I think, audible. For, in expressing sympathy for the farmers, the exclamation expresses sympathy for the Italians, Aeneas' enemies: the voice feels for them—unlike Aeneas himself at this time.[4] It is in fact a telling point to recall that Aeneas did once feel for his enemies (or his imminent enemies as they then were) in precisely these words (8.537, 'heu quantae miseris . . .').[5] But much has happened since then, and humanity in war is easier to utter than to practise, a point which this poem is among other things concerned to make.[6] Anyway, this comment, at variance with the hero's sympathies, seems distinctive: a further voice. Vergil (I would be inclined to say) reveals *his* difference from *his* hero.[7] Discreet evidence of sympathy with Turnus is somewhat similarly shown in the dream simile of 12.908ff.[8]

Comparison with Vergil's source for 12.451ff., Homer, *Il.* 4.275ff., shows no such intervention there—a fact which highlights (should it be necessary) the deliberateness of Vergil's policy. Comparison helps to bring out other points. Here is the Homeric simile:

ὡς δ' ὅτ' ἀπὸ σκοπιῆς εἶδεν νέφος αἰπόλος ἀνὴρ
ἐρχόμενον κατὰ πόντον ὑπὸ Ζεφύροιο ἰωῆς·
τῷ δέ τ' ἄνευθεν ἐόντι μελάντερον ἠΰτε πίσσα
φαίνετ' ἰὸν κατὰ πόντον, ἄγει δέ τε λαίλαπα πολλήν,
ῥίγησέν τε ἰδών, ὑπό τε σπέος ἤλασε μῆλα·

Just as when from some vantage-point a goatherd sees a cloud moving over the sea before the blast of the West Wind; and to him being afar off it seems blacker than pitch, as it passes over the sea; and it drives a mighty storm; and he shudders at the sight of it and drives his flocks beneath a cave . . .

In Homer the storm is sighted by a goatherd who fearfully drives his goats to *safety*. Vergil changes the image to farmers

[4] So it would seem reasonable to infer from the indiscriminate slaughter that ensues at 12.494ff.
[5] See Pöschl, 76ff., refuting misunderstandings of the exclamation.
[6] Cf. 'Vergil and the Politics of War', esp. 193, 201–3.
[7] Cf. the comment of G. Williams, 168, which seems to me rather naïvely conceived.
[8] The simile derives from Homer, *Iliad* 22.199f., but is adapted most interestingly: see the perceptive remarks of Pöschl, 166, Steiner, 72–5; a summary in Rieks, 1089f. But these scholars miss the discreet sympathy intruded by the first-person 'uidemur'.

apprehensive at the imminent *destruction* of their crops. Comparison with Homer therefore focuses and emphasizes the pitiable position of the 'agricolae' (and through them the Italians). But there is a more important point.

Why does Vergil change 'goatherd' (his version of which would be, I suppose, 'pastor') to 'farmers'? This is an example of a tactic that occurs quite frequently in Vergil's text, and one for which the poet prepares us carefully. The language and associations of the simile, the 'agricolae', 'sata', and so on, recall the *Georgics*; and Vergil is alluding to and building upon what he had established in that poem.[9] In the *Georgics* he had explained a path of peace and morality through the figure of the farmer; he presented the farmer, in a war-ravaged world, as the embodiment, or rather the possible embodiment, of a peaceful, Italian morality.[10] Therefore, for Vergil and for readers of the *Georgics*, the 'agricola' with his crops was a significant and sympathetic figure. Often Vergil exploits this fact, this sympathetic significance that has accrued to the 'agricola' and his

[9] On allusion in general, see Ch. 3. Vergil prepares us for allusion to the *Georgics* in the *Aeneid*, and for other important tactics, by the way he manages the first three similes in the poem. They all surprise, and in consequence instruct. Unexpectedly, the first (1.148–53) is drawn from Roman political life. This suggests to us the important point that a political significance is available in the mythical narrative of the poem: cf. Pöschl, 21f. (the simile productively fools us, too, for it suggests that we will find a poem more clear-cut in its issues than we in fact find; see below, n. 55). The second simile (1.430–6) is also unexpected: it quotes the *Georgics*. This must make us ask: is the fact that Vergil *quotes* significant? Is he *alluding* to the *Georgics*? The only effective way to answer this is to try it out. Does a supposition of allusion benefit the *Aeneid*? We find that it does. The fact that the bees symbolized an ordered type of collective society in *Georgics* 4, but one which was not in all senses attractive (cf. Griffin, 'The Fourth Georgic'), makes them a useful shorthand in the present context of the *Aeneid*; it is also relevant to remember that the society symbolized was totally dependent on its monarch (*Georg.* 4.211ff.). The fact that Vergil displays in such a proud and prominent position that he is prepared to exploit the text of the *Georgics* prepares us for other perhaps less obvious examples; other clear examples are the similes at 12.103–6, involving quotation (see Ch. 6 pp. 237–8), and 2.304–8; cf. W. W. Briggs, Jr., *Narrative and Simile from the Georgics in the Aeneid* (Leiden, 1980). In the third simile of the poem (1.498–502) we eventually find what we probably expected at the beginning, an adaptation of Homer. But this too has its surprises—instructive ones; it provides details for us to puzzle over; and when we have puzzled over them, compared the original Homer with Vergil, and so on, we should have learned to be responsive to Homeric allusion—and to other Vergilian tactics: see below, Ch. 3 n. 41.

[10] Cf. my remarks in *Quality and Pleasure in Latin Poetry*, eds. T. Woodman and D. West (Cambridge, 1974), pp. 47–9, and in my introduction to Cecil Day Lewis's translation of *Eclogues* and *Georgics* (Oxford, 1983).

world—and not just in similes. It is, for example, particularly troubling and tragic when Allecto's war in Book 7 flares up not just between Trojans and Italians, but between Trojans and Italian 'agrestes'. And if in this simile the Italians are depicted as 'agricolae', we know that sympathy expressed for them is not only keen but has particular point. The simile discreetly suggests that Aeneas' imminent destruction of the Italians, however necessary or forced upon him, will destroy those who have the potential to embody essential qualities of peace and morality. That is what 'agricola' may connote to a reader acquainted with the *Georgics*. While, therefore, the drama, the epic voice, simply presents the return of our respected and imminently victorious hero, a further voice, operating now by allusion (to the *Georgics*), calls attention to the fact that his imminent victims are potentially valuable citizens. And consider the general fact that Aeneas' advance is pictured as a storm. Storms have supplied potent illustrations of destructive, irrational passion since the great opening scene of the poem.[11] The basic imagery here therefore voices the opinion that the passion of the advancing hero is disquieting.

To make my final and, I think, most striking point in connection with this simile, I must bring into play two neighbouring passages: the beginning of Aeneas' speech to Ascanius just preceding his re-entry into battle (435f.), and the phrase that leads us out of the simile, 'ductor Rhoeteius', the periphrasis which is chosen for Aeneas at this time (456).

Here are lines 435f., the beginning of Aeneas' speech:

> disce, puer, uirtutem ex me uerumque laborem,
> fortunam ex aliis . . .

Learn valour [virtue, excellence—'uirtus' is a difficult and ramifying word][12] from me, my son, and true endurance of toil. From others learn good luck.

---

[11] Cf. Pöschl, 13ff., 30ff., 152–4; Otis, 68f., 79f., 227ff., 259.

[12] See the useful discussion of K. Büchner, 'Altromisch und horazische Virtus', in *Römische Wertbegriffe*, ed. H. Oppermann (Darmstadt, 1967), 367–401. On the ethical expansion of the word, which originally meant manliness, courage, see 386ff. (Lucilius 1326ff. is an interesting passage); the word would inescapably have ethical connotations in Vergil's time and context. In the light of what is to come in Book 12 of the *Aeneid*, here is a suggestive quotation, Publilius Syrus 690 Duff = 682 Meyer = S48: 'supplicem hominem opprimere uirtus non est, sed crudelitas'; see further below, Ch. 4 pp. 205–6.

In Medias Res: Examples Various   9

It is a striking instruction, in some senses not un-Stoic, but in its totality not quite what we might expect from Aeneas—whom many critics see as the Stoic-Augustan hero at this stage in the action.[13] It is not the utterance of a man adjusted to his lot—but that is hardly new for Aeneas. The grimness of tone perhaps is. And it reminds one of another hero. It and the rest of Aeneas' speech bear some resemblance to Hector's prayer for his son in *Il.* 6.476ff.; but much more obvious is the recall of the tragic Ajax's last words to his son in Sophocles' play *Ajax*, 550f., lines which are based on Hector's words, but which are more arrogant:

ὦ παῖ, γένοιο πατρὸς εὐτυχέστερος,
τὰ δ' ἄλλ' ὁμοῖος.

My son, may you be luckier than your father, but otherwise the same [i.e. courageous, enduring, etc.].

Vergil's text is obviously echoing this Ajax—but perhaps in Accius' translation of Sophocles rather than Sophocles himself (*trag.* 156 'uirtuti sis par, dispar fortunis patris').[14] The recall, in fact, is striking enough for one to feel that allusion is in play: Vergil is alluding to Ajax and wishing us to pick up the allusion. Why? From the work of scholars such as W. S. Anderson and G. Knauer, we can gather that Vergil constantly, by allusion, represents his characters as new versions of other, usually Homeric, heroes. This is a topic I shall develop in a later chapter; indeed the pattern of allusion I am about to trace is part of a larger pattern, as I shall there demonstrate. For the moment it suffices to say that at this point in the narrative Aeneas is being represented, at a certain level, as playing the role of the tragic Ajax. And this is significant, and disturbing. As Aeneas re-enters the battle, presented by the epic voice as a hero bent on establishing peace and the common good, we have the troubling, allusive suggestion of something quite dif-

---

[13] e.g. Heinze, 271ff., esp. 276–80; Otis, 317 ('the "reborn" hero is a truly Roman hero who stands in the great line that includes Hercules, Romulus and Augustus'). On Aeneas' speech at 12.435ff., see Ch. 4 pp. 191–3. Aeneas was Stoic-Augustan at the beginning of the book (see above), but things are changing—not for the first time.

[14] But Accius' context may have been different from Sophocles': Ajax going out to battle rather than Ajax about to commit suicide. See H. D. Jocelyn, *CQ* 15 (1965), 127–9.

ferent: a relentless, passionate hero, whose essentially selfish obsession with honour led to madness and suicide.[15] A disturbing further voice.

As yet, of course, the suggestion of an Ajax in Aeneas is not large; it would welcome confirmation. For this, let us return in the first place to the simile and to its source (Homer, *Il.* 4.275ff., above). Here too allusion is operative.

We should ask ourselves: what is the context of Vergil's Homeric source? Often Vergil expects us to bear the context of his source in mind and to apply it when reading his new fabrication. In our own passage (we should remind ourselves) Aeneas drives his columns back to war and attracts a storm simile. In the Homeric source two homonymous heroes lead their phalanxes back to war and attract the original storm simile; the simile is, it is true, strictly tied to the phalanxes, but the heroes' names command the beginning and end of the simile. And the name? The 'Aiantes', the two Ajaxes:

ἦλθε δ' ἐπ' Αἰάντεσσι . . .
τὼ δὲ κορυσσέσθην, ἅμα δὲ νέφος εἵπετο πεζῶν.
ὡς δ' ὅτ' . . .
τοῖαι ἄμ' Αἰάντεσσι διοτρεφέων αἰζηῶν
δήϊον ἐς πόλεμον πυκιναὶ κίνυντο φάλαγγες

He [Agamemnon] came to the Aiantes. . . . These were armed, and there followed with them a cloud of foot-soldiers. Just as when from . . . beneath a cave; so with the Aiantes moved the dense phalanxes . . .

Allusion, now working through the Homeric simile, reinforces the suggestion that behind Aeneas we might sense Ajax.

Finally, 'ductor Rhoeteius', the periphrasis given to Aeneas in the sentence that returns us from simile to narrative. This confirms the allusive point, and makes the further voice undeniable. Vergil, as is well known, uses antonomasia like this with great care; the effect, for example, of 'Anchisiades' in 10.822 is well known.[16] But 'ductor Rhoeteius' is a surprising periphrasis

[15] Cf. B. M. W. Knox, *The Heroic Temper* (Berkeley and Los Angeles, 1966), 28–30, 41–3. Note that I (and Vergil) emphasize the *tragic* Ajax: Homer's Ajax was rather different, at times quite the team man.
[16] See Otis, 340; also Warde Fowler (*Site of Rome*, 88) who recalls having the implication of the patronymic explained to him by H. Nettleship. The perception is in essence as old as de la Cerda (cf. Conte, *Il genere*, 136).

(it is applied only here to Aeneas[17]), for it seems to lack sufficient function. R. D. Williams (7–12) glosses the epithet 'Trojan' (i.e. he takes it to be a synecdoche); and this so far as it goes is not inept. Rhoeteum was a place on the Troad, and it is suggestive that Roman Aeneas[18] should get a Trojan periphrasis at this stage of the poem (contrast 12.166, 'pater Aeneas Romanae stirpis origo'). But if Vergil meant *only* 'Trojan', why not say so? What is the key? We must investigate this place Rhoeteum further.

Rhoeteum was in fact the name of a town and, when used loosely, its adjacent territory and coastline in the Troad. The place had its ups and downs in history, but the most famous thing about it was an association that is now predictable. Here was the tomb and shrine of—Ajax. The earliest reference to this which I have to hand is in an epigram of Antipater of Sidon (*Anth. Pal.* 7.146; the epigram refers to the contest for Achilles' arms; Ajax's defeat in this led ultimately to his suicide):

Σῆμα παρ' Αἰάντειον ἐπὶ 'Ροιτηΐσιν ἀκταῖς
θυμοβαρὴς Ἀρετὰ μύρομαι ἑζομένα,
... διὰ κρίσιν ὅττι Πελασγῶν
οὐκ ἀρετὰ νικᾶν ἔλλαχεν, ἀλλὰ δόλος.

By the tomb of Ajax on the Rhoetean shore I, Virtue, sit and mourn, heavy at heart . . . because in the judgement court of the Greeks not Virtue but Fraud triumphed.

The tomb at Rhoeteum is also mentioned by, among others,[19] Lucan (9.962f., 'Graio nobile busto / Rhoetion'), Lucian (*Charon* 23), and Quintus Smyrnaeus, who affectingly describes Ajax's cremation and burial in a mound 'not far from the Rhoeteian shore' at the end of Book 5 of his epic. And a final, very interesting, reference suggests that the association of Rhoeteum with Ajax was not only large but topical, and thus easy for Vergil's readers to pick up. Marcus Antonius had

---

[17] The other occurrences of the epithet *Rhoete(i)us* in Vergil are: *Aen.* 6.505, 'Rhoeteo in litore' (the site of the cenotaph of Deiphobus); 5.646, 'Rhoeteia . . . Dorycli coniunx'; 3.108, 'Teucrus Rhoeteas primum est aductus in oras'. The name of the place does not occur as a substantive in Vergil. One could have a shot at seeing significance in these other uses.

[18] We recall in particular Anchises' 'tu . . . Romane, memento' (6.851), addressed to Aeneas as well as to future Roman generations: cf. Ch. 5 p. 214.

[19] See further W. Leaf, *Strabo on the Troad* (Cambridge, 1923), 156f.

purloined Ajax's statue from the shrine at Rhoeteum and moved it to Alexandria. After Actium, Augustus had returned it, together with other Antonian loot, to its proper home. His policy of returning loot was one that Augustus was sufficiently proud of to record in the *Res Gestae* (24). The details concerning Rhoeteum come from Strabo, 13.1.30:

Then there was Rhoeteum, a city situated on a hill, and adjacent to Rhoeteum a low-lying shore on which are a tomb and temple of Ajax and a statue of him, which was taken by Antonius and carried off to Egypt; but Augustus Caesar gave it back again to the Rhoeteians, just as he gave back other statues to their owners.

So the suggestive allusion continues in the phrase 'ductor Rhoeteius'; indeed it becomes quite sharp. And, evocative of the dead and therefore the tragic Ajax, it confirms the particular respect in which Aeneas is being allusively associated with him. He is being associated with Ajax the tragic figure.[20] While therefore (as I adumbrated above) the epic voice presents us at this point of the narrative with Aeneas the selfless Roman hero returning to battle to secure victory, peace, and the common good of Italians and Trojans alike, a further voice naggingly insinuates a quite different message: that there is still something of an Ajax in Aeneas, a hero honour-obsessed and doomed. Nor is the insinuation totally absurd. And this, together with the preparatory allusions to Ajax, seems to me to be a very pleasing example of the way in which Vergil intrudes a further voice. There is enough of a puzzle in the text (especially in 'ductor Rhoeteius' itself) to encourage the eager *habitué* to probe the style, to find the allusion—and hence to unearth a disquieting message, a message that maintains other disquieting messages already delivered: by imagery (farmers threatened by a storm) and by discreet intervention ('heu miseris'). A further voice is definitely and distinctly there, in the background of this section of the text. But it is not forced upon us, by any means. This is Vergil's usual and tactful way. The reader may follow the main lines of the drama undisturbed, if he wants to; he may listen merely to the epic voice. But he has the option of complexity, the option of disquieting comment and disturbing opinions.

[20] See above, n. 15.

2. Imagery and linked imagery; invention and arrangement, and not resisting implications: Juno, Allecto, Venus, Amata, Dido

In Book 7 Juno dispatches the Fury Allecto to Latium. The great consort of Jupiter wishes her to foment war in order to obstruct Jupiter's plan, to hold up the marriage of Aeneas and Lavinia, to delay the alliance of Trojans and Italians. Allecto picks out Queen Amata as her first tool, intending to make her a passionate partisan of Turnus as Lavinia's future husband. It is a good choice. Amata is already passionately seething at the prospect of Lavinia's being married to Aeneas—as Vergil describes in a vivid, perhaps colloquial, image (7.345, 'coquebant', lit., '[cares] were cooking' her)[21]—and Vergil's gods and demons are shrewd enough to 'work with' existing propensities in the mortals they wish to manipulate (Ch. 2 s. 2). Actually, Amata is a particularly good choice; and the way Allecto works on her to make her Turnus' passionate partisan is brilliant.

The beginning of Allecto's enterprise is described thus (7.341 ff.):

> exim Gorgoneis Allecto infecta uenenis
> principio Latium et Laurentis tecta tyranni
> celsa petit, tacitumque obsedit limen Amatae,
> quam super aduentu Teucrum Turnique hymenaeis
> femineae ardentem curaeque iraeque coquebant.

Thereupon Allecto, instilled with Gorgon poisons, first seeks out Latium and the lofty halls of the Laurentine king; and she laid siege to Amata's silent threshold. Female anxieties and anger over the arrival of the Trojans and the marriage of Turnus were already making the fiery queen seethe....

The language of Allecto's assault deserves attention. 'Obsedit limen Amatae' introduces a military metaphor, 'siege' (cf. 2.441, 'obsessumque acta testudine limen'; 802 f., 'Danaique obsessa tenebant / limina'). That in itself is not particularly striking. However, if we allow time for Vergilian insinuation to

---

[21] Cf. Catull. 83.6, where I think 'coquitur' not 'loquitur' should be read.

work, something very striking emerges. With a certain *frisson* we must realize that there is a touch of *erotic* military metaphor here. It was not traditional for Furies to beset 'limina'. Although a variety of reasons might be cited to explain why Vergil decided to place Allecto at the threshold,[22] we must remember that the 'limen' is a key feature of Latin erotic poetry: it was the central stage-prop in that very popular scene, the 'excluded lover', 'exclusus amator'.[23] Military imagery is also a characteristic of Latin erotic literature ('militia amoris'),[24] and the image of 'siege' itself featured in that selfsame 'excluded lover' topos: excluded lovers were said to 'lay siege' to their beloveds.[25] Most relevant to compare with our passage are the following: Ovid *Ars* 2.526, 'quid nostras obsidet iste fores?' ['why does that fellow besiege our doors?']; and, involving 'limen' as well as 'obsideo', Ov. *Amores* 1.9.19 (a poem on the 'militia amoris'): 'ille graues urbes, hic durae limen amicae / obsidet' ['the soldier besieges cities, the lover besieges the threshold of his hard-hearted girl-friend']. That Vergil's text insinuates an erotic siege may seem a strange suggestion, but the insinuation is there: Vergil is making some kind of serious, perverse use of an image that is normally romantic or frivolous.[26] A final consideration clinches the point. The phrase 'obsedit limen' is coupled with 'AMATAE'. And 'amatus', 'amata', as a substantive or quasi-substantive, means 'beloved'.[27] In this connection we should remember, of course, that Vergil's original readers did not have capital and small letters, so that nothing automatically marked off 'Amatae' as a proper name: the text that met their eyes was OBSEDITLIMENAMATAE. And an additional and very relevant fact is that the name 'Amata' for Latinus' wife is more than

---

[22] See Pease on 4.473.

[23] See F. O. Copley, *EXCLUSUS AMATOR: A Study in Latin Love Poetry* (Baltimore, 1956), 35f., 75ff.; more refs. and bibliography in *Mnemosyne*, 27 (1974), 264 n. 8.

[24] See R. O. A. M. Lyne, *The Latin Love Poets* (Oxford, 1980), 71ff.

[25] As well as the passages mentioned in the text, cf. e.g. Ter. *Eunuch.* 771ff., and Hor. *Odes* 3.26.6–8. At Ov. *Rem.* 691, 'artibus innumeris mens oppugnatur amantum', the image is applied as it were psychologically—interesting in view of what follows.

[26] As he does on other occasions: see below and Ch. 4 p. 195.

[27] *TLL* 1.1959.69ff.: e.g. Livy, 30.14.1; Ov. *Met.* 3.405.

likely Vergil's innovation;[28] if this is the case, then the reader had no familiarity with the name to dull his sensitivity to the word. And it is also very relevant to remark that this is the first time that Amata's surprising name occurs in the *Aeneid*[29]—the *Aeneid* itself has not accustomed us, desensitized us, to it.

We have, therefore, strange information provided by a further voice (exploiting ambiguity and a hinted metaphor): the perverse and paradoxical insinuation that Allecto is in some sense some kind of horrible lover laying 'siege' to Amata—a demon-lover indeed. What do we infer from this strange, hinted image? It cannot work exactly like the conventional image in 'militia amoris' (lover besieges beloved in order to induce latter to sleep with former). We might hazard several deductions. But one implication seems to me unavoidable. If Allecto lays siege to Amata in terms that are erotically coloured; and if the siege is then successful, as it is, and results in Amata's being fired with a violent passion: I think we must deduce that this passion, resulting from an erotic siege, is itself erotic in nature. The passion which is whipped up in Amata and which she proceeds so vividly to display is erotic.

Once we have grasped this, we can see the brilliance of Allecto's plan. What she has done is to identify and 'work with' (cf. Ch. 2 s. 2) a passion which Amata incipiently feels for Turnus, and make her into a Phaedra figure: probably (I think we should infer) an unconscious one, but a Phaedra figure nonetheless. And what more fanatical partisan could Turnus have than the queen who was, without properly knowing it, actually in love with him?

But this may seem a challenging thesis that I am propound-

---

[28] Fabius Pictor is often cited as evidence for the name 'Amata'. I think this is unfounded. I think we may deduce from Servius *auctus* on 12.603 that Fabius Pictor reported that the queen's mode of suicide was to starve herself to death (= Fabii Pictoris *Latini Annales* fr. 1 Peter)—though only one MS of the *auctus* actually attributes the information to Fabius Pictor; on this MS however, the *Floriacensis*, see the Harvard Servius vol. iii, p. viii. But I do not think we can deduce that Fabius transmitted the name actually as Amata. He is not being cited for nomenclature. Servius *auctus* is quoting information from him (on the mode of death) for a character to whom he himself naturally refers by the name that is familiar to him (Vergil's); I imagine that Fabius used the older name for the queen which we find in Dionysius of Halicarnassus (Amita): cf. *RE* 1.1751.11ff., Fordyce on 7.343.

[29] Vergil regularly delays identification of a character; this is a technique familiar from early Greek poetry: see Heinze, 377, Hopkinson on Callimachus, *Dem.* 32.

ing.[30] It can be supported in three main ways—and the point was, I think, understood by Propertius.[31] First, the way Amata's passion is described following Allecto's assault, in Book 7 and subsequently, provides more evidence that this passion is an erotic one, directed towards Turnus. Secondly, the role in which the further voice casts Amata (Phaedra) may not immediately square with our presuppositions about how an Augustan poet would cast an ancestral Italian queen; but it does, in fact, square with one of the main literary traditions with which Vergil works—and with his own demonstrable literary taste. Thirdly, there is a very significant parallel and precedent in the *Aeneid* for what happens here in Book 7: not only for Allecto's mode of operation (exploiting sexual passion) but also for the manner in which its beginning is described (erotic siege). As often in the *Aeneid*, scenes in the first half of the poem get replayed in interesting ways in the second.

I take up the first point. The insinuations of the further voice are in fact quite insistent. A signal to the effect that Amata's passion is erotic is contained in the simile at 7.378ff., where Amata's mad movements under the impulse of Allecto are compared to a top being whipped by boys. This is a simile to which I shall shortly return, but for now we may remember that it is one which readers of Tibullus (1.5.3f.) knew to be suited to the effects of the actions of *Amor* on a lover. The erotic nature of Amata's passion is also heavily suggested by 7.355f., an earlier description of Allecto's assault:

> ossibus implicat ignem,
> necdum animus toto percepit pectore flammam

It [i.e. the serpent that Allecto hurls] entwines fire in her bones. Not yet has her spirit absorbed the flame throughout her breast . . .

Line 356 is echoed from Ariadne's 'eros' in Catullus, 64.92; while 'ossibus implicat ignem' is the exact and striking phrase used of Dido's love at 1.660 (and the phrase occurs only at these two places in the poem); and the language—'ossa' and

---

[30] But cf. J. W. Zarker, *Vergilius*, 15 (1969), 2–24; J. Foster, *LCM* 2 (1977), 121f.; Giancotti, in M. Gigante, 445.

[31] Propertius clearly echoes Vergil's account of Allecto's assault on Amata in his description of Vesta's manipulation of Tarpeia at 4.4.68ff. Equally clearly, the passion in Tarpeia which Vesta 'works with' (cf. Ch. 2 s. 2) is erotic (cf. *Hermes*, 99 (1971), 376–8).

'ignis' in combination—is naturally erotic.[32] The passionate Amata recalls the passionate Dido. And that is what she does again, in particular at 12.55ff. I shall be considering this passage in detail later on (see pp. 116–7). For the moment, I summarize: at 12.55 ff., when Amata appeals to Turnus, she sounds like his lover: she sounds, in fact, like Dido appealing to *her* lover, Aeneas—and thus exposes her feelings. Bringing these passages together, I think we have to admit that we are dealing with more than a figment of my overheated imagination. We are dealing with a persistent insinuation of Vergil's, a further voice: there is something erotic, something sexual about the emotions which Amata displays in regard to Turnus, in particular after Allecto's attack. Or, in other words, there is something of a Phaedra in her. In this connection we should note the mode of suicide which the queen eventually chooses, despairing at the apparent death of Turnus. According to Vergil, but against the tradition,[33] she hangs herself: a 'degrading death' ['informe letum'], as Vergil calls it (12.603), befitting the desperate, the self-disgusted: Jocasta, Phaedra, and— according to Vergil—Amata.[34] They all hang themselves. And, by the by, Vergil's line describing Amata's suicide is based on, we might say it alludes to, Homer's description of the death of Epicaste (Jocasta), at *Od.* 11.271.

Comparisons with Jocasta and Phaedra have virtually made my second point for me. The epic, or at least the Homeric, tradition may not bulge with perverse women; but tragedy, especially Euripidean tragedy, does. And, as is well known, tragedy supplies Vergil with much of his ethos, and not a little of his material.[35] In addition, perverse women and unnatural love were naturally to the taste of the Roman Callimacheans,

---

[32] See Lyne on *Ciris*, 163 and 164, with bibliography.
[33] See Servius *auctus* on 12.603.
[34] Soph. *OT* 1263; Eur. *Hipp.* 802. The degradation of death by hanging is stressed in the *Odyssey*: 22.462, 472. It can, of course, be forced upon an innocent who has no other resources: Antigone, Soph. *Ant.* 1221 f.; contrast Deianeira, Soph. *Trach.* 886, and Canace in Eur. *Aiolos* (T. B. L. Webster, *The Tragedies of Euripides* (London, 1967), 159). (Cf. further E. Fraenkel, 'Selbstmordwege', *Philologus*, 87 (1932), 470–3 = *Kleine Beiträge*, i, 465–7.)
[35] Cf. Quinn, 324–49; F. Muecke, *AJP* 104 (1983), 134–155 with bibliography; and further items in W. Suerbaum's bibliography in *ANRW* 31.1, ed. W. Haase, 134f. and 267f.

the 'Neoteric' poets[36]—and to these poets belonged Vergil's original schooling and younger inclinations.[37] Nor are other signs of a continuing interest in such topics absent from the *Aeneid*.[38]

And now to my third point, that there is precedent in the *Aeneid* for Allecto's mode of operation and the manner in which its beginning is described. Amata, I have said, recalls Dido. And Allecto recalls Venus. The parallel, fully stated, is as follows: the chain of influence Juno–Allecto–Amata (Book 7) recalls Venus–Cupid–Dido (Book 1), with Allecto playing much of the role of Venus as well as Cupid.[39] Allecto certainly recalls Venus, in action and imagery. Her plan and actions as regards Amata are a kind of perverse replay of Venus' plan and actions as regards Dido.

Erotic military imagery clothed the assault of Allecto. Erotic military imagery is prominent in the story of Dido and is specifically employed for Venus' attack on her. This is how Venus tells Cupid of her intention to inflame Dido with love (1.673):

> quocirca capere ante dolis et cingere flamma
> reginam meditor . . .

Wherefore I plan to forestall the queen with guile and lay a ring of fire around her . . .

She, like Allecto, wishes to manipulate a victim with passion, 'working with' existing propensities—and patently here it is erotic passion that is at issue. And she uses, as Vergil uses for Allecto, an image of erotic *siege* (this is the clear implication of the words 'cingere flamma': see Austin ad loc.). But, as with Allecto so with Venus, the object of the siege is not to provoke the besieged to love the besieger (as in the conventional image of 'militia amoris'), but to love someone else: in Dido's case, Aeneas. And Cupid sets about the fulfilment of his mother's

---

[36] See R. O. A. M. Lyne, *CQ* 28 (1978), 182.

[37] See esp. *Eclogue* 6, with O. Skutsch, *RhM* 99 (1956), 193–5, an article which is still indispensable.

[38] Cf. Cycnus at 10.188ff., Cydon at 10.325, and Nisus and Euryalus in Book 9 (Ch. 6 pp. 228–9).

[39] The more obvious and first recall effected by the Juno–Allecto sequence in Book 7 is of Juno-Aeolus at the beginning of Book 1. Then comes this more disconcerting second parallel.

wishes, using on her instruction poison ('uenenum', 1.688), among other devices: another detail common to and linking the Venus–Dido and Allecto–Amata scenes (7.341, 354). So a parallel between the two scenes can be detected. It supports my interpretation of Allecto's 'obsedit limen Amatae'. It does something else. If we detect a parallel between Allecto and Venus, this surely puts Augustus' divine ancestress in a somewhat disturbing light: a further voice again insinuates, using invention and arrangement (the structural similarity organized between Books 1 and 7, Venus and Allecto) as well as imagery (the shared image of erotic siege). On Venus and Allecto, see further below.

A further voice, working by *linked* imagery (cf. Ch. 4 s. 12), has more to say to us about this Venus–Dido episode. Venus lays siege to Dido: we read on and we find that this is the beginning of a line of linked military imagery giving colour and character to the tragic love story of Dido.[40] At 4.434, for example, Dido talks of herself as 'uictam' ['conquered']. At 4.330 she uses the phrase 'capta ac deserta' ['captured and desolate'], to suggest her plight: evocative of a sacked city, this phrase proves in retrospect to be tragically apt. The ant simile of 402 ff. ominously intrudes into the Trojan departure the tones of a rapacious Roman army on the march—not a sympathetic characterization.[41] And finally the tragic culmination, occurring in the simile attached to the lamentation that greets news of Dido's death. It is indeed as if the city were being sacked (4.669–71):

> non aliter quam si immissis ruat hostibus omnis
> Karthago aut antiqua Tyros, flammaeque furentes
> culmina perque hominum uoluantur perque deorum.

[40] Cf. F. L. Newton, 'Recurrent Imagery in *Aeneid* IV', *TAPA* 88 (1957), 31–43.

[41] Note 'populant . . . it nigrum campis agmen praedamque . . . conuectant . . . agmina cogunt castigantque moras'; an Ennian echo (502 Sk.) reinforces Roman 'color'. The Trojan departure is lent harsh tones by this simile. Klingner, 450, comments pertinently; R. G. M. Nisbet (*PVS* 18 (1978–80), 53) reacts to the simile thus: 'There could be no better description of the legalised destructiveness of the Roman army with its requisitioning of corn . . . organised supply-columns, and discipline on the march . . .'. Contrast La Penna, who finds it ornate and extraneous (liii), 'minuziosa', and justified only by the need for a pause during all this high drama and emotion (lxvi); contrast too G. Williams, 189: 'The ant-simile has the detachment and humour of the poet's own voice . . .'; an odd comment, in more than one way.

Just as if Carthage or ancient Tyre were falling, the enemy pouring in, and furious flames rolling on over the roofs of men, over the roofs of gods.

This is how devastating Dido's death is: as if destruction were upon the city—compare Hector.[42] But the simile is, as I say, the culmination of a line of linked images, and the significance of the linkage is the point to interpret now.

Venus 'lays *siege*' to Dido in Book 1: eventually Dido dies amidst lamentations such as might attend the *sack* of her city. There is indeed a detectable link. The one event seems to lead inexorably to the other: a line of imagery finds its conclusion. And it is most important to see that the simile of the sack issues out of linked military imagery, starting with Venus' words in 1.673ff.: it is important to see that Venus' 'siege' leads to Dido's 'sack'. It shows what Venus' action finally results in: her action in inflaming Dido (the siege) leads to Dido's death and the despair of her citizens (the sack). That has implications. If Venus actually foresaw all this, she was indeed vicious. But if, as I think we have reason to believe (pp. 23–7), she did not, if she was simply trying to secure Dido's friendliness towards Aeneas, it is still troubling: it means that she deployed her weapons with cruel irresponsibility, uncaring as to their power. . . . Inferences like these may be made if, once more, we consider Vergil's imagery, and the way he carefully links imagery. To put it in the terms I favour: the information delivered by the epic voice—the facts of the drama, the plot—tells us only that Venus 'helps' Dido, by 'working with' her, to fall in love with Aeneas; a further voice, operating by linked imagery, ties Venus into Dido's suffering and death and asks us to consider the implications of that connection. We shall see this happening on another occasion (Ch. 4 s. 12).

There is another problem in Book 4 which I may suitably confront now, a feature of the Dido narrative which, so far as I know, no commentator adequately explains—but which can be illuminated in the light of what has just been established. I have

---

[42] The simile is based on the one attached to the lamentations attending the death of Hector at *Iliad* 22.410f. Allusion is operative and the simile suggests (besides all the things I discuss in the text) that Dido is in the eyes of her citizens as Hector was in the eyes of his: beloved, indispensable, noble, and so on.

in mind Dido's, and Vergil's, references to 'exuuiae', 'spoils', and objects associated with these 'spoils'. The relevant passages are three. First, 4.494–7, where Dido orders the construction of the pyre thus:

> tu secreta pyram tecto interiore sub auras
> erige, et *arma* uiri thalamo quae fixa reliquit
> impius *exuuiasque* omnis lectumque iugalem
> quo perii, super imponas.

Do you in the centre of the palace secretly raise up a pyre skywards, and on it place the man's *arms* which, impious one, he left hanging[43] in my chamber, and all the *spoils*, and the marriage-bed which brought my doom.

Next, when the pyre has been constructed and the bed placed on top, Dido herself places various objects on it (507f.):

> super *exuuias ensemque* relictum
> effigiemque toro locat . . .

And on the bed she places the *spoils* and the *sword* that was left behind and an effigy . . .

Finally, at 645 ff. Dido climbs the pyre and is described thus:

> et altos
> conscendit furibunda rogos *ensemque* recludit
> Dardanium, non hos quaesitum munus in usus.
> hic, postquam *Iliacas uestis* notumque cubile
> conspexit, paulum lacrimis et mente morata
> incubuitque toro dixitque nouissima uerba:
> 'dulces *exuuiae*, dum fata deusque sinebat,
> accipite hanc animam meque his exsoluite curis.'

Frenzied she climbed the lofty pyre and unsheathed the Dardan *sword*, a gift not sought for such a use. And here she caught sight of the *Trojan clothes* and the well-known bed; and she stayed a while in tears and remembrance; and then she flung herself on the bed, and spoke her last words: 'sweet *spoils*, sweet while fate and a god allowed it, receive this my life, and release me from these cares.'

Let me, to begin with, explain the reference of certain key words in these passages, in the most economical way which fits the facts (we can, I think, be much preciser than commentators allow). First, when Dido refers to 'arma', 'arms', in the first

---

[43] See below, n. 45.

passage, she seems particularly to have in mind the 'ensis', the sword, which is what actually appears on the couch—in the event, she puts it there herself; Servius *auctus* on 4.495 has an explanation of why she should use the general term which is far from despicable: 'she applied the general word, lest by mention of the sword alone her design should be betrayed.' This sword, we are specifically told in the third passage, was a gift, 'munus', from (presumably) Aeneas. Next, the 'exuuiae' seem basically to be the 'Iliacas uestes', the 'Trojan clothes', mentioned in 648, although in this last passage—unlike the other two—Dido also seems to subsume under the term the sword she was given. And these 'Iliacae uestes' are, I think, also gifts from Aeneas to Dido: they are the gifts mentioned in 1.647 as 'munera Iliacis erepta ruinis' ['gifts snatched from the ruins of Troy'], which were in fact some luxurious clothes that had once belonged to Helen. (With nice and convincing symmetry, therefore, gifts are reciprocated: Aeneas gives Dido clothes and a sword and she does likewise to him, 4.261–4.) So (in summary): Aeneas has given Dido a sword as a present; he has also given her some clothes, which, as the one-time property of Helen, some might regard as inauspicious, not to say tactless, gifts;[44] and these Dido refers to as her 'spoils', 'exuuiae', and she gathers them to herself in the last moments of her life. I translate 'exuuiae' as 'spoils', unlike other commentators and translators,[45] partly because I doubt whether a poet like Vergil would often or ever use the word without exploiting at least the connotations of this its main sense. But mainly I translate it thus because the sense works well, indeed superbly, in the context.

It fits into the line of military imagery already identified in the love story of Dido. Spoils feature in conventional erotic

---

[44] Pöschl, 180, sees that the gifts are inauspicious, but he misses what seems to me the fair point that Aeneas might have chosen a more tactful present. Buchheit, 189, thinks that Vergil indicates in these gifts Dido's 'guilty longing for *Pergama* and *inconcessos hymenaeos* with Aeneas'!

[45] But see now R. G. Basto, *AJP* 105 (1984), 333–8, esp. 338; but Basto does not see the relation, which is crucial, to 'militia amoris'. Basto also argues (336f.) most seductively that 'fixa' in 4.495 has connotations of spoils: Dido hangs Aeneas' sword in her bedroom as a trophy indicating his change from warrior to lover. But I think this depends on Dido's being the agent of 'fixa', and this surely is difficult. Although at the moment I find Basto's final conclusions difficult to accept, I should stress that this is a stimulating article.

military imagery ('militia amoris'), in a variety of nuances, and in more or less coarse ways.[46] Vergil himself has in fact already, before the references to 'exuuiae', adapted the image to his own purpose in the Dido story. Juno uses it, commenting in a nastily ironic way on Venus' successful inflaming of Dido (4.93f.): 'Splendid indeed', she says, 'is the renown, and rich the *spoils* you win, you and your boy' ['egregiam uero laudem et spolia ampla refertis / tuque puerque tuus']. Dido's example is not coarse like some of the erotic poets', nor is it nastily ironical like Juno's. But it is 'militia amoris', fitting into the line of military imagery ('siege' to 'sack'). What we must do is imagine Dido, there, in her last moments, with Aeneas' sword and the clothes of Helen, Aeneas' ominous, tactless gifts, δῶρα ἄδωρα. Dido, and then Vergil after her, refers to these things which remain to her from Aeneas, which she seems to treasure, as her 'spoils'. The pathetic and bitter irony of that is, I think, only too clear. For Dido is saying, Vergil is saying, that she is the possessor of the proceeds of erotic victory. Nothing could be more awfully wrong, and presumably Dido is drawing attention, Vergil is drawing attention—by pathos, by irony—to exactly that fact. For consider the proceeds of her erotic victory: a hated adulteress's clothes and a sword with which to kill herself.[47] Consider her 'victory', implied in the word 'exuuiae'. She is not the victor in love's war, but the vanquished, the catastrophically vanquished—as the simile of the sack of the city which I discussed above is promptly about to underline. The use of 'exuuiae' ties pointedly into that line of imagery.

And so, if we probe the use of the word 'exuuiae', allow its implications to work, we can once again find Vergil suggesting, commenting: commenting on the pathos of Venus' victim, on the pathos of (it might also be said) Aeneas' victim—a further voice. We shall shortly hear more insinuations on the same topic.

I return now to a question raised above. Military imagery tied Venus directly into the suffering and death of Dido. But did Venus mean to produce such calamity? Or did she simply,

---

[46] Cf. Catull. 66.14; Prop. 2.14.27f., 3.13.12; Ov. *Am*. 1.10.29.
[47] Cf. Ov. *Her*. 7.195 and Sil. 8.148f. on Aeneas' gift of the sword.

unwittingly—but with cruel irresponsibility—administer via Cupid an overdose of 'uenenum'? An answer to this can be found via Juno–Allecto–Amata, the scene recognized above to be parallel to Venus–Cupid–Dido. In the process we shall find another disturbing parallel between that nasty team and the emperor's divine ancestress.

The simile which describes the effect of Allecto on Amata (cf. above, p. 16) runs as follows (7.377–84):

> immensam sine more furit lymphata per urbem.
> ceu quondam torto uolitans sub uerbere turbo,
> quem pueri magno in gyro uacua atria circum
> intenti ludo exercent—ille actus habena
> curuatis fertur spatiis; stupet inscia supra
> impubesque manus mirata uolubile buxum;
> dant animos plagae: non cursu segnior illo
> per medias urbes agitur populosque ferocis.

In frenzied abandon Amata rages throughout the great city. Just as at times a top spins under a whirled whip; boys intent on the game urge it around an empty court; it, driven by the whip, is borne on in great circles; the youthful throng bend over the whirling boxwood, puzzled and amazed; their blows give it life: with no slacker course is Amata driven through the midst of the city and its proud people.

We have learnt to expect 'multi-correspondence' in Vergilian similes,[48] and up to a point it is easy to demonstrate the correspondences here. For example, the whip corresponds to Allecto's snake, the 'anguis' of line 346, and Allecto herself corresponds to the boys, the 'youthful throng'; Amata provoked into maddened movement by Allecto's snake is figured as the whipped top. If we find it incongruous that Allecto and her vicious assault should be compared to boys in a game, the incongruity is only apparent, and the explanation of it productive. For, to Allecto, the cruel attack *is* a game; it is fun: she is the demon who, as we have been told, takes pleasure in evil (7.324–6); and the boys' innocence in their game can be construed as an ironic underlining of Allecto's malice. But there is one detail that may seem emphatically not to correspond:

---

[48] Cf. D. A. West, *JRS* 59 (1969), 40 ff.

'stupet inscia', the youthful throng's puzzlement, their lack of understanding. In the simile itself it is explicable, if unexpected. The boys do the whipping and can see the effect that their whipping produces (the spinning of the top); but they are puzzled, ignorant, 'inscii', as to how *that* action produces *this* engaging result—and are therefore fascinated. But in what sense could 'inscia' apply to Allecto, who is figured through the boys? Surely she is in no doubt as to what is happening, and how, and why? And pressure is in fact put on us to explain this detail because it seems a deliberate reversal of one in the simile to which Vergil is very probably referring, Tibullus 1.5.3f.:

> namque agor, ut per plana citus sola uerbere turben
> quem celer assueta uersat ab arte puer.

For I am driven, like a top whirling over a flat surface, which an agile boy drives with his customary skill.

Vergil's boys' ignorance is, I say, explicable; but Tibullus' boy, who is said to proceed with practised and conscious artistry, is more obvious, and Vergil has changed him. Why? Why does he so deliberately and strikingly wish to impute a measure of ignorance to Allecto, figured in his boys? In what sense could Allecto be thought of as 'inscia' and amazed ('stupet')? In the following way.[49]

The job given to her by Juno was to disrupt the peace, foment war, spoil the projected marriage of Lavinia to Aeneas. Allecto's first target was Amata: she cast a snake into her to make passion in her flare up for Turnus. It was a brilliant plan, as we have said, serving Juno's purpose well. But what was not enjoined upon her and not part of her plan—it was not necessary—was that Amata should rave madly round the city. That effect of her assault Allecto neither planned nor foresaw. She overdosed the queen. This is what 'inscia' in the simile tells us. But the simile also tells us that Allecto was pleased by this unexpected bonus. The fact that *that* action (the assault with the snake) produced *this* engaging result (Amata as a whirling dervish) puzzles but fascinates her: 'stupet'. So she watches.

[49] For a different attempt to interpret the 'inscia manus', see G. Williams, 63.

Allecto watches her top. And then, as it is so fascinating, she decides to apply even more stimulus (385 ff.).[50]

With Juno–Allecto–Amata, compare Venus–Cupid–Dido. In 1.664 ff. Venus announced her intention to make Dido fall in love with Aeneas as a measure to ensure her friendliness towards Aeneas and Aeneas' consequent safety. To this end she instructed Cupid to 'breathe hidden fire into Dido and deceive her with poison'. He did so, and Dido duly became passionately in love. But what was not enjoined upon him—it was not necessary—was that Dido should be sufficiently maddened as to rave like a Bacchant through the city (4.300 f.), and finally, in the extremity of despair, to commit suicide. That was an effect which, as I think we can now see clearly, was neither planned nor foreseen by Venus. We cannot say that Venus gained any pleasure from it, as Allecto did from her unexpected achievement. But, like Allecto, Venus caused an overdose to be administered, and the text certainly does not tell us that she regretted the consequences. It was a case of cruel, divine irresponsibility, a piece of irresponsibility which not only contributed to Dido's death, but had nearly disastrous implications for her son. Venus does not come well out of the Dido story by any account. But, in particular, what do we make of this goddess who overdoses with an irresponsibility and an effect like the Fury's? The troubling thought that occurred to us earlier (p. 19) may now be reformulated; the parallel in the stories of Allecto and Venus is closer than we thought—and,

---

[50] So I understand the text (but I find myself in disagreement with the commentators). I take the 'false Maenadism' section (385–405), ending 'reginam Allecto stimulis agit undique Bacchi', to involve a further assault by Allecto. The situation in this further stage is, I think, like that with Venus and Aeneas at 12.554 ff. (below, pp. 70–1). The text tells us the following two facts. (*1*) After raving through the city, Amata essays a *greater* craziness and wickedness (386), snatching Lavinia into the mountains, indulging rites and so on; but she gives her mad and impious impulses a cover: she feigns the authority of Bacchus, 'simulato numine Bacchi' (385). (2) Allecto does something in addition: she goads Amata with a powerful but false Bacchism. That seems to be the sense of 405: the Fury Allecto attacks with 'goads of Bacchus', but since she is a Fury and not Bacchus they cannot be the genuine article. Two 'facts'; but which is the truth? Is Amata responsible for her greater madness and phoney Bacchism? Or is Allecto? After my discussion below (Ch. 2 s. 2) the problem will be a familiar one, and the answer evident. We should infer that Allecto 'works with' a potential in Amata, in this second as in the first stage of her assault. Human and divine are interacting and interdependent.

indeed, reinforced by yet more invention.[51] Vergil intrudes a questioning voice by discreet manipulation of invention and arrangement (as well as imagery, etc.), and we must not resist the implications. Venus will occupy us again shortly.

3. Linked motifs; dramatic irony; invention, arrangement, and not resisting implications; allusion: Evander, Hercules, Aeneas, Augustus, Venus and Vulcan

On the divinely forged shield of Aeneas, Augustus is depicted with light beaming from his temples. Vergil phrases it thus (8.680): 'geminas cui tempora flammas / laeta *uomunt*' ['His exultant temples *vomit* forth twin flames']. The metaphor used here for the radiation of light is very remarkable; no close parallel can be adduced before Vergil.[52] The phrase 'flammas [or something very similar] uomere' occurs on four other occasions in the *Aeneid*, three of them in Book 8, like the one just quoted. They are as follows. First, Aeneas' divinely made helmet (8.620): 'terribilem cristis galeam flammasque uomentem' ['A helmet terrifying in its crests and vomiting flames']. Secondly, further back in the book, Evander describes Cacus as more or less literally 'vomiting' fire in his battle with Hercules (8.259): 'incendia uana uomentem' ['vomiting futile fires']. Similarly, at 8.198f.: 'atros / ore uomens ignis' ['vomiting black fire from his mouth']. And we may compare another phrase in Evander's description of Cacus (8.252f.), 'faucibus ingentem fumum . . . / euomit' ['he vomits forth vast smoke from his maw']. The fourth example of 'ignem [*vel sim.*] uomere' is attached to Aeneas' shield which he holds aloft as he arrives by sea to assist the beleaguered Trojans (10.271): 'uastos umbo

---

[51] Venus in Book 4 is allusively compared to Dionysus and, in large part as a result of her actions, Dido becomes 'Bacchic': 4.301 'bacchatur' (and note the following simile): see Ch. 4 p. 197. Allecto is explicitly said to usurp Bacchic power and to goad Amata into acting the Maenad: 7.385ff., above, p. 26. Allecto and her effect are more explicitly, more concretely 'Dionysiac', but the parallel which Vergil has organized is clear—and troubling. Note too that Dido's perception of herself as an Orestes at 4.471–3 might cast Venus in the role of Fury (i.e. an Allecto figure). Note in particular 4.473, 'ultricesque sedent in limine Dirae' and 7.343, 'obsedit limen Amatae'. (In the Orestes simile of 4.471–3, note 'scaenis', which is, among other things, a most remarkable 'signal' to another text: cf. Ch. 3 p. 103).

[52] In pre-Vergilian uses the phrase 'ignem uomere', *vel sim.*, is confined to fire-breathing monsters and volcanoes: see Wigodsky, 'The Arming of Aeneas', 214. Wigodsky, 214ff., has some stimulating comment on the passages I discuss in this section.

uomit aureus ignis' ['Its golden boss vomits forth awesome fires'].

Clearly these passages are linked by their imagery, perhaps better to say, by their motifs. It is particularly hard not to make connections in Book 8. Puzzlement at such strange *metaphors* for Augustus and Aeneas should spur us to associate them—and then to remember that Vergil had *literally* described the monstrous Cacus twice in such terms, and a further time in a phrase closely resembling the others. Why should our heroes be equipped with imagery that recalls the monstrous Cacus? How do we interpret the pattern? A further voice is jogging us to questions.

Some context is necessary. First we should remind ourselves of the structure and strategy of Book 8. In it three great struggles are assembled and associated: Aeneas' coming struggle with Turnus, Hercules' destruction of Cacus (related by Evander), and Augustus' victory over Antony and Cleopatra (depicted on the shield).[53] All seem, or may seem (and I think Vergil wishes them initially to seem), ideal and exemplary instances of civilized heroes vanquishing the powers of passion, madness or brutishness, powers which threaten civilization.[54] All seem—to use the terms that the *Aeneid* encourages us to use—exemplary instances of 'pietas' defeating 'furor', in the *Aeneid*'s past, present, and future.[55] The exemplary Hercules appears to prefigure the exemplary Aeneas, who prefigures the

---

[53] Cf. Otis, 330ff.; Galinsky, *The Herakles Theme*, 141ff.; Wigodsky, 'The Arming of Aeneas', 219; Wlosok, *Die Göttin Venus*, 66, with n. 53 containing full bibliography.

[54] The way I describe the Hercules–Cacus episode in this paragraph is how it appears to, e.g., Otis (n. 53).

[55] The *Aeneid* encourages us to see a simple polar opposition between the typical and essential Roman virtue of 'pietas' on the one hand and mad passion, 'furor', on the other in two commanding and programmatic passages. The first simile of the poem (1.148–53), drawn strikingly from political life and suggesting a political interpretation of the poem's mythical events (cf. above n. 9, Pöschl, 21f.), opposes the statesman 'pietate grauem' to the seditious 'uulgus' among whom 'furor arma ministrat'. Jupiter's great prophecy then ends with a vision of 'Furor impius' in bonds (1.294–6). (After this we might expect to see such a polar and simple opposition reflected in the events of the *Aeneid*—and in an episode like Hercules–Cacus. But as the events of the *Aeneid* unfold, they teach us that a distinction along these attractive lines is not easily realizable in practice. And the paradigmatic Hercules–Cacus episode turns out, against our expectations, to be a paradigm of this same lesson.)

exemplary Augustus: Hercules (and Aeneas) are mythical paradigms for an idealized Augustus. Such, I think, may well be the way in which the episode first appears to us. We should remember that Hercules in Vergil's time was paraded both as a benefactor of civilization[56] and (and simultaneously) as a paradigm of Augustus: Horace, influenced by a tradition of ruler-panegyric, several times uses Hercules' heroic example as an illustration of and comparison for his ruler;[57] and Vergil himself had already compared both Aeneas and Augustus to Hercules, and the Hercules he adduces for Augustus (6.801f.) also brings to mind the Hercules of ruler-panegyric.[58] In addition we should note that Vergil has elevated Cacus into a monstrous figure like that of 'Furor' in Jupiter's prophecy (1.294).[59] All these facts help to suggest an idealized and

[56] Cf. Cic. *ND* 2.62, *Tusc.* 1.28f., *Off.* 3.25; Horace in n. 57 and Seneca in n. 70. This was probably the Stoics' Hercules, though the evidence on Hercules in pre-Senecan Stoicism is annoyingly sparse. It is to be noted that Hercules the benefactor of civilization was interpreted by some, including it seems Roman (but not earlier) Stoics, as having earned divinity because of his benefactions: he was thus a useful paradigm for more prudent panegyrists of Augustus (see n. 57). Cicero reports deification in the passages above, though he is circumspect in his phrasing in each case. In *ND* he reports the deification of Hercules, and assigns the same history to Castor and Pollux, Aesculapius, Liber, and Romulus as well; in *Tusc.* that of Hercules plus Castor and Pollux, Liber, and Romulus; in *Off.*, that of Hercules alone. For Cicero's cautious phrasing note e.g. *ND* 2.62, 'suscepit autem uita hominum consuetudoque communis ut beneficiis excellentis uiros in caelum fama ac uoluntate tollerent' ['human experience and general custom have made it a practice to raise distinguished benefactors to heaven through fame and gratitude']. See further E. V. Arnold, *Roman Stoicism* (London, 1911), 233, 296; M. Pohlenz, *Die Stoa*, vol. ii (Göttingen, 1949), 140f. Lucr. 5.22ff. seems to me, *pace* B. Frischer, *The Sculpted Word* (Berkeley, 1982), 225ff., to presuppose a Stoic hero Hercules considered by his followers to be literally or metaphorically divine.

[57] Hercules the deified benefactor is represented as an analogue for Augustus, also eventually to be deified: *Odes*, 3.3.1ff., 3.14.1ff., *Epist.* 2.1.5ff. (To state or imply divinity after death is quite cautious panegyric: Horace had been less cautious back in *Odes*, 1.2). The basic comparison of ruler to Hercules and to other heroes and deities (like Castor, Pollux, Dionysus) seems to have been popularized in panegyrics of Alexander: see Austin on *Aen.* 6.801ff., and (with full bibliography) C. O. Brink, *Horace on Poetry: Epistles Book II* (Cambridge, 1982), 39–42. Horace is also clearly influenced (esp. in 3.3) by a Stoic Hercules and by the Roman Stoic version (if such it be) of Hercules' and other heroes' deification (see n. 56). But I imagine that contamination between the 'philosophical' and 'panegyrical' Hercules had occurred before Horace.

[58] On Vergil's comparison of Aeneas and Augustus to Hercules (implicit or explicit) see Galinsky, *The Herakles Theme*, 132ff. On his comparison of Augustus to Hercules at 6.801f. see Austin ad loc.

[59] See Fordyce on 8.184–279; Galinsky, *The Herakles Theme*, 142.

paradigmatic significance, indeed a propaganda significance, for the Hercules–Cacus episode of Book 8. The deified benefactor Hercules prefigures Aeneas; and he prefigures Augustus, soon similarly to be deified. The way Evander himself introduces the hero also suggests ideal and paradigmatic significance for the episode.[60]

Horace, if I may digress for a moment, prefigures Augustus and his victory over Antony in another paradigm, the battle of Jupiter and the Giants.[61] From it he draws the following conclusion (*Odes* 3.4.65ff.):

> uis consili expers mole ruit sua:
> uim temperatam di quoque prouehunt
> in maius . . .

Force that is devoid of 'rational judgement' falls headlong under its own weight: force that is 'advised, controlled' the gods join in promoting to greater things . . . [I have glossed, rather than translated 'consilium' and 'temperatam' in order to bring out important implications.]

Pithily and conveniently phrased, this can be seen as a manifesto of the *means* of warfare employed by a civilized hero. More specifically, it is Horace's manifesto of the means of warfare adopted by a civilized Roman hero, in particular, of course, by Augustus himself. Force that is advised, controlled, rational (the colouring is Stoic), this is the means of warfare operated by the Augustan hero (whose *end* is peace and civilization). Irrational force (employed by barbarians like Antony) brings about its own destruction.[62]

I have digressed to Horace partly because he provides a convenient formula for assessing the *Aeneid* and its Stoically burdened, *pius* hero in the theatre of war. 'Vis temperata' is the means we should expect our self-subordinating, proto-Augus-

---

[60] See below, p. 33.
[61] See E. Fraenkel, *Horace* (Oxford, 1957), 281 f.
[62] I give parallels and context for this type of military philosophizing or 'image-making' in my article 'Vergil and the Politics of War'. Cf. Anchises at 6.852 f., quoted above, p. 4. When Anchises and others advocate clemency ('parcere subiectis') as well as the warring down of the proud, they are spelling out an important aspect of 'advised force'. It is part of 'advised force' to know when not to use it: force must be judiciously employed *and* judiciously refrained from if 'foedus' and peace are to be achieved. See further Ch. 4 p. 187 and 'Vergil and the Politics of War', 195.

tan Aeneas to employ; it is in effect what Anchises orders Roman Aeneas to employ (6.851–3);[63] and indeed it is what Aeneas himself seems eager to try to employ (note e.g. 8.537–40, 11.108ff., 12.176ff.).[64] But, of course, in the heat of battle, at crucial points, he cannot. Furious, inadvised passion dominates him in a sequence of killings in 10.517ff.; at the end of the poem he is 'furiis accensus et ira / terribilis': at these times the force he employs (his *means* of warfare) is indistinguishable from his opponents'—though his *aim* may ultimately be different. This, in fact, is one of the points Vergil is concerned to make in the battle narrative of the *Aeneid*: 'uis' is indivisible, Horace and the propagandists have it wrong—and the *Aeneid's* own neat, polar opposition of 'pietas' and 'furor' is, in this respect at least, too neat.

We return to Book 8, first to the account of Hercules. Scrutinizing the description of Hercules' conflict with Cacus (190–267), we find that he too in his conduct is as 'furens' as anyone in the poem.[65] So he prefigures Aeneas surely enough, but not as an idealized paradigm for a paradigmatic Aeneas (and Augustus), but as a real foretaste of what Aeneas will really be like; Vergil tempts us into thinking he will give us propaganda, but in fact delivers truth. Hercules' and Aeneas' aims in combat may be very different from Cacus' and Turnus', but their means are, perhaps because they must be, fairly similar: 'uis' is indivisible. Another detail in the book suggests the same point: Vulcan forges Aeneas' weapons for him; but Vulcan, according to Vergil, is also Cacus' father.[66]

And now we can return to the linked 'vomiting' motifs. The fiery light beaming from Aeneas and Augustus must among other things symbolize their power;[67] and Augustus is associated with his prototype by the shared image. But the image also

[63] See n. 62.
[64] See 'Vergil and the Politics of War', esp. 192ff.
[65] Galinsky, 'The Hercules–Cacus Episode', has useful things to say on this episode, particularly on the connections between Cacus and Turnus (esp. p. 35). But we disagree in this particular respect. He detects a change to 'uis temperata' in Hercules after 8.232. I do not see it. Hercules tears Cacus' cavern apart, rains boughs and rocks as large as mill-stones down upon him, hurls himself through the fire and smoke, and throttles him till his eyes start out. Is not this a continuation of Hercules 'furens'? Cf. Wigodsky, 'The Arming of Aeneas', 215.
[66] 8.198. This is Vergil's invention: see Fordyce on 8.184–279.
[67] Cf. Wigodsky, 'The Arming of Aeneas', 216.

acutely raises the question of 'uis' again. In fact, it imputes to both Aeneas and Augustus some of the monstrous force of Cacus: for Cacus' characteristically monstrous action (vomiting fire) is vividly reflected in the imagery that attaches to the power of our august heroes. The point we have already noticed is again being made, but now most emphatically—by a further voice operating through linked motifs. Necessary though it may be, force is not comfortably distinguishable along Horatian lines—far from it: force on the 'right' side may not only be as passionate as the enemy's, but monstrous like an enemy's; and the linked motifs extend the application of that lesson beyond Aeneas down to Augustus himself. Of course Cacus' fire is 'uanus' and 'ater' as the fire of Aeneas and the refulgent Augustus is not; and this may signify the different aims to which the force, typified in each case by the fire, is directed. But the striking verb 'uomo' associates the three situations more than the epithets distinguish them, and the point sticks: the means, the force deployed by each protagonist, is or will be force, similar and unpleasant (the unpleasant resonance of 'uomo' is not to be ignored). The insinuation then recurs in 10.271 when Aeneas makes his spectacular return to the beleaguered Trojans. He comes as a saviour, but we should not be surprised by ugly and violent means on his part: the boss of his shield 'vomits fire', recalling a monster.

In a further voice therefore, exploiting linked motifs, Vergil puts insinuations into his narrative, and comments thereby on comfortable Stoic and Roman dogmas concerning force. But what are we supposed to make of Evander? There is a comment on him too. Evander talked of Cacus as 'incendia uana uomentem' and so on, and it is clear that Evander thought he was choosing vividly brutal phrases for a vividly brutal monster, a monster quite different from the saviour Hercules—and, of course, from the saviour Aeneas. However, Vergil, building on Evander's choice of words, is soon to insinuate that the division between heroes and monsters is not quite so clear-cut as Evander appears to imagine; and in retrospect the attitude of Evander may seem rather naïve, even gullible. If indeed we reread Evander's 'incendia uana uomentem' and so on, which in Evander's view befits a monster, in the light of 8.620ff., which contain the same phraseology applied to Aeneas and

Augustus, an effect quite close to *dramatic irony* (Ch. 5) can be felt: Evander's words mean more and different things to us than they do to him. We may detect in this irony a further voice making an insinuation about Evander: an advocate of the simple life, he is a little simple in other respects too. This simplicity is evidenced in two other ways.

The first concerns Hercules again. Evander seems to regard him as a saviour, a hero who came for their salvation; he seems to view him almost as Hercules the Benefactor, the Stoics' Hercules.[68] That seems to me the clear implication of the way Evander describes him,[69] when he explains to Aeneas the reason for the solemn celebrations being performed in his honour (8.185ff.):

> non haec sollemnia nobis,
> has ex more dapes, hanc tanti numinis aram
> uana superstitio ueterumque ignara deorum
> imposuit: saeuis, hospes Troiane, periclis
> seruati facimus meritosque nouamus honores.

No groundless superstition ignorant of the gods of old imposed on us these solemn rites, this customary feast, this altar to a mighty deity: saved from savage dangers, Trojan guest, do we perform and renew the worship due.

Note too how he describes the arrival of Hercules on that fateful day (200f.):

> attulit et nobis aliquando optantibus aetas
> auxilium aduentumque dei.

For us, too, time brought a god's advent and aid, in answer to our prayers.

That surely is also language that befits a saviour: someone who arrived to deliver them. Well, did he? Yes and no.

Certainly Hercules destroyed the Arcadians' monstrous enemy. But his *motive* in doing so was not the Arcadians' salvation, as Evander's own evidence then shows; and in this he

---

[68] Cf. above, p. 29 and below, n. 70.
[69] And Evander persuades, e.g., Fordyce. In his note on 8.184–279 he writes: 'Hercules comes to Evander's people as a deliverer (189 "seruati").'

is quite unlike the Beneficial or Stoic Hercules.[70] Hercules was in fact *leaving* Pallanteum, as Evander tells us, with no intention of tackling Cacus at all—until, in the process of his departure, the lowing of his oxen was answered by one of those that Cacus had stolen (8.213–18):

> interea, cum iam stabulis saturata moueret
> Amphitryoniades armenta abitumque pararet,
> discessu mugire boues atque omne querelis
> impleri nemus et colles clamore relinqui.
> reddidit una boum uocem uastoque sub antro
> mugiit et Caci spem custodita fefellit.

Meanwhile, when Amphitryon's son was already moving the well-fed herds from their stalls, and was preparing his departure, the oxen lowed on leaving, filling the grove with their plaint, quitting the hills in clamour. One heifer returned the cry, and mooed in the depths of the cavern, and in her captivity baffled Cacus' hopes.

That was what made Hercules tackle Cacus: the discovery that Cacus had stolen four of his herd, four of the 'spolia', the spoils he had won by slaying Geryon, spoils of which he was proud, 'superbus' (202). Incidentally, therefore, in the process of exacting vengeance for the stealing of his spoils, Hercules became the Arcadians' deliverer. He did not intend to. I do not therefore think he quite merits the way Evander presents and honours him. Misled by gratitude and relief, Evander sees only the deliverer and saviour, where we—on Evander's own evidence—can see a different figure: a mighty Hercules swayed by fierce emotion, who is a benefactor by accident. Again, Evander is shown to be slightly gullible. A much funnier demonstration of his simplicity is shortly to follow. But before that there is a point to be drawn out. We remember that in the

---

[70] The Beneficial Hercules' disinterested motive is stressed by Cicero and Seneca. Cic. *Off.* 3.25, 'est secundum naturam pro omnibus gentibus . . . conseruandis aut iuuandis maximos labores molestiasque suscipere imitantem Herculem' ['it is in accordance with nature to undertake the greatest toils and hardships, for the sake of aiding or saving the world, imitating Hercules']. Sen. *Ben.* 1.13.3, 'Hercules nihil sibi uicit; orbem terrarum transiuit non concupiscendo, sed iudicando quid uinceret, malorum hostis, bonorum uindex, terrarumque marisque pacator' ['Hercules conquered nothing for himself; he crossed the world, not in greed, but, in judging what to conquer, an enemy of the wicked, a defender of the good, a peacemaker on land and sea'].

structure of the book Hercules prefigures Aeneas who prefigures Augustus. In Book 8 we see Hercules fiercely exacting vengeance for the theft of his spoils; and we see that, in the process of doing so, he removes a public enemy. There are some scholars who believe that at the end of Book 12 Aeneas removes a public enemy. That, I think, is questionable, but the parallel is possible. What is certain is that Aeneas, no more than Hercules, was motivated by a desire to remove a public enemy. He acted out of a fierce impulse to avenge Turnus' taking of spoils. The parallel in this respect is, although very far from exact, perceptible. Hercules in fact prefigures Aeneas rather more closely than we thought (in *ends* as well as *means*); and I think the parallel is suggestive and thought-provoking.[71]

Venus and Vulcan

Vergil has already provoked me to say disrespectful things about Venus. Before I proceed to the Venus and Vulcan scene and find myself further provoked, it might be timely to recall or stress certain facts. Venus was the reputed ancestress of the Julian *gens*. The dictator Julius had honoured her with a temple in his new forum. She was exploited in the propaganda of Augustus.[72] One might expect Rome's great epic to defer to her and assign to her dignity, benevolence, magnificence. In fact—as we have already seen—this is not the case. The explicit action (the epic voice) as well as further insinuating voices present her in roles that are traditional but hardly flattering, paralleled but not quite, one would think, what her Julian claimants would wish to promote. It becomes quite clear that Vergil is not fond of this goddess,[73] in spite of her illustrious associations. There could be many reasons for that.

In the story of Dido we have already seen Venus displaying some of the viciousness of the Aphrodite of Euripides' *Hippolytus*—and we shall see more of that. In 1.227ff., by way of

---

[71] Cf. my comments on the end of the poem, Ch. 4 s. 10.
[72] See Weinstock, 80ff.; R. Syme, *The Roman Revolution* (Oxford, 1939), 66 n. 3; A. Wlosok, *Die Göttin Venus*, 118ff.
[73] I take a very different view of Vergil's Venus than, say, A. Wlosok: note e.g. *Die Göttin Venus*, 115, where Venus is described as 'die Erscheinungsform der göttlichen Gnade'. Klingner, 406, and Putnam, 174, offer perceptive comment.

contrast, she is as plangent as the Aphrodite of *Iliad* 5. In 8.370ff., her scene with Vulcan, she reveals the devious sexuality which fuelled such stories as *Od.* 8.266ff. (the affair with Ares). Some have found the scene regrettable because of its lack of morals or dignity.[74] This is to discount Vergil's sense of humour—which does exist. It also discounts the fact that Vergil presents no god (with perhaps one exception) as consistently dignified, or indeed, in our terms, as consistently respectable. Gods, including very important gods, display dubious morality. They permit themselves licence not necessarily permitted to mortals, by them or indeed by mortals themselves. Morality is one of those crucial areas where (cf. life and death) gods reveal their difference from men (cf. below, pp. 84ff.). The Venus and Vulcan episode already hints at this difference, but with humour and irony. It also shows up Evander again.

The point is in essence as follows. Just before the Venus–Vulcan scene, in 8.362ff., Evander, king of the poor Arcadians, the people who occupy the site of Rome in exemplary and symbolic simplicity,[75] has (true to his principles) enjoined upon Aeneas Stoical hardiness, Stoical simplicity. 'Dare to scorn wealth,' he says, 'and come with no asperity to poverty' ['aude, hospes, contemnere opes . . . rebusque ueni non asper egenis']. And, to put his message in a nutshell, he employs this grandly religio-philosophical instruction:

> aude, hospes, contemnere opes, *et te quoque dignum finge deo* . . .

Dare to scorn wealth and *do you too* [like Hercules, who has just been talked of] *mould yourself to be worthy of god* . . .

To be Stoically hardy—despising wealth and so on—is, for

---

[74] Cf. Macrobius 1.24.6f. Coleman, 162, remarks: 'The lofty seriousness of the theodicy that on the above [i.e. his own] interpretation underlies the whole divine participation in the narrative is on a number of occasions [e.g. in the Venus–Vulcan scene] dangerously undermined by the anthropomorphic realism with which the gods are portrayed.' This, intended as adverse criticism, neatly demonstrates how dangerous but easy it is to maintain preconceived ideas—and how it is imperative not to resist implications. K. W. Gransden's view of the episode (*Virgil: Aeneid Book VIII*, Cambridge, 1976, 29) is that 'One may also see the Venus–Vulcan episode as evolutionary allegory', a rather desperate resort.
[75] Cf. e.g. Pöschl, 69f.

Evander, to follow divine principle. Simplicity and fortitude are in his view virtues esteemed by God; and to aspire to them is to aspire to divinity.[76] Immediately adjacent to Evander's instruction, Vergil exhibits gods in a scene of seduction and opulence. The irony is surely clear: clear, humorous, and instructive.[77] The gullible Evander has a view of God which Vergil's organization of scenes shows to be emphatically misplaced. This is a fine example of arrangement, 'dispositio', the task of deciding when and where to deliver a certain piece of information, in order to affirm a point or suggest implications. Vergil has decided to juxtapose these two scenes, that juxtaposition has implications, and we must not resist those implications: a further voice is speaking to us. In retrospect the arrangement causes us to sense something like dramatic irony in Evander's confidently pious words, which underlines his gullibility. Meanwhile the irony of the 'dispositio' emphasizes the difference between men and gods, which some men misunderstand. Gods do not have and do not have to have the same morals or standards as principled men. They may make all sorts of demands of men, and commit men to a desperately earnest world; but for their part they manifest a lack of earnestness, an

---

[76] The phrase 'te quoque dignum finge deo' is not, however, pellucid. 'Deo' in particular has caused difficulty. Sen. *Epist. Mor.* 18.12f. cites the phrase in support of Stoic doctrine and interprets it Stoically: man should—by, e.g., despising wealth—conform to the divine reason which directs the universe; in so doing he becomes 'worthy of God'. Fordyce ad loc. doubts whether Vergil had such ideas (on which see further Eden ad loc.) in mind. I think the Latin imposes an interpretation like this, or not too far from this; and our proper question should be, 'did *Evander* have such ideas in mind?' The answer to that is: very likely. They suit his Stoical and rather monolithic *Weltanschauung*. 'Deo' cannot refer to Hercules for the reason cited by Fordyce, R. D. Williams (7–12), and Eden ad loc.: 'quoque'. An interpretation in antiquity (quoted by Servius *auctus*) was that deo = 'immortalitate'. As Eden succinctly remarks, 'this is implied by the phrase, but not expressed.'

[77] It is instructively misunderstood by Coleman (163): 'The spectacle of an adulterous beauty-queen calculatingly turning her charms on a long-suffering husband would have delighted Callimacheans . . . but [it] gravely detracts from the seriousness of the surrounding narrative. Evander has just taken leave of Aeneas with the lofty moral advice: "aude hospes, contemnere opes . . .".' Again (cf. above, n. 74) this is meant as adverse criticism of Vergil, and is a spectacular example of implications being missed. Slightly closer to the truth is G. Williams, 152. Seneca twice quotes Evander's words in support of Stoic arguments (*Epist. Mor.* 18.12, referred to in n. 76, and 31.11); I doubt therefore whether he perceived any irony.

Unernst.[78] They may compel men to earnestness and indeed to morality, but they themselves are unconstrained. Implications like these emerge. The topic will occupy us again (Ch. 2).

I proceed to detail. First, and incidentally, I should like to draw attention to an example of one of Vergil's minor but effective narrative techniques. Heinze has shown,[79] picking up a hint preserved in a note of Servius,[80] how Vergil's descriptions of dawn are often adapted to the mood of the succeeding scene. Here the description of *night* is adapted to, indeed heralds, the mood of the coming scene. The fall of night is described in a phrase and image used only this once by Vergil (8.369): 'Nox ruit et fuscis tellurem *amplectitur* alis' ['Night rushes down and *embraces* the earth with dusky wings']. 'Amplectitur', especially in the immediate proximity of 'At Venus' (370), has an obvious erotic resonance, and sets the reader's mood for what follows. Indeed, it anticipates the 'amplexus' of 388 and 405.

Next I substantiate my point about divine opulence and Evander's gullibility. Venus and Vulcan have a 'golden chamber' ['thalamo . . . aureo'] (372) and 'soft coverlets' ['mollibus . . . stratis'] (415) on their bed. This would surely have shocked the proudly 'pauper' Evander who occupies a 'humble dwelling' ['angustum tectum'] (366), who beds Aeneas down on 'leaves' (note the verbal parallel: 'stratis . . . foliis', 367f., 'mollibus e stratis', 415), and preaches poverty and simplicity as divine conditions. The irony (the insinuating voice) is surely evident. But now let us turn to the interesting and sensuous drama that takes place in these opulent surroundings.

Venus wishes Vulcan to forge arms for her son. Similarly, Thetis in *Iliad* 18.369ff. had had to ask Hephaestus to make armour for Achilles. Thetis had no need to resort to persuasion: Hephaestus was already in her debt and willing to do whatever she asked. Venus, however, has much need of her

---

[78] I am taking over K. Reinhardt's term. A surprising amount of Reinhardt's comment on the *Unernst* of the Homeric gods has, I think, validity for the gods of the *Aeneid*: see *Das Parisurteil* (Frankfurt, 1938), esp. 12–14 and, on the theomachy, *Die Ilias und ihr Dichter* (Göttingen, 1961), 446f.

[79] Heinze, 366ff. The point is taken up by Pöschl, 171f., but implicitly denied by La Penna, lxxxvii.

[80] Servius on *Aen.* 11.183.

In Medias Res: Examples Various

powers of persuasion, for hers is a ticklish situation. Vulcan is her husband and Aeneas is her son by another man. She needs to tread deftly, exploiting all her talents (and in so doing she recalls not only Thetis but the sexually guileful Hera in the 'Deception of Zeus', *Iliad* 14.153ff.).

Her request is carefully phrased and pitched, a model *suasoria*,[81] combining reason (displayed through *exempla*), flattery, deference, and pathos. In addition she 'breathes divine love into her words'. Lines 373–86:

> incipit et dictis diuinum aspirat amorem:
> 'dum bello Argolici uastabant Pergama reges
> debita casurasque inimicis ignibus arces,
> non ullum auxilium miseris, non arma rogaui
> artis opisque tuae, nec te, *carissime coniunx*,
> incassumue tuos uolui exercere labores,
> quamuis et Priami deberem plurima natis,
> et durum Aeneae fleuissem saepe laborem.
> nunc Iouis imperiis Rutulorum constitit oris:
> ergo eadem supplex uenio et sanctum mihi numen
> arma rogo, *genetrix nato*. te filia Nerei . . .'

Breathing divine love into her words, she says: 'while the Argive kings were with war devastating Troy's doomed towers and its citadels fated to fall by hostile fire, I asked no aid for the sufferers, nor weapons from your skill and resource, nor, *dearest husband*, did I wish to task you and your labours in vain, although I owed much to the sons of Priam and often wept over the harsh trials of Aeneas. Now by Jupiter's orders he has settled on Rutulian shores. So I come as a suppliant, and ask a deity who is holy to me for arms, *a mother for her son*. The daughter of Nereus [Thetis] was able to persuade you . . .'

A model *suasoria*: actually, it is *nearly* a model *suasoria*. It is not perfect for its specific purpose, for it does not immediately achieve its aim. Vulcan in response is described as 'hesitating', 'delaying' ['cunctantem']. Why? There can only be one reason. He is disinclined to make arms for his wife's bastard offspring. When Venus allowed the pathos of her situation to generate the moving collocation 'genetrix nato' ['a mother for her son'], it seems that her 'carissimus' and legitimate 'coniunx' felt pique rather than pity and was not therefore immediately persuaded: 'carissime coniunx' and 'genetrix nato' are amusingly (from the

---
[81] See Eden on 8.374ff.

reader's point of view) juxtaposed, and Venus' slight *faux pas* revealed. But where speech did not immediately persuade, actions, the embraces of the goddess of love, do (387ff.):

> dixerat et niueis hinc atque hinc diua lacertis
> *cunctantem* amplexu molli fouet. ille *repente*
> accepit solitam flammam . . .

So spoke the goddess and, as he *hesitated*, she put her snowy arms about him and fondled him in soft embrace. *Suddenly* he felt the familiar flame . . .

And Vulcan proceeds to declare his enthusiastic willingness to do what Venus wants, and does what she wants—after enjoying (406) the love-making implicitly promised in the embrace of 388.[82]

I think it is already clear that the scene has and is meant to have its funny aspects. Details will be mentioned in a moment. It is appropriate to interpose this thought: such amusing immorality, amusing ingloriousness, permissible among gods, is not permitted to mortals like Aeneas, who are committed by gods to morality, earnestness, and glory. Scenes like these can make his fate seem that much more pitiable, that much more *unfair*. Why should the *ernst* Aeneas have to be *ernst*, and do the biddings of *unernst* gods? Vergil's invention intrudes a further voice.[83]

I point to some details in the humour. First, a Vergilian insinuation, effected by allusion. The enthralled Vulcan is described thus (394): 'tum pater aeterno . . . deuinctus amore' ['the father Vulcan, shackled by eternal love']. This is based on Lucretius' vivid description of Mars' captivation by Venus (1.33f.):

> in gremium qui saepe tuum se
> reicit aeterno deuictus uulnere amoris . . .

Mars who, conquered by the eternal wound of love, often flings himself back into your lap . . .

So, even as Vergil describes Venus' overwhelming effect on her

---

[82] On the interpretation of 406, 'coniugis infusus gremio', see H. D. Jocelyn, *LCM* 9 (1984), 20f.

[83] I develop this topic in Ch. 2. As we shall see, grander gods than Venus and Vulcan are similarly *unernst*.

In Medias Res: Examples Various

husband, he alludes to the most famous of her illicit affairs: behind her principled approach to her husband (if it can be called that), we sense, amusingly, her unprincipled embrace of the god of war—a pleasing further voice. (Lucretius uses the word 'deuictus', 'conquered', of the god of war, producing a witty paradox. Vergil's 'deuinctus' is aurally very similar and thus does not impede the allusion. But why has he changed the image? Perhaps to produce another paradox, and to emphasize Vulcan's discomfiture. When Vulcan discovered the affair of Venus and Mars, he engineered it so that they were caught in shackles. Here Venus shackles him.)

There is surely humour, too, in the contrapuntal positioning of 'cunctantem' (the result of Venus' speech) and 'repente' (the result of Venus' embrace). A lot of words got Venus a little way; her touch is immediate in its successful effect. The contrast between the effect of word and action is amusingly underlined by the placing of the two key words.

And there is humour in Vulcan's reply (395 ff.):

> 'quid causas petis ex alto? fiducia cessit
> quo tibi, diua, mei? . . .
> . . .
> et nunc, si bellare paras atque haec tibi mens est,
> quidquid in arte mea possum promittere curae,
> quod fieri ferro liquidoue potest electro,
> quantum ignes animaeque ualent—absiste precando
> uiribus indubitare tuis.'

Why do you look so far back for a plea? Where, goddess, has your faith in me gone? . . . And now, if you are preparing for war, and this is your intention, whatever devotion in my craft I can promise to you, whatever can be achieved by iron and molten electrum, whatever fire and bellows may avail—Oh, cease by entreating me to distrust your powers!

In the long and increasingly excited sentence that begins 'et nunc si', Vulcan is in fact so excited that he gets his grammar wrong. I think that the grammatical anomalies of 'uiribus indubitare tuis' (the odd dative, the new and perhaps clumsy compound) may be meant to reflect the excited confusion of the aroused god. More importantly and definitely, the series of clauses constructed in 'breathless asyndeton' and concluding with 'quantum ignes animaeque ualent' runs into anacoluthon:

the syntax collapses in the god's impatience. Eden, from whom the phrase 'breathless asyndeton' comes, comments well (on 8.401 ff.): the series of clauses is 'each one the subject or object of a verb which should follow them, but does not, because Vulcan is carried away by his emotion and substitutes a quite different main clause'. And then he quotes the prolix but often acute Victorian commentator, James Henry, who writes: 'in the midst of his protestation, and just as he was going to say "All this and more I promise you" or "All this and more I swear to you" he stops short, breaks off . . . and simpers: "Demand no more as a favour what you have the right and power to command."' Henry's phrasing is, of course, imaginative. But he has his finger on an important point. Vulcan's comportment suggests he accepts a role-reversal here, one amusingly deleterious to his dignity: a sexual role-reversal.[84] Venus the female and wife does not in his view have to 'precari'; therefore she can, as would more naturally suit the husband and male, command. And to Venus the female he attributes the 'uires', a 'strength' or 'power', which is very masculine in its connotations.[85]

This point is confirmed in the following lines, which describe Vulcan getting up to do his wife's bidding (407–15):

> inde ubi prima quies medio iam noctis abactae
> curriculo expulerat somnum, *cum* femina primum,
> cui tolerare colo uitam tenuique Minerua
> impositum, cinerem et sopitos suscitat ignis
> noctem addens operi, famulasque ad lumina longo
> exercet penso, castum ut seruare cubile
> coniugis et possit paruos educere natos:
> *haud secus* ignipotens nec tempore segnior illo
> mollibus e stratis opera ad fabrilia surgit.

Then, so soon as rest had banished sleep in the mid-course of departing night, *at the time when* a woman whose burden it is to support life by distaff and Minerva's humble work awakes the embers and slumbering fire, adding night to her day's work, and keeps her slave-girls

---

[84] Cf. Catull. 68.135 ff. where Catullus in respect of Lesbia compares himself to Juno in respect of Jupiter. (I assume that Hertzberg's 'contudit iram' in 139 conveys the sense if not the letter of what Catullus wrote (thus Goold); but see C. W. Macleod, *CQ* n.s. 24 (1974), 83 = *Collected Papers*, 160 f.)

[85] Cf. *OLD* s.v. *uis*, e.g. 20 a and c, and note Isidore's etymology (11.2.17): 'uir nuncupatus, quia maior in eo uis est quam in feminis: unde et uirtus nomen accepit: siue quod ui agat feminam.'

working by lamplight at their long allotment of spinning, so that she can keep her husband's bed chaste and rear her little sons: *even so*, and no more slothful at that hour, did the god of fire rise from his soft couch to the work of his smithy.

The *cum* clause which defines the (very early) time of day unexpectedly, or shall we say slily, turns into a simile—'haud secus'; a simile that is full of funny similarities and pointed dissimilarities.[86] First, we now find Vulcan explicitly compared to a woman ('cum *femina* . . . haud secus'); so that the hint of sex role-reversal becomes concrete. And among three identifiable sources for the temporal clause/simile[87] is one (Apoll. *Arg.* 3.291 ff.) in which the amorous Medea is the subject:

ὡς δὲ γυνὴ μαλερῷ περὶ κάρφεα χεύατο δαλῷ
χερνῆτις, τῇπερ ταλασήια ἔργα μέμηλεν,
ὥς κεν ὑπωρόφιον νύκτωρ σέλας ἐντύναιτο,
ἄγχι μάλ' ἐγρομένη· τὸ δ' ἀθέσφατον ἐξ ὀλίγοιο
δαλοῦ ἀνεγρόμενον σὺν κάρφεα πάντ' ἀμαθύνει·
τοῖος ὑπὸ κραδίῃ εἰλυμένος αἴθετο λάθρῃ
οὖλος Ἔρως·

Just as a poor woman, whose task is the spinning of wool, heaps dry twigs round a burning brand so that she may make ready flame beneath the roof at night, having woken very early; and the flame is roused up wonderfully from the small brand and consumes all the twigs: so coiling round her heart, blazed baneful Love . . .

So *allusion* further confirms the sex-reversal—and reminds one of Vulcan's humbled erotic condition. Humour can then be seen in the comparison between the luxuriously situated Vulcan and the poor woman, who in fact embodies the sort of virtues that Evander esteems, and thinks divine; in this respect, humorous contrast is what strikes us. And, in particular, humour can be seen in the motive attributed to the woman in the temporal clause/simile ('so that she can keep her husband's bed chaste and rear her little sons'). Again we are struck by a very pointed contrast: Vulcan is playing the role of 'femina' opposite the dominant Venus, but his chance of preserving a

---

[86] For a rather different interpretation of this simile see G. Williams, 128. For Fordyce's view see below.
[87] Homer, *Il.* 12.433 ff., Apoll. *Arg.* 3.291 ff., 4.1062 ff.

chaste bed is long since gone; and the reference to 'nati' is, in the present circumstances (remember 'genetrix nato'), sly on Vergil's part. Vergil has fun at the expense of the devoted, subordinate, and cuckolded Vulcan. The 'cum . . . haud secus' clause (which Fordyce on 8.408ff. calls 'curiously inappropriate in the context as an indication of time and incongruous when it is turned into a simile') is splendidly amusing. So is the whole scene: we accept the implications. However (I stress again), these gods, so funny and immoral in their own conduct, may influence a mortal world in which, for some, such indulgences are excluded, excluded by divine ordinance. And that has troubling implications. Vergil's invention of humour involves a serious further voice.

4. Characterization and apparent lack of characterization; 'negative' invention: Dido, Juno, Priam and Hecuba, Aeneas

It is, I think, vain to pretend that Vergil characterizes with the sure vividness that Homer manages.[88] For this there are various reasons. One is simply the presence and operation of further voices: the degree to which the text is reflective and self-preoccupied. I have stressed the 'optional' nature of the intrusions (questions, comments, criticisms, etc.) which Vergil works into the texture of his poem; and in the last chapter I shall demonstrate how remarkably Vergil still contrives to adhere, or to appear to adhere, to Homeric narrative principles. Nevertheless, a text so densely reflective cannot present characters with the requisite objectivity—leaving them sufficiently alone—for them to stand on their own feet and live as convincingly as Homer's characters do. In this respect the *Aeneid* does not bear comparison with the *Iliad*.

This is the necessary introduction to the following statement. Vergil can characterize admirably: not like Homer, but admirably, exploiting action and word. It is an important point to establish. We shall then be properly placed to assess puzzles

---

[88] For a very generous view of Vergil's characterization, see R. G. Austin, *P. Vergili Maronis Aeneidos Liber Secundus* (Oxford, 1964), xviff. Conte has some suggestive comments in this connection, discussing the relatively undramatic nature of the *Aeneid*: *Il genere*, 72ff.; he is particularly provocative on Aeneas, 86ff. See further Ch. 4 p. 148.

that the figure of Aeneas, who can seem curiously uncharacterized, presents. We shall not simply dismiss such puzzles, invoking Vergil's incompetence or lack of interest.

Dido

Dido is a good illustration of Vergil's ability to characterize. She has, of course, been discussed frequently in the past; so I shall confine myself to some relatively unobvious comments. A first point to notice is a simple item in the action of Book 4, which characterizes her eloquently and unexpectedly.

In 365 ff. Dido delivers her terrible, hate-filled tirade against Aeneas which starts 'nec tibi diua parens': 'no goddess was your mother . . . Caucasus bristling with hard rocks gave birth to you, Hyrcanian tigresses gave you suck . . .'. She ends the speech with a vivid vow to haunt him after she herself is dead, and fearsome words promising his punishment. Then she breaks off, turns away, and leaves. It all sounds pretty final. One does not, I think, expect her to approach Aeneas again, much less to supplicate him; the pride she has so often displayed would surely (one would think) prevent such an action. But not so. There is an unexpected turn of events, and by it we find the queen characterized, characterized (to be more exact) in her relationship with Aeneas. Dido reveals that *in extremis*, in these particular extremes, she is prepared to stoop, and, moreover, to a pathetic and desperately reduced appeal: she says, amongst other things (433 f.):

> tempus inane peto, requiem spatiumque furori,
> dum mea me uictam doceat fortuna dolere.

'For empty time I ask, rest and respite for my madness, until my fortune schools me through defeat to sorrow'.

But the characterization is finely tuned. Dido sends this plea via her sister Anna ('i soror atque hostem supplex adfare superbum' ['go my sister and address my haughty enemy in suppliance'], 424). She does not humble herself in person. The queen will stoop, but not so low.[89] That is nicely judged. Action, and inaction (Vergil's invention), characterize the queen.

---

[89] La Penna (lxvi) has it half right. He remarks of the overture via Anna: 'la passione non solo strazia la donna, ma umilia l'orgoglio della regina'.

46   *In Medias Res: Examples Various*

Action and words characterize her in the scene just preceding her suicide. Here are her 'nouissima uerba' (651 ff.):

> 'dulces exuuiae, dum fata deusque sinebat,
> accipite hanc animam meque his exsoluite curis.
> uixi et quem dederat cursum Fortuna peregi,
> et nunc magna mei sub terras ibit imago.
> urbem praeclaram statui, mea moenia uidi,
> ulta uirum poenas inimico a fratre recepi,
> felix, heu nimium felix, si litora tantum
> numquam Dardaniae tetigissent nostra carinae.'
> dixit, et os impressa toro 'moriemur inultae,
> sed moriamur' ait. 'sic, sic iuuat ire sub umbras.
> hauriat hunc oculis ignem crudelis ab alto
> Dardanus, et nostrae secum ferat omina mortis.'

'Sweet spoils—sweet while god and the fates allowed it, receive this my life and release me from these sorrows. I have lived, and I have finished the course which Fortune gave, and now a glorious shade of me will go beneath the earth. I have established a noble city and beheld my own walls. I took vengeance for my husband, exacting punishment from the brother who was my foe. Happy, ah! too happy, had but the Dardan ships never touched our shores.' So she spoke, and pressing her lips to the bed, cried, 'I shall die unavenged, but let me die. Thus, thus go I gladly to the shades. Let the cruel Dardan's eyes drink in this fire from the deep, and let him carry with him the omen of my death.'

Dido's use of the term 'exuuiae', 'spoils', discussed above (pp. 20 ff.), discloses bitterness, and a sense of her own pathos. The epithet 'dulces', 'sweet', suggests continuing love. But Dido is now in full control of her feelings: she sees and faces facts, perceives and accepts (for example) the qualification 'while god and the fates allowed'. And such calmness persists. Gone now are the furious assertions of betrayal and maltreatment to which earlier speeches of hers have accustomed us; she is content and able to let her case more or less rest on its assured merits. The wild 'woman scorned' regains queenly composure and dignity; and the fact that she does so contributes much to the tragic impact of her death:[90] we need to respect Dido as well as to pity her, to be profoundly moved when she dies.

---

[90] As Pöschl, 119 f., appreciates.

In Medias Res: Examples Various

Dignified, she recalls her large achievements in tones of measured and merited pride.[91] She adverts to the destruction and chaos introduced into her life by the Trojan arrival, with sorrow and feeling, but sobriety—so different from her previous furious accusations. And the hate produced by her betrayal, which we saw so much of earlier, has been tempered; it has been mastered—but it has not been expunged. She no longer seems to have such vivid enthusiasm for the revenge her hate desired, and certainly no confidence in it (contrast 625, 'exoriare aliquis nostris ex ossibus ultor' ['Arise some avenger from our bones!']). But that does not mean that she no longer wants it. This is evident in her resigned words 'moriemur inultae, sed moriamur' ['I shall die unavenged, but let me die']: it is obviously a matter of regret to Dido that she lacks her vengeance. But simultaneous with these residually hostile words there is something else, a marvellous touch. In the same moment that Dido suggests her continuing *hate* ('moriemur inultae'), we see her continuing *love*. Vergil characterizes by action as well as speech, making Dido reveal an acute ambivalence of the most plausible kind. She kisses the bed she lies on, that is to say, the 'marriage-bed'—'os impressa toro', a heart-rending and (to me)[92] unmistakable gesture. And an extraordinary but very believable ambivalence is maintained in her final sentence, 'hauriat hunc oculis ignem crudelis ab alto / Dardanus', a line whose significance the commentators all miss. The surface sense is, of course, clear: Dido wants Aeneas to *see* the flames of her death, to have some knowledge of what he has done, and carry the ill omen of it along with him. There is some pathos as well as vindictiveness in that. This pathos is then reinforced by a bitter *double entendre*. Consider 'hauriat hunc oculis ignem'. The metaphor 'let him drink in with his eyes the fire' refers in the first place to Aeneas' *seeing* the flames of the pyre (cf. Pease on 4.661); but the metaphor also suits, indeed it

---

[91] She speaks rather like a Roman general in his *elogium*: cf. E. Fraenkel, *Kleine Beiträge zur klassischen Philologie*, vol. 2 (Rome, 1964), 73, 140f., 223; Pöschl loc. cit.; Klingner, 461; also Austin on 4.653ff.

[92] But it has been quite staggeringly misunderstood. One critic believed that Dido bit the bed in rage: see Pease ad loc., who himself interprets correctly and supplies several illuminating parallels for this loving gesture (e.g. Alcestis at Eur. *Alc.* 183). Servius has the right answer ('quasi amatrix').

more naturally suits, an erotic sense:[93] it suggests the sense 'drink in with the eyes the fire of *love*', i.e., 'feel love'. We must see Dido's emphasis on 'hunc'—'at least let him drink in *this* fire', she says; and she means, to paraphrase clumsily, 'if he could not feel love for me, at least let him see the *consequences* of that failure, namely the flames of my death': 'if he could not feel love for me, if he could not drink in fire in *that* sense, at least let him drink in *this* fire', i.e. 'let him perceive the fire of my pyre, the consequences of his failure to love me'. Grim ambiguities or concealed senses are, by the by, characteristic of the speech of Dido (we have to do here with a character's habit and idiosyncrasy, not just an author's).[94] In this same speech (651f.), 'dulces exuuiae . . . accipite hanc animam' suggests at first sight no more than 'receive my life',[95] *vel sim.*, i.e. a passive version of 'animam dare' (Conington – Nettleship and Pease compare *Georg.* 4.204, *Aen.* 10.854). But Dido has in mind the blood she is going to give up, as comparison of 9.349 and 10.908 and indeed common sense must reveal. In what other way could clothes (which are included among the 'spoils' which she apostrophizes) receive her life?

I have mentioned one indication of Dido's persisting love for Aeneas (her kissing the marriage-bed). There is another sign of it in this scene, indeed a demonstration of it: a confused, perhaps half-unconscious demonstration, but for all that a most spectacular one—it is in Dido's nature to make the grand gesture, and in her death she remains true to type. I refer simply to the *manner* of her death. Dido thought up the device and strategy of the pyre in the first place to conceal under a pretence of magic her real intention to kill herself. But conceal-

---

[93] See Lyne on *Ciris* 163. Note in particular Vergil's use of the metaphor for the loving Dido at 1.749, 'longumque bibebat amorem'. 1.749 guarantees that metaphorical 'drink' is the sense here. On the troublesome 'haurio' see D. A. West, *CQ* 15 (1965), 271–80: it may be that a sense of metaphorical drinking for 'haurio' precedes such a literal sense; the basic force of the verb seems to be 'to take by scooping', 'to draw'. For 'eyes' in an erotic context, see Eur. *Hipp.* 525f. with Barrett's note; Hor. *Odes* 1.36.17 with Nisbet-Hubbard; Prop. 3.10.15; Ov. *Am.* 2.19.19 with Brandt ad loc.

[94] See the examples adduced and explained in exemplary fashion by Pöschl, 113–5 (including 4.384, 'sequar atris ignibus', 436, 'cumulatam morte remittam'). Cf. Aeschylus' Clytemnestra: see W. B. Stanford, *Aeschylus in his Style* (Dublin, 1942), 119f.

[95] Klingner, 461, translates 'nehmt hin dies mein Leben . . .'.

ment could have been achieved in a much less bizarre and elaborate way, and what moved Dido to select this precise scheme was its other function: as the mode of her death. Dido organizes, therefore, a very particular and surely expressive way to die. What is she trying to express? Let us consider it. Dido ends up committing suicide in the flames of a pyre, on which is the marriage-bed of her 'husband' (as she would say) and on which there is even the effigy of her 'husband' (4.508). So whatever other gesture Dido is making, whatever else is in her mind—and clearly one of these things is to obliterate Aeneas and all his works as well as herself—Dido's action also involves a suggestion of suttee: the Eastern custom of widows burning themselves to death on the pyres of their husbands, the devoted fanatical death sought, in Greek mythology, by Evadne.[96] The 'effigies' of Aeneas is only an 'effigies', but it is of Aeneas, and Dido dies with it in flames, on a pyre. With dreadful vividness, therefore, but pathetically, uselessly, and I suppose half-unconsciously, Dido protests herself an Evadne— as Aeneas sails away, alive and well. Dido makes her last grand gesture; and Vergil characterizes by action.

So: nobility, pride, pathos, love, hate, extraordinary ambivalences; and (it should be added) courage. Vergil characterizes by action and by word, with invention and arrangement: organizing *this* speech and *these* actions at *this* time, and so giving us a richly coloured Dido who could have been described very differently.

Juno

Aeneid 7.291 ff.:

> stetit *acri fixa dolore*.
> tum *quassans caput* haec *effundit pectore dicta*:
> 'heu stirpem inuisam . . .
> . . .
>
> quin etiam patria excussos infesta per undas (299)
> ausa sequi et profugis toto me opponere ponto.
> *absumptae* in Teucros *uires caelique marisque*. . . .

---

[96] For a contemporary reference to Eastern suttee and to Evadne, see Prop. 3.13.15–24.

>   Mars perdere gentem   (304)
> immanem Lapithum ualuit, concessit in iras
> ipse *deum* antiquam *genitor* Calydona Dianae,
> quod scelus aut Lapithas tantum aut Calydona
>   merentem?
> *ast* ego . . .
>   . . .
>
> non dabitur regnis, esto, prohibere Latinis,   (313)
> atque immota manet fatis Lauinia coniunx:
> at trahere atque moras tantis licet addere rebus,
> at licet amborum populos exscindere regum.
> hac gener atque socer coeant mercede suorum:
> sanguine Troiano et Rutulo *dotabere*, uirgo,
> et Bellona manet te pronuba. nec face tantum
> *Cisseis* praegnas ignis enixa iugalis;
> quin idem Veneri partus suus et Paris alter

Juno stood pierced with keen anguish. Then shaking her head she poured forth these words from her breast. 'Alas, hated stock . . .

Nay more, when they had been thrown out of their country I lacked no courage in pursuing them as their foe over the waves and confronting the exiles all over the deep: against the Teucrians has been spent all the power of sea and sky . . .

Mars could destroy the Lapith's huge race; the father of the gods himself yielded ancient Calydon to Diana, to satisfy her wrath—though in respect of what great sin did the Lapiths or Calydon deserve it? But I . . .

It will not be given me to keep Aeneas from kingdom in Latium—I grant it—and by fate Lavinia abides unchangeably his bride. But to put off matters and to bring delay to these great events, that I can do; I can destroy the nations of both kings. At such price paid by their people let the father-in-law and son-in-law be united. You, maiden, will be given a dowry in Trojan and Rutulian blood, and Bellona awaits you as bridal matron. It was not only the daughter of Cisseus [Hecuba] who was pregnant with a torch and brought forth marriage fire. Nay, Venus too has the like in her offspring, a second Paris . . .

Vergil gives his gods and goddesses as well as his mortals individual characterization. To illustrate this I offer some very selective comments on the way Juno's entry into Book 7 is managed.[97] At the same time I shall demonstrate Vergil's skill in characterizing by diction: by deft choice between words of

---

[97] I discuss this passage fully in my paper 'Diction and Poetry in Vergil's *Aeneid*', 67 ff.

different stylistic register, he lends vitality and idiosycrasy to one of his divine figures.

A goddess, to appear a goddess, ought to radiate grandness, epicality, qualities *other* than those of our own every-day experience. To this end Vergil describes Juno in the majestic terms of Poetic Diction, and elevates some of her own direct speech similarly: so that language resonant with the connotations of the epic world and untainted with the connotations of things every-day ensures our realization that this is a heroic goddess. Examples of such Poetic Diction (grecism, archaism, and, in particular, Homericisms and Ennianisms) are italicized in the quotation above: '*acri fixa dolore*', '*quassans caput*', '*effundit pectore dicta*', and so on.[98]

Poetic Diction thus helps to suggest the grand *otherness* of the goddess Juno. But Juno makes no pretence at any grand morality. That is the compelling and frightening thing about many of Vergil's gods, Juno in particular (cf. Ch. 2): the way she combines the grandness and power of divinity with the mean motivations and methods of the nastiest of mortals. Her self-righteous appeal to the example of the Lapiths and Calydon, for instance (304-7), is flagrantly dishonest: as Juno well knew, Calydon had very definitely offended Diana, and the Lapiths had offended Mars;[99] whereas Aeneas and his band of Trojans, far from offending Juno, had assiduously honoured her. More acutely, Juno's majestic, dignified archaism 'dotabere' (318)[100] viciously clothes the cruellest of predictions—concerning someone who is completely innocent as regards her, who might indeed reasonably have been her protégée.[101] That combination of diction and content gets right at the essence of the goddess Juno—which, until we are used to it, is rather a paradoxical essence.

Other sorts of diction can bring out this paradox—Vergil has other ways of characterizing his compelling divine creation. Juno's divine and heroic stature, her otherness compared with us, is guaranteed by a norm of Poetic Diction; and much of her nastily human emotion is appropriately, and effectively, 'digni-

---

[98] See Appendix 1 for full information on the Poetic Diction in this passage.
[99] See Horsfall, review of Fordyce, 222.
[100] I infer it to be an archaism from the existence of 'dotatus': see Appendix 1.
[101] Cf. Buchheit, 147.

fied' in the same way. But not always. We sometimes hear the great Juno uttering not only nastily human sentiments but speaking in all too nastily human *tones*: sometimes she permits herself to descend devastatingly from dignified propriety to the diction of the streets. That is disturbing for us—more disturbing perhaps than seeing her viciously doling out suffering in the grand manner; or it is disturbing in a different way. It brings into sharper focus what a frightening mixture this mean-minded almighty is.

An unobtrusive example is 'excussos' (299). In Vergil's time this verb was, I think, quite colloquial, certainly unpoetical (though one would not believe it from the commentaries and dictionaries, which badly mislead us). It is a very vigorous word meaning 'throw out', 'shake out', and, because of its (colloquial) vigour, was suited to comedy; but it was largely and in significant ways avoided in other poetry before Vergil. If we turn to prose we find that Cicero has quite a penchant for it (and how and why he uses it can usually be appreciated and explained); but Sallust and the austere Caesar eschew it. So, with 'excussos', Juno speaks vigorously, bluntly, like us: she speaks of her mighty vengeance in familiar, even crude, terms—a most individual goddess.[102]

Similarly in line 317. For Juno's brutal remark about the cost of Aeneas' and Latinus' settlement, Vergil has her select the word 'merces'. Statistics do not immediately provide a neat label for this word. But distribution figures plus consideration of the contexts of its occurrences, and comparisons with the better mannered 'pretium', point to its being on the prosaic side.[103] It was the word used when one wished to refer in a specific, every-day, mercenary way to wages, or to the price of something. The aura of business attached to it; it was the brother of 'merx'; and naturally, therefore, it occurred more often in prose. Poets preferred to cover much of its ground with, among other words, 'pretium'; when they did use 'merces' it was for its mercenary, every-day effect. Thus Juno. She perceives her vile plan clearly and she states it with blunt clarity: like us, in our business moods.

[102] For an analysis of 'excutio', see Appendix 2.
[103] See Appendix 2.

In Medias Res: Examples Various

The climactic example of this means of characterization occurs in 319f. Here Juno builds on Hecuba's famous dream to make her cut at Venus. The normal story was that Hecuba *dreamed* she was pregnant with a flaming torch; and the dream was then *interpreted* to mean that her child would be the destruction of Troy. Juno more vividly, more unpleasantly, says that Hecuba *was* pregnant with a torch and *actually* brought forth 'marriage *fire*'; and, she says, even so Venus.

An unpleasant conceit—and unpleasantly uttered. Juno descends abruptly to almost offensive diction, unobserved by Vergil's commentators. After bestowing upon Hecuba a grand, poetical patronymic ('Cisseis'), she speaks of her pregnancy with a word ('praegnas') which was to Roman ears so bluntly specific in its indelicate signification that it was rigorously avoided by poetry; even a semi-technical writer such as Lucretius—or Vergil himself in the *Georgics*—selected the discreeter 'grauidus' (or 'fetus'); and prose too exhibits clear doubts as to the propriety of 'praegnas'[104]—just as Victorian and indeed much later English prose preferred drawing-room circumlocutions to the word 'pregnant'. So Juno speaks coarsely (that must be the impact of the word in a heroic context) of the pregnancies she loathes. Goddesses often hate in epic; but Juno expresses her hatred with the crudity of tone that might characterize a crude and hating mortal. And that is a striking effect. Juno is singularly unpleasant, colourfully nasty, a vividly drawn figure: the product of Vergilian characterization.[105]

Priam and Hecuba

The deaths of Polites and Priam at the hand of Pyrrhus in Book 2 make a famous scene, and the characterization of Priam at this point—his bravery, pathos, dignity, love—is finely handled and patent enough. I wish to offer just a few comments on the cameo that opens the scene (2.515–25). A summary of it, and its context, runs as follows. The aged Priam has donned arms to make a pathetic last gesture. Hecuba and her daughters sit in sanctuary at the central altar of the palace. A simile deriving from Homer (cf. *Il.* 21.493f.; see Austin ad loc.) amplifies their

---

[104] Full figures on 'praegna[n]s' in Appendix 2.
[105] Vergil's intentions at 10.704f., where 'face praegnas Cisseis' occurs in the narrative, are not yet perspicuous to me.

pitiable weakness. Priam arrives and Hecuba begs him not to fight. Vergil's lines are as follows:

> hic Hecuba et *natae nequiquam* altaria circum,
> praecipites atra *ceu* tempestate columbae,
> condensae et diuum amplexae simulacra sedebant.
> ipsum autem sumptis Priamum iuuenalibus armis
> ut uidit, 'quae mens tam dira, miserrime coniunx,
> impulit his cingi telis? aut quo ruis?' inquit.
> 'non tali auxilio nec defensoribus istis
> tempus eget; non, si ipse meus nunc adforet Hector.
> huc tandem concede; haec ara tuebitur omnis,
> aut moriere simul.' sic *ore effata* recepit
> ad sese et sacra longaeuum in sede locauit.

Here around the altar sat Hecuba and her daughters, to no avail, like doves swept before a dark storm, huddled together and clasping the images of the gods. But when she saw Priam clad in youthful arms, she said, 'my most wretched husband, what so dread a thought drove you to gird on these weapons? Where do you rush to? The hour needs not such assistance nor defenders like that, not though my own Hector were now here himself. Come here, I beg you. This altar will protect us all, or you will die with us.' Thus did she utter, and drew the aged man to her and placed him on the holy seat.

First, the dignity as well as the pathos of the scene is to be appreciated. Dignity is imparted by language—in much the same way as heroic status was imparted to Juno. The Homeric simile of the doves does indeed suggest the weakness and vulnerability of Hecuba and her daughters; but it *is* a Homeric simile, with Homeric epic resonance. And other diction, which I have italicized, derives from the Roman epic tradition, bringing with it dignified Roman resonances, and ensuring the heroic status of the little cameo.[106]

---

[106] On the archaism 'nequiquam' see Austin on 1.707. Subst. '[g]natus' and '[g]nata' are Ennian poetical usages: cf. Enn. *Ann.* 44 Sk.; *Sc.* 82, 291 V. Vergil's phrase 'nate dea' (*uel sim.*) is also poetical (and perhaps Ennian). Livy offers quite striking evidence that 'natus', 'nate dea', continued to belong firmly in poetry. Although he can accommodate more Poetic Diction than most historiographers, he dislikes this. He has huge quantities of 'filius' and 'filia'; and also of the past participle of 'nascor' in orthodox use. But seeking parallels for subst. 'natus' and 'nata' and for the epical formula 'nate dea', I find only two: 1.7.10 and 1.23.1; both are heightened contexts. (But counting is a little difficult, since the 'nate dea' formula is grammatically comparable with such prosaic phrases as 'seruus serua natus', and it is difficult to draw a line: e.g. 1.56.7, 'sorore regis natus').

In Medias Res: Examples Various

But within this epic context, Vergil allows ordinary and touching human pathos to assert itself; and his heroic figures are humanly and individually characterized. When Hecuba speaks to Priam, she not only utters tender sentiments, she employs tender tones. The turn of phrase 'quae . . . aut quo' (519f.) is colloquial, intimate Latin (the tone is impossible to reproduce in English), likewise her crucial appeal, 'huc tandem concede' (523).[107] The heroic queen reveals her ordinary and gentle humanity, in language as well as sentiment. She is characterized. And not only in herself: by the sentiments *and* tones, gently and ordinarily human, which she thinks fitting to utter to Priam, she is characterized in her relationship with Priam. And when Priam complies (temporarily) with her request, he too reveals his humanity and is characterized in his relationship with Hecuba: by the fact that she persuades him. Vergil might well have had him refuse and stand firm in futile bravado from the beginning.[108] Instead, an epic king is made real, humanized and characterized in relation to his queen. We observe therefore, once more, that Vergil can characterize admirably, by action and word. Not only that: he can characterize a relationship—one person in an affective relationship with another.

Aeneas and 'negative' invention

I now direct our thoughts to a problem; and in this case I must preserve my answer entirely for a later chapter. The problem is this. Given that Vergil can and does characterize admirably—and not only individuals, but individuals in an affective relationship—why is Aeneas at times so uncharacterized, particularly in the matter of affective relationships? (Dido's relationship with Aeneas is partly characterized—above, p. 45—but, as we shall see, not his with her.) Why does Vergil, who demonstrably knows the craft of characterization by both action and word, so often deny his services to his hero? Why does Vergil's inventiveness desert him at crucial moments in his hero's life? Obviously it does not. We have to do with what I have called

---

'ceu' is an Ennian archaism: *TLL* s.v. init: '*inde ab* ENNIO *apud poetas praeter scaenicos priscos; in oratione pedestri primum ap.* SEN. *nat.* VI 24,4, *deinde* . . .'. For 'ore effata', cf. Enn. *Ann.* 203f. Sk.; Austin on *Aen.* 2.524.
[107] See Austin on 2.523; *TLL* 4.7.75ff.
[108] This vital point is missed by Quinn, 3ff., though his discussion is otherwise quite interesting. See too his *Latin Explorations* (London, 1963), 229–38.

'negative invention': at key moments Vergil's invention provokingly includes *silence*. And a further voice is operative, providing implications which are not to be resisted.

APPENDICES TO CHAPTER 1
Note: figures for Vergil do not include occurrences in the Vergilian *appendix*; but figures for Caesar do include the *Fortsetzer*.

1. Analysis of Poetic Diction in Aeneid 7.291 ff.

Fixa dolore: a vividly metaphorical phrase with Homeric and, probably, Ennian resonance.

(*a*) The metaphor is that of a 'telum' of pain. The following literal uses of 'figo' illustrate the image: *Bell. Alex.* 30.6, 'diuersis . . . telis nostri figebantur'; Verg. *Aen.* 9.493, 'figite me', 10.382 etc. It is Vergil, incidentally, who popularizes this use of 'figo' for 'transfigo': *TLL* VI.715.37 ff.

(*b*) Vergil is the popularizer, indeed virtually the initiator, of our metaphorical use of 'figo'. We may compare a passage like Cic. *Orat.* 89, '[orator] aduersarios figet', or *ND* 1.93; or cf. Catullus' lively, imaginative picture (allegory rather than metaphor) at 116.7 f.; and there is further precedent in Latin idiom in the frequent image represented by e.g. Plaut. *Pers.* 25, 'sagitta Cupido cor meum transfixit' (which Lucretius adapts, rationalizing it, in 2.360); cf. too Lucr. 3.305 below. But other parallels for our metaphorical use of 'figo' are lacking, and the phrase itself is without a close parallel at all—until the Vergilian imitators: Val. 3.74, etc. (*TLL* VI.718.82 ff.). The freshness of the use of 'figo' (in the literal sense (*a*) behind the metaphor, as well as in the metaphorical sense (*b*)) ensures that the impact of the metaphor is fresh and powerful. (Vergil's line *Aen.* 11.645, 'hasta . . . duplicatque uirum transfixa dolore' will remind us of the way in which it was powerful.)

(*c*) The phrase is fresh and powerful—but it may too have inherited Latin epic colouring. Cf. Lucretius' use of 'perfigo': 3.305, 'nec gelidis torpet telis perfixa pauoris'. Inevitably we think of a common Ennian source (for the principle see Norden, *Aeneis Buch VI* (3rd ed., Berlin, 1926), Anhang 1, especially p. 371); and Lucretius' context might suggest it. If Vergil did know an Ennian phrase with 'perfigo', his change to 'figo' would be explicable not only for the vividness analysed above. It was in his manner to like simple verbs: see Austin on *Aen.* 1.20, 2.98; Williams on 5.41; Leumann-Hofmann-Szantyr on 2.298–300.

(*d*) The striking nature of the metaphor and its possible Latin epic

In Medias Res: Examples Various 57

tone has been established. But for the reader familiar with Homer, the phrase also introduces Homeric resonance: it recalls *Il.* 5.399.

quassans caput: a calque of the Homeric Poseidon: *Od.* 5.285. (But it is something else too. 'quasso' is more colloquial than 'quatio', and 'quassans caput' is demonstrably an old colloquial phrase for a movement of pain or anger (*TLL* III.390.34ff.). Vergil suggests Juno's Homeric status but simultaneously shows her in a vividly familiar gesture. Quite often he will 'protect' colloquialism or vivify Poetic Diction in this sort of way: see 'Diction and Poetry', 75, 78, 80.)

effundit pectore dicta: an Ennian phrase. See Enn. *Ann.* 553 Sk., 'effudit uoces proprio cum pectore sancto'. Cf. Albinovanus Pedo, 15, 'obstructa in talis effundit pectora uoces'; Verg. *Aen.* 5.482, 723 and 8.70. As well as other poets, prose writers, in particular Cicero, take up 'effundere uoces', *vel sim.* (e.g. Cic. *Flacc.* 69, *Att.* 16.7.5); but I think it is clear that they pick it up for its epic resonance: full instances at *TLL* V.2.223.76ff., 224.4ff. (Cicero likes 'fundo' of speech too, but interestingly it is for him a word particularly suited to the utterance of poets: *Fin.* 4.10, 'aliud est enim poetarum more uerba fundere, aliud ea quae dicas ratione et arte distinguere', de Orat. 3.194, *Tusc.* 1.64.)

absumptae . . . uires caelique marisque: it can be argued that this has Ennian resonance.

absumptae uires: TLL s.v. 'absumo': '*verbum deest apud* CAES. (*semel* BELL. ALEX.), NEP., TIB., LUCAN., PERS., PETRON., MART., *vitatur a* TER. (*semel* [but it is in fact thrice]), CIC. (*semel* Quinct., *bis* carm.), SALL. (*semel*), PROP. (*semel*), QUINT. (*semel*), *qui omnes praeferunt* consumo; *adamant* PLAUT. (*nusquam* cons.) et TAC. (*septies decies* abs., *duodecies* cons.)'. I also count getting on for 100 examples of 'absumo' in Livy against 41 of 'consumo'. Further figures are 'absumo/consumo': Enn. 0/0; *Trag. frag.* 1 (Acc. 564)/0; *Com. frag.* 0/0; Catull. 2 (64.242, 65.14)/0; Lucr. 1/6; Verg. 7 (*Aen.* 6)/7 (*Aen.* 5); Hor. 2 (*Odes* 1, *Epist.* 1)/5 (*Serm.* 3, *Epist.* 2); Ov. 14 (*Met.* 6)/22 (*Met.* 8). The implication of these figures is not conspicuous. But perhaps what attracts Tacitus and Livy is some quality of archaism. Note Plautus' predilection; no example survives in Ennius, but note Accius. Other facts are consonant with such an assumption. Observe Horace; observe too Catullus, both of whose examples occur in passages of high style.

TLL I.220.3ff. (cf. Wölfflin, in *Archiv.* 7 (1892), 192 f.) parallels the collocation of 'absumo' and 'uires' at Lucr. 4.1121, 'adde quod absumunt uires', Verg. *Aen.* 7.301, Ov. *Ars* 2.439, *Met.* 1.543, *al.*, and subsequently. I suggest it is an old epic phrase (cf. 'fixa dolore' (*c*)) which Lucretius applies with sardonic grandness to lovers wasting their strength. There is support in Lucretius' context (other epical language) for supposing this to be an epic phrase; and the fact that Lucretius normally uses 'consumo' suggests that 4.1121 employs a special, a borrowed, phrase. (Such tone would not be inappropriate in *Ars* 2.439: a four-line simile.)

caelique marisque: '-que' . . . '-que' is Ennius' calque of the Homeric τε . . . τε and it tended to retain its epic tone (see the excellent note of K. F. Smith on Tibull. 1.1.33). One suspects that 'caelique marisque' (cf. too *Aen.* 5.802) was an Ennian line-ending.

deum genitor: on the genitive plural in '-um' (archaic) see Fordyce on *Aen.* 7.189. Cf. Enn. *Ann.* 444 Sk., 'o genitor noster Saturnie maxime diuum'; Cic. *carm. frg.* 3 (*de consul.*).32 'deum genitor', etc.: several poets follow in Ennius' footsteps: *TLL* VI.2.1818.65ff.

ast: see Fordyce on *Aeneid* 7.308.

dotabere: according to our information (as far as I can see) Vergil is the first writer certainly to use the finite verb 'doto'; conceivably it was used on a very old inscription that survives: *TLL* V.1.2056.33. But we must assume, I think, that the finite 'doto' pre-existed the familiar 'dotatus'. I imagine Vergil knows it from an old poetic text; his use then encouraged a resurgence. Vergil's particular metaphor ('sanguine') was taken up by Christian and later writers: *TLL* V.1.2056.66ff. Metaphors with 'dos', 'dotatus' are old and common, but nothing like Vergil's 'sanguine' can be found.

Cisseis: this grand patronymic may have been used of Hecuba by Ennius and Pacuvius: see Servius on *Aeneid* 7.320: 'Cisseis: regina Hecuba filia secundum Euripidem Cissei [cf. Hec. 3] quem Ennius, Pacuuius et Vergilius sequuntur.' Ennius tells the story of Hecuba's dream that she was pregnant with a torch in his *Alexander*: Sc. 35ff.V = 50ff. J.

2. Some Unpoetical Diction in Aeneid 7.291ff.

excutio: the comment in *TLL* s.v. '*usitatum est dactylicis et* SEN. *trag.*' is misleading, to say the least. Here are some facts and figures on occurrence: Plaut. 9; Ter. 2; Enn. 0; *Trag. frag.* 0; *Com. frag.* 0; Lucil. 1 or 2 (837M = 939W is very unlikely); Lucr. 2; Cic. *poet.* 0; Catull. 1; Prop. 1 or 2 (2.16.27 is very doubtful); Tib. 1; Hor. 4 (*Serm.* 3, *Odes* 1); Vergil 22 (all in *Aen.*); Ov. 65 (*Am.* 8, *Met.* 24); Luc. 24; Sil. 20; and other post-Vergilian poets are fond of it; Sall. 0; Caes. 0; Liv. 7; Cic. 23 (*Orat.* 13, *Rhet.* 1, *Phil.* 6, *Epist.* 3); Petron. 8.

The poetical pattern before Vergil is clear: a matter of the occasional example, particularly in the lower genres. Lucil. 1064M =

1037W is pleasant to quote to show the force of the verb: 'ipso cum domino calce omnis excutiamus' ['let's kick out the whole crowd, host and all!' (Warmington)]. Tibullus' one example and Horace's one example in the *Odes* occur, significantly, in connection with the potentially comic topos of the excluded lover: *Odes* 3.9.19, 'si flaua excutitur Chloe / reiectaeque patet ianua Lydiae'; Tibull. 2.6.12, 'excutiunt clausae fortia uerba fores' (a wittily unexpected object is provided by 'uerba'). I infer that the word was too vigorous and colloquial to be poetical before Vergil. Its persistent colloquialism is shown by Plautus at one end of the figures and Petronius at the other. What happens in poetry after Vergil is a phenomenon which is often repeated. Vergilian usage sets a precedent, gives authority, *legitimizes*. (It is interesting that Ovid uses the word comparatively rarely in the early *Amores*: six of the eight examples are provided by the refrain in *Am.* 1.6.) The popularity of the word with Cicero is due not only to the fact that oratory and dialogue can accommodate the occasional vigorous word of familiar speech—in a way that more austere examples of historiography (Sall., Caes.) cannot: it is significant that many of Cicero's examples are in a *metaphor* which *Cicero* seems to have invented: *TLL* V.2.1312.79ff., 1313.7ff. (*i.q. examinare, perquirere, explorare*).

merces: some facts and figures from the poets: Enn. 0, Lucr. 0, Catull. 0. Prop. has 4 examples (none in Books 1 and 2): of these 3.4.3 seems to exploit prosaic tone and sense very obviously; and the other three can be interpreted along the same lines without great difficulty. Tibull. 0: note 'pretium' in an analogous function at 1.9.33, 52; 2.4. 14, 33, 39. Horace has 11 examples of 'merces', 5 in the Odes—which should not surprise us given his penchant for prosaic diction (Axelson, *Unpoetische Wörter* (Lund, 1945), Ch. 4; but this is an unsympathetic account); nor, of course, should the satirist Juvenal's 12 examples surprise us. Vergil has four careful uses of the word; a function for prosaic tone in each case can be discerned: besides *Aen.* 7.317, see *Ecl.* 6.26, *Georg.* 2.62, 4.150. Vergil has 9 examples of 'pretium' (all in the *Aen.*) covering the same ground as 'merces'. Further figures for 'merces': Ov. 18 (5 in *Met.*), Luc. 19, Val. 0, Stat. 5, Sil. 7. A certain legitimizing effect (see above) is probably visible here, though Ovid and of course Lucan have positive reason for bluntness.

praegnas: the bluntly prosaic tone of this word can be swiftly demonstrated. Here are the figures for a series of authors who use 'praegna[n]s' and/or 'grauidus'. The figures speak for themselves. Note these are total figures (thus metaphorical uses of the words are included), and no account is taken of 'grauis' and 'fetus' (which would in fact strengthen my point). So the demonstration, though sufficient, is rough and ready. 'Praegna[n]s/grauidus': Plaut. 8/19; Ter. 2/5; Enn. 0/1; *Trag. frag.* 0/3; *Com. frag.* 3/1; Lucr. 0/4; Cic. *poet.* 0/2; Prop. ?1 (a very unsure emendation introduces it at 4.7.79: when one observes the tone of the word, the emendation seems even more unsure)/0; Hor. 1 (*Odes* 3.27.2, where an ugly sound is clearly being sought)/2; Verg. 2 (our phrase is repeated at 10.704)/14; Ov. 0/31; Luc. 0/2; Juv. 3/0; Varr. *Rust.* 14/0; Cic. *Rhet.* 1/1, *Phil.* 3 (all in the *De Div.*, which needs precisely technical words at times)/3 (but of these 3 cited by Merguet's *Lexikon* in *Phil.*, 2 occur in a quotation from Cicero's own *De Cons.*, and the other is in a *Trag. frag.*), *Epist.* 1/0, *Orat.* 2/2; Liv. 0/2.

2
Gods and men

Invention, arrangement: not resisting implications

When I talked of Venus, Vulcan, and Allecto in the previous chapter, I may seem to some to have made assumptions about the gods of the *Aeneid* that need to be justified. Other scholars have very different views in this respect, as I shall shortly acknowledge. In this chapter, therefore, I shall present my view of the religion of the *Aeneid* in a more orderly fashion, but with the intention of focusing particularly on Jupiter: Jupiter and his relationship with other gods, Fate, and man. At the same time I shall be illustrating the workings of further voices in the text of the *Aeneid*.

1. Introduction; Homeric continuity

It is possible to interpret the gods of the *Aeneid* in tidy and, so to speak, undisturbing formulae. For some, the religion of the *Aeneid* is, at bottom, Stoic:[1] a single provident Fate guides the world, and the gods to whom separate names are attached are aspects of this one divinity. For others the gods (several of them anyway) are to be interpreted symbolically:[2] when Venus apparently acts upon Dido in Book 1 and Allecto apparently acts upon Amata and others in Book 7, these are figurative representations of what goes on in the hearts of men. Another scholar sees the gods and Fate as 'technical devices' of the poet, intended among other things to disclose his own authorial

---

[1] Cf. Bailey, esp. 204ff., Heinze 291ff.; Otis is not far from such a view: 226ff., esp. 227.
[2] Cf. Heinze again, 304ff.; Quinn 316ff., calling the phenomenon 'Parallel divine and psychological motivation', and building on incorrect views of Homeric religion; Klingner, 514, on Amata and the role of Allecto: 'Dies alles liesse sich sehr wohl auch "psychologisch" darstellen'; Pöschl, 29ff. on Allecto; cf. R. D. Williams, 'The Purpose of the *Aeneid*', 37.

views.[3] But others do grant that the gods of the poem *are* gods, separate beings with their own separate wishes and capacities;[4] gods, who, in the believable world of the *Aeneid*, live, move, and have their believable being—unpredictable, partial, powerful, and, therefore, frightening; but these scholars allocate a special, quasi-Stoical and supreme role to one of them, Jupiter. This last viewpoint is far closer than the other's to the truth. But it is not the whole truth. In search of the whole truth, I revert to the beginning of the poem.

I quote some key passages (1.8ff.):

> Musa, mihi causas memora, quo numine laeso
> quidue dolens regina deum tot uoluere casus
> insignem pietate uirum, tot adire labores
> impulerit. . . .
> urbs antiqua fuit . . .
> Karthago, Italiam contra Tiberinaque longe
> ostia . . .
> quam Iuno fertur terris magis omnibus unam
> posthabita coluisse Samo. . . .
>
> progeniem sed enim Troiano a sanguine duci
> audierat Tyrias olim quae uerteret arces;
> hinc populum late regem belloque superbum
> uenturum excidio Libyae; sic uoluere Parcas.
> id metuens ueterisque memor Saturnia belli,
> prima quod ad Troiam pro caris gesserat Argis—
> necdum etiam causae irarum saeuique dolores
> exciderant animo; manet alta mente repostum
> iudicium Paridis spretaeque iniuria formae
> et genus inuisum et rapti Ganymedis honores:
> his accensa . . .

O Muse, relate to me the reasons, for what injury to her divinity, or wherein pained in anger, did the queen of the gods drive a man so illustrious in piety to go through so many misfortunes, to face so many toils. . . .

There was an ancient city, Carthage . . . confronting Italy and far away Tiber's mouth . . . which Juno is said to have cherished above all other lands, holding even Samos less dear . . . But she had heard that

---

[3] G. Williams, 4ff., 17–20, sees the gods functioning as a 'figure' for 'authorial intervention', and fate functioning as various 'figures' and 'tropes'.

[4] Camps, 41ff.; Coleman (who, however, has reservations about the success of Vergil's religious system: see Ch. 1 nn. 74, 77); La Penna, lxxvff.

a race was springing from Trojan blood to overthrow the Tyrian citadels; that from this source would come a people wide in power and proud in war for the downfall of Libya; for such was on the scroll of the Fates.

The daughter of Saturn, fearing this and mindful of the old war which she had first waged at Troy on behalf of her beloved Argives—nor yet had the reasons for that wrath and her fierce pain then faded from her memory; deep in her heart remains stored away the Judgement of Paris, and the injustice of her beauty scorned, the hated race, and the honour done to ravished Ganymede—inflamed by these things, Juno . . . [harried the Trojans]

The first thing that should strike us is how Homeric the ethos and religion of the poem seems.[5] Juno loves a city, the city of Carthage—and proleptically hates another, the city founded by Trojans destined to rise (12ff.); and she hates, fiercely and personally (9ff., also 7.310ff.), the hero Aeneas, and his people, and pursues them relentlessly over the oceans (29ff.). This hatred of hers is clearly explained by the poet—and some of its Homerically unmoral character might, I think, have surprised Vergil's readers (cf. below, pp. 94–5). She hates them partly because of her love for Carthage, threatened by the future Trojan nation (19ff.), and partly because she feels that insult has been done to her *timē*, her honour or status, in the matter of the Judgement of Paris and the affair of Ganymede; note the implications of the words 'spretae' and 'honores': Juno felt her beauty had been *scorned*, and resented the *honour* done to Ganymede; and she is none too pleased either about the parentage (Jupiter) of Dardanus—that is the point behind 'genus inuisum', the 'hated race' (28). Hence the Trojans and their leader are hateful to her.

I continue a little way further into the poem, in summary. In the first major scene (50ff.) Juno suborns Neptune's lieutenant Aeolus to rouse up a storm against Aeneas, offering him as a bribe a pretty girl. Aeneas is battered, despairs (81ff.). But (124ff.) Neptune notices that something is amiss in his territory, and is outraged by this encroachment upon his 'imperium' (138); he dresses down Aeolus and the insubordinate winds,

---

[5] Cf. La Penna, Camps, Coleman, and Boyancé, 18ff., who much underestimates it; Coleman thinks (163) that the anthropomorphic realism of Aeolus, Juno etc. hazards a religious system intended to be serious: see Ch. 1 nn. 74, 77.

and calms the storm. In this way Aeneas is enabled to reach land. It should be stressed[6] that Neptune does not act out of a sense of justice or pity: he simply resents the encroachment on his area of command (on Neptune see further below, p. 99). Anyway, with Aeneas on land and temporarily safe, Venus, his mother and protectress, approaches Jupiter and tearfully implores his aid (227 ff.). Jupiter has in fact just turned his eyes, hitherto averted, to the chaos on earth and is troubled (223 ff.). He listens to Venus, smiles, and answers (254 ff.) in a speech which I shall consider shortly.

The Homeric parallels for all this may be listed briefly: I do so simply to remind us how Homeric in motive and topic this divine action is. Vergil's chief source is, of course, Odysseus' entry into the *Odyssey* in Book 5. Poseidon hates Odysseus fiercely and personally, pursuing him relentlessly over the oceans, because of the blinding of his son, the Cyclops—he acts therefore like Juno, though his motive is different. In particular, he rouses up a storm against Odysseus. The battered hero despairs (5.299 ff.), but is given divine assistance out of the blue (by Leucothea, 5.333 ff., and, subsequently, others), and reaches land (5.451 ff.). Meanwhile a divine protectress, Athena, has implored aid on his behalf from Zeus (1.45 ff., 5.7 ff.). I said that Poseidon's motive was different from Juno's: but in the *Iliad* we can find a goddess motivated very similarly to her. Hera—Juno's Greek counterpart—loves some cities (Argos, Sparta, and Mycenae), and hates another, Troy (4.51 ff.); and she hates it because of the insult done to her in the Judgement of Paris (24.28–30). Hera, too, suborns a lesser deity, this time Sleep, to further her ends (in the 'Deception of Zeus', 14.224 ff.). And it is Zeus who characteristically turns his eyes away from, or towards, some particular action (see below).

The parallels could be multiplied but are not particularly important. What is important is, as I say, to realize how similar the religion of the *Aeneid* is (up to this point) to much of the *Odyssey*'s and just about all the *Iliad*'s: how similar the nature of the gods seems, how similar the relations between gods and men. In both poems the heroes are operating in a polytheistic

---

[6] *Pace* Otis, 229.

world, a world influenced by powerful but wilful gods, acting not in concert, not apparently concerned with what we could call justice, but motivated by love, hate, status. And, a point I should like to stress, such a religion is not implausible; on the contrary it is plausible, though far from comforting. To many people (especially in the ancient world) it may well seem that there are supernatural powers, powers beyond their control, affecting their lives; and it may well seem that there is no rhyme or reason to such powers. For example, storms assail this person and not that; love, madness, plague attack and incapacitate us, indiscriminately, paying no apparent heed to justice or the lack of it. Why? How do these immense, inexplicable phenomena occur? And why here and not there, now and not then? I think a natural, ready, and economic explanation *is* to assume that there is a plurality of capricious or partial gods. It is certainly a more ready explanation than to suppose that all such phenomena are caused by one god, and a benevolent one at that.

But there are, of course, striking differences as well as similarities between the gods in the Homeric poems and the gods in the *Aeneid*.[7] One of these is perhaps unexpected: the gods dominate the opening of the *Aeneid* far more than they do the opening of the *Iliad* or the *Odyssey*—or perhaps it is more prudent to say that they occupy relatively more space.[8] Another important point is that Juno and, to a lesser extent, Venus have a *historical* sense, they have an eye to posterity, in a way that Homeric gods do not. And Vergil's gods display a greater reluctance to mingle with men. But the most important difference rests with the notion of Fate, 'fatum', in the *Aeneid*, to which I shall attend in a moment.

But first I should like briefly to consider and dismiss the theory of 'gods as symbols', gods as figurative representations of what happens in the hearts of men. In the process of dismissing it we shall come upon a significant fact about Vergil's gods. But how do we dismiss it? How do we show that what seem to be divine interferences in the action of the *Aeneid* are *not*

---

[7] Cf. e.g. Coleman, Boyancé, 23 ff., with bibliography.
[8] Klingner, 386.

symbolic, figurative representations? Vergil is cagey enough to make the facts and their interpretation far from self-evident. Take this passage, 12.554 ff.:

> hic mentem Aeneae genetrix pulcherrima misit
> iret ut ad muros urbique aduerteret agmen
> ocius et subita turbaret clade Latinos.
> ille ut uestigans diuersa per agmina Turnum
> huc atque huc acies circumtulit, aspicit urbem
> immunem tanti belli atque impune quietam.
> continuo pugna accendit maioris imago: . . .
>   'urbem hodie, causam belli, regna ipsa Latini . . .
>   eruam . . .'

Hereupon his most beautiful mother inspired Aeneas with the intention to advance to the walls, to turn his column on the town, and confound the Latins more swiftly with sudden disaster. He, while tracking Turnus here and there through the armies, turning his gaze this way and that, caught sight of the city, untouched by all the warfare, peaceful, unharmed. Straightway a vision of a greater battle inflamed him . . . [and he said] 'Today, I shall overthrow the city, the cause of the war, the very kingdom of Latinus . . .'

Vergil simply sits Venus' inspiration and Aeneas' vision side by side. Does not the former indeed sound rather like a symbolic or figurative representation of the latter? How do we show that it is not? My answer to this problem is set out in the next section.

2. 'Working with'

Gods in the *Aeneid* effect a change in degree if not in kind in the humans they work upon, which is explicable only if we accept the fact of external and supernatural interference. It is to be noted that there are *two* important points contained in that sentence. The gods do effect a change, but it is in degree rather than kind. To put it another way: they *play on emotions already present*; they *work with* susceptible humans to produce, or to try to produce, the ends they desire.[9] When Nisus contemplates his bold enterprise at 9.184f., he is made to phrase a stimulating but over-simple question:

---

[9] Cf. La Penna, n. 4, who would, so I infer, be sympathetic with my view. Contrast, e.g. G. Williams, 20ff.: the gods 'are not needed'.

> dine hunc ardorem mentibus addunt,
> Euryale, an sua cuique deus fit dira cupido?

Is it the gods who put this passion in men's minds, Euryalus, or does each person's fierce desire become his god?

This is to see the issue in unreal 'either/or' terms (is it divine or human motivation?).[10] In fact, when the gods are observable, what happens is a blend of the two alternatives—and more interesting than either: the gods 'work with'. As parallels for what I am suggesting happens in the *Aeneid*, one might compare (though the situations are by no means exactly comparable) Dionysus' manipulation of Pentheus in Euripides' *Bacchae*, or the way divine justice may seem to 'work with' predispositions in Aeschylus' Agamemnon, and other occasions in Greek literature;[11] then one might contrast Lyssa's effect on Euripides' Heracles, or for that matter Apollo's on Patroclus in *Iliad* 16.

In advance of evidence for this thesis I should like to make three points. First, the fact that the gods are made to operate like this contributes further to the plausibility of the religion of the *Aeneid*. For does not our experience of human nature constantly offer us changes in degree that might seem, though only in degree, inexplicable? Changes like Heracles' occur infrequently in life, and in literature verge in consequence on the implausible. But changes in degree are, though 'inexplicable', frequent: youths merely amorously inclined become 'inexplicably' crazed with love overnight. Sports fans merely aggressive in their partisanship become 'incomprehensibly' violent. Frequent phenomena in life (such changes in degree) do therefore require special explanations—and some would

---

[10] R. D. Williams (7–12) remarks on 9.184f. 'A good deal of the divine symbolism in the *Aeneid* revolves around this question—e.g., did Allecto drive Turnus to frenzy, or is his frenzy symbolised in Allecto?' Nisus' over-simple question has misled many commentators.

[11] Cf. E. R. Dodds, *Euripides, Bacchae* (Oxford, 1944), 163: 'the poet shows us the supernatural attacking the victim's personality at its weakest point—working upon and through nature, not against it.' What contributes to Agamemnon's decisions and disaster? A 64,000-dollar question of course, but 'working with' might be a useful formula; the comments of K. Reinhardt, *Aischylos als Regisseur und Theologe* (Bern, 1949), 15ff. are in this connection very suggestive. Cf. too Aesch. *Pers.* 742.

say, not implausibly, supernatural explanations. Vergil's explanation is: gods, pervasive and active: 'working with'.

My second point is really a suggestion, something to bear in mind as we read the poem. If gods operate by playing on emotions already present, it is presumably because they need to operate this way. To exploit available emotions successfully might require talent and originality. We would expect gods to possess talent and originality, and we should be able therefore to discern such qualities in their actions. We have already seen one spectacular example. Assaulting Amata, Allecto is stimulated to an ingenuity of which Lyssa simply has no need.

Thirdly, if crucial events are produced by the interaction and indeed interdependence of divine plans and mortal inclinations, how do we apportion responsibility? The answer of course is that the Vergilian system—characteristically—forbids exact apportionment, and precludes easy answers. It offers only a sliding scale on which the extremes (total human or total divine responsibility) are *pace* Nisus rarely if ever evident, and each reader on each occasion must make his own assessment. Responsibility in the *Aeneid* is a grey area; and many of us might think that to be a true reflection of the facts of life.

Now some examples. We have observed the ingenuity of Allecto's assault on Amata—the way she 'works with' the queen's passion. Consider, too, Turnus, attacked in his sleep. He is brooding on what is happening in Latium: as he tells the disguised dream-apparition of Allecto (7.436ff.), he knows the Trojans have arrived and it is not to be imagined that he is afraid . . . ; meanwhile, he says, the old priestess (for Turnus thinks Allecto is the priestess Calybe) should mind her own business . . . There is a certain menace in Turnus' words, in his cool reference to his own deliberations as well as in his scornful dismissal of 'Calybe'. He was clearly going to react in some way to Aeneas' interference. But how? In response to 'Calybe's' rebuttal, Allecto is enraged and tries harder: she reveals her demonic self, flings a torch into him, and Turnus' brooding deliberation—from which *something* would certainly have resulted—is translated into a mad fury. Allecto 'works with' Turnus. How much of Turnus' subsequent furious career would have happened without Allecto and can therefore be put down to his personal account? We cannot say, not for sure. The fact that Allecto 'works with' a potential in Turnus produces a grey area as regards responsibility. And as with Amata, so with Turnus; Allecto acts with intelligence and ingenuity. This is Vergil's description of her actual assault (7.456f.):

> sic effata facem iuueni coniecit et atro
> lumine fumantis fixit sub pectore taedas.

Having spoken thus she hurled a firebrand into the young man and fixed in his breast a torch smoking with black light.

Note the emphasis on Allecto's 'torch', referred to by two different words within two lines, 'fax' and 'taeda'. Vergil makes her use a different weapon from that used in the assault on Amata, and emphasizes the fact. Why? There is an insinuation of imagery, which reveals Allecto's perception and policy. Torches are symptomatic of violence and warfare. On one level, therefore, Vergil is simply arming Allecto with another suitable weapon (and see 7.337). But torches also typify and may symbolize the wedding ceremony (note in particular in Book 7 lines 322 and 388). The language (a further voice) is indicating to us that Allecto has grasped the issue that most angers Turnus (the frustration of his marriage to Lavinia) and now works on the emotions connected with that to turn them into fury for war. The simile which then ensues (7.462ff.: Turnus compared to a simmering cauldron brought to the boil) suggests external interference nearly as much as Amata's top simile did.[12]

Another and obvious example. Venus clearly has malleable material to work with in the shape of Dido. Dido is generous and sympathetic by nature, lonely and exposed in situation, and feels an immediate affinity with Aeneas himself (see especially 1.615ff.). She is obviously vulnerable to love. But the poison of Cupid produces out of this vulnerability a 'uulnus', a wound, disease, madness (1.712, 4.1ff.): a passion quite differ-

---

[12] External interference, but interference with emotion already existing. The image is of a *simmering* pot being brought to the *boil* (brushwood is added to a cauldron already 'seething' ('undantis', 463), which then in consequence 'boils' (465)): a good illustration of 'working with'. Although a top is predisposed to whirl, Amata's simile suggests more external manipulation and control than Turnus' does. The sources of the cauldron simile are Hom. *Il.* 21.362ff. (allusive function?) and, as D. P. Fowler points out to me, Lucretius' account of anger, 3.294–8.

ent in degree than would have resulted naturally (but *how* different? we cannot tell).

Consider too Juno in 5.613ff. Via Iris disguised as Beroe she plays on the despair and weariness of the Trojan women, seeking to induce them to burn the ships. The plan eventually works. But not before the bogus Beroe has flung the first torch *and* been exposed as a god by Pyrgo, and her own spectacular exit. How on earth do we apportion blame here? What would the women have done without divine interference? We cannot say. Even Vulcan seems to get into the act here ('furit immissis Volcanus habenis / transtra per et remos et pictas abiete puppis' ['with reins freed, Vulcan rages over the thwarts, the oars, and the painted poops of pine'], 5.662f.). Or is he just a figure of speech? When gods 'work with' mortals, the question of responsibility can get inextricably entangled, and life is rendered difficult and mysterious for humans—and for their interpreters. But, I repeat, it seems to me a far from implausible way of representing causation.

My penultimate example will be what is one of the most famous interventions in the *Aeneid*: when Jupiter dispatches Mercury to Carthage in order to jolt Aeneas back to his duty (4.219ff.). We find the same formula: 'working with'. But this time a god works with—it might be said—good and constructive instincts. Jupiter via Mercury prods an Aeneas already inclined to be prodded. For, as he tells Dido (4.353f.), his conscience had been troubling him in respect of Ascanius (added to which, visions of Anchises had appeared to him in dreams, admonishing him, 351ff.). So whose is the responsibility for his departure? Here too it is a grey area. We each must make our own assessment of how much applause is due to Aeneas, how much to Jupiter, for the abandonment of the queen. (But the choice of *how* the parting should be conducted, can, as we shall see (Ch. 4 ss. 5, 6), be more definitely attributed—and assessed.)

We can now return to 12.554ff. Frustrated by his inability to corner Turnus, Aeneas conceives the disturbing but effective idea of attacking the Latin city. Or does he conceive it? There is the part played by his mother to contend with; she, Vergil tells us, 'inspired him with the intention'. When I referred to this passage above, I said that Vergil seems simply to sit the one

Gods and men

beside the other, the divine inspiration beside the human conception. Now we can see that the scene fits into a pattern. True, the process whereby Venus 'works with' Aeneas is not spelled out. But the ingredients are the customary ones—divine and human, interacting (we should infer), and interdependent. The responsibility for the plan? Choose your point on the sliding scale. One thing, however, is certain. Vergil does not want us to miss Venus' contribution. The plan is shrewd and effective but not particularly pleasant, and Vergil comments on the insidious goddess's participation with an irony, calling her at this precise juncture 'pulcherrima', 'most beautiful' (honourable, excellent: the word has ramifying implications)—and Vergil chooses major figures' epithets with great care.[13]

'Vergil comments.' To put this in my customary and cautious terminology, a further voice intrudes an opinion about Augustus' dislikeable ancestress.

3. Jupiter and Fate

It is time now to attend to the place of fate, 'fatum', in the *Aeneid*, which, at first glance anyway, strikes an extremely unHomeric note.

Fate is mentioned in the very second line of the poem. Aeneas' migration to Italy was, we learn, 'fated'; and, in Italy, he had a fateful purpose: to establish the Trojans in a city, to introduce their gods, and thus to lay the foundations of Roman civilization (1.1–3 and 5–8):

> Troiae qui primus ab oris
> Italiam fato profugus Lauiniaque uenit
> litora . . .
>   dum conderet urbem
> inferretque deos Latio; genus unde Latinum
> Albanique patres atque altae moenia Romae.

the man who first came by fate an exile from the coasts of Troy to Italy and Lavinian shores . . . [buffeted etc.] until he should found a city and bring his gods to Latium; whence came the Latin race, the Elders of Alba, and the walls of lofty Rome.

These are indeed unHomeric notes. 'Fate', of course, remains a

---
[13] Cf. Ch. 1 p. 10.

constant theme of the poem. What does it mean? How does it affect our view of Vergilian religion?

Jupiter's reply to the tearful Venus throws crucial light on the significance and scope of fate, and is illuminating in other ways (1.254ff.). I quote the opening of it, together with its introduction:

> olli subridens hominum sator atque deorum
> uultu, quo caelum tempestatesque serenat,
> oscula libauit natae, dehinc talia *fatur*:
> 'parce metu, Cytherea, manent immota tuorum
> *fata* tibi; cernes urbem et promissa Lauini
> moenia, sublimemque feres ad sidera caeli
> magnanimum Aenean; *neque me sententia uertit.*
> hic tibi (*fabor* enim, quando haec te cura remordet,
> longius, et uoluens *fatorum* arcana mouebo)
> bellum ingens geret Italia populosque ferocis
> contundet moresque uiris et moenia ponet . . .

The creator of gods and men smiled at her, with the expression wherewith he calms sky and storms, and lightly he kissed his daughter and then spoke thus: 'Spare your fear, lady of Cythera, your people's fate abides unchanged; you will see the city and the promised walls of Lavinium, and you will raise great-hearted Aeneas to the stars of heaven; no purpose has changed me [i.e. my purpose has not been changed by anybody else's]. But, since this care nags you, I shall speak and, unrolling the scrolls, reveal the secrets of fate: this your son will wage a mighty war in Italy, will crush fierce peoples, and set up city walls and civilized institutions for men . . .

And Jupiter goes on to prophesy the salient moments of what is to be called Roman history, down to and beyond the triumphant time of Augustus.

Jupiter thus confirms that Aeneas has a historic and fated purpose: his struggles are the first step on the way towards a vast and magnificent future. So all is not, it appears, emotion and wilfulness on the divine plane. There seems to be a plan for the world, conceived in heaven and overseen from there, a grand and (especially if you are a Roman) a good plan: law, peace, empire, Rome. And this is what is 'fated'. It is also clearly something closely connected with Jupiter.

First, let us be precise about 'fate' and 'fatum'. This word shifts slightly in signification, depending on its context in the poem, but it has a definite and crucial main area of sense. We should scrutinize the opening of the passage just quoted. Jupiter expounds the 'fatorum arcana', the 'secrets of fate', which are as we have seen a grand plan for the world: empire, peace, and so on. If the 'secrets' are fate's, then the plan is fate's: it is fate who has conceived the grand and good plan for the world. This is to introduce a Stoic or quasi-Stoic notion.[14] For the Stoics believed in a planning and guiding fate. They labelled this provident divinity Nature, or God, or Providence, or Fate, indifferently—but often Fate; and Vergil's language, the way he presents Jupiter's prophecy here, irresistibly brings to mind this Stoic idea of a provident and overseeing Fate. And this is the most important sense of 'fatum' in the *Aeneid*, the sense which affects the poem's religion most radically: 'fatum' or 'Fatum' is the Divine Will that has a grand plan for the world and oversees its realization. This is what I would call the word's primary sense—a 'cosmic' and 'active' sense. Then by an easy shift it also has what one might call a 'cosmic' and 'passive' sense: it can signify *what* is willed, the plan as well as the planner. It may signify what is willed for a city or a people—this, I think, is its sense in 257f., 'manent immota tuorum / fata' ['your people's fate abides unchanged']; and it can also signify what is willed on a much smaller scale: Fate's allocation to an individual, what is in store for him, his 'moira'.

What of the relation of Jupiter and his Will to Fate and Fate's plan? This is another point in which Vergil differs radically from Homer. In the *Iliad* there is both a 'passive' fate, 'moira', and an 'active' 'Moira'.[15] But 'Moira' possesses a much more limited province than 'Fatum' (it decides in particular when a man is to die; and passive 'moira' is limited similarly). And it is distinct from Zeus. The coexistence of Zeus and 'Moira' is arguably a religious anomaly, but it is one which Homer puts to spectacular dramatic effect at *Iliad* 16.431ff. and 22.167ff. It is not, however, an anomaly or effect which Vergil wants. In fact, the passage I have quoted seems to be doing its utmost to *identify* Fate with Jupiter and his Will.[16] A first point: Jupiter

[14] Cf. Heinze, 293ff.; Boyancé, 46ff.; Bailey, 208ff., esp. 220ff.
[15] Cf. A. W. H. Adkins, *Merit and Responsibility* (Oxford, 1960), 17–23.
[16] Thus Heinze, loc. cit.; Camps, 42f.; Bailey, loc. cit. Boyancé, 47ff., is more cautious. *Contra* La Penna, lxxvi f.

administers Fate's scrolls: he, like Fate, 'uoluit' (1.22, 262). More substantially, it is hard to differentiate Jupiter's statement 'manent immota tuorum fata' from his statement 'neque me sententia uertit', the statement that no purpose has changed his purpose: the 'fate' of Venus' people *depends* upon his 'purpose'; it is he who wills it. Thirdly, as my italics above show, Vergil twice uses the verb 'fari' of Jupiter as he expounds fate in close collocation with the word 'fatum'. What he is doing is putting into relief the etymological connection of verb and noun[17] (which can hardly be reproduced in English), and thereby suggesting that the two ideas—the Jupiter who 'utters', 'fatur', and Fate (the 'Utterance' or 'Utterer')—are indissociable. We can therefore draw the following conclusions. There seems to be a divinity providently directing the world of the *Aeneid*: Fate. And Jupiter and his Will are identifiable with that Fate. In sum, therefore, not only is an entirely unHomeric philosophical dimension added to Vergil's inherited Homeric religion: one, and only one, of Vergil's gods is much redrawn compared with his Homeric counterpart. The authoritative, far-seeing, provident Jupiter sounds—on the face of it at least—very much unlike Homer's Zeus.

Minor complications need hardly delay us here. For example, another god's will, besides Jupiter's Will, may be termed 'fatum' or 'fata' (8.292); somewhat more enigmatically Fate, *the* Will, can be termed 'fata deum'. But these are not points I wish to pursue now.

I should like to take up, however, that specification *one*: one of Vergil's gods is much redrawn compared with its Homeric counterpart. But the others are surprisingly little altered (though cf. above, p. 65), and the *Aeneid* must not be forced into a false cohesion. The poem remains definitely *poly*theistic. Jupiter, it appears, has a will and a plan, also called 'fatum'. Jupiter seems provident—in addition he has the ability to foresee that his plan will be accomplished, and thus can attempt to reassure Venus. But that does not mean that the other gods do not exist; and it does not mean that they necessarily contribute to his plan, or approve it, or are part of it. Remember Juno. That vicious goddess is going to do all she can to prevent

[17] Varr. *Ling.* 6.52; Boyancé, 39.

Jupiter's Will, or at least to make its agents suffer in the process. So, Providence there is; but there is also wilfulness, pride, self-regard, malice, *divine* wilfulness, pride, self-regard, and malice; and these work alongside or in actual opposition to Providence. This complex cosmos is what Aeneas has to contend with as he tries in particular to obey Providence, to accomplish the Will of Jupiter: 'to follow Fate' as Vergil and indeed the Stoics would say.[18] And in that connection I must stress a vital point: free will. The *Aeneid* does *not* adopt the Stoics' determinism—a doctrine which the Stoics themselves found not a little unrealistic. Humans are vulnerable to divine interference as described above (s. 2 'Working with'); but they also have their measure of freedom, and bear a measure of responsibility, as was also explained above. In Aeneas' case, he may be told what to do, and helped by divine messages, even messengers; and Jupiter may be able to foresee that he will eventually, more or less, do it. But the task is still his.[19] And we, the readers, perceive its difficulties and pains.

4. Jupiter

I have established that Fate and Jupiter's Will appear to be synonymous; Jupiter is, as it were—or in effect—Providence, a providential god, but faced with the wilfully hateful Juno, the emotional and sometimes cruel Venus, the prickly and inscrutable Neptune, and others. But is this picture of Jupiter correct? Is it the whole picture? Not so, by far: he is a much more interesting figure than I have so far sketched.

The first thing we ought to reassess is that Will of his, that provident plan outlined in 1.257ff.: Rome, empire, peace, morality and law, to rise out of the ashes of Troy, the achievement of heroes. Jupiter seems perspicuous in his intentions, his plan clear and good; none of the inscrutability that Homer's Zeus displays, none of the mystery that attends Zeus' *boulē*— Zeus, we remember, had a 'plan', a mysterious one that seems to widen in compass and darken in purpose as the poem

---

[18] Cf. 5.709; Sen. *Epist. Mor.* 107.11; R. D. Williams on 5.709f.
[19] In this connection Adkins' remarks, op. cit., 118ff., on prophecy are worth rereading.

progresses.[20] Or has Jupiter's plan some inscrutability? Consider this: Jupiter's plan of course starts from, it rises out of, the destruction of Troy. It is therefore a relevant question to ask *why* Troy was destroyed.[21] I concentrate on the motives of the divinities concerned, those who were most lethal in their hostility to Troy. There is what we might call an 'Iliadic' answer to the question; and, perhaps surprisingly (below, pp. 94–5), we find that the *Aeneid* is in substantial agreement with it. Troy's especial enemies were Poseidon/Neptune, Pallas Athena and Hera/Juno. Poseidon/Neptune's hostility was due to the fact that he had been defrauded of payment by Laomedon (*Iliad* 21.436ff., *Aeneid* 5.810f.; on Neptune see too below, p. 99); Pallas Athena and Hera/Juno were hostile because of the Judgement of Paris (*Iliad* 24.27ff., *Aeneid* 1.26–8); and in Juno's case there were other grudges too (above, p. 63). But the *Aeneid*, perhaps developing a hint in the *Iliad*,[22] introduces a complexity.

Let me quote the apocalyptic vision which Venus vouchsafes to Aeneas, showing Athena, Juno, and Poseidon venting their hatred on the doomed city (2.608ff.):[23]

> hic, ubi disiectas moles auulsaque saxis
> saxa uides, mixtoque undantem puluere fumum,
> Neptunus muros magnoque emota tridenti
> fundamenta quatit totamque a sedibus urbem
> eruit. hic Iuno Scaeas saeuissima portas
> prima tenet sociumque furens a nauibus agmen
> ferro accincta uocat.
> iam summas arces Tritonia, respice, Pallas
> insedit nimbo effulgens et Gorgone saeua.
> ipse pater Danais animos uirisque secundas
> sufficit, ipse deos in Dardana suscitat arma.

---

[20] Cf. J. Griffin, *GR* 29 (1982), 130. Whatever our impression of Zeus' plan at the end of *Iliad* 1, we will find it changed and widened by the events in the poem and in particular by Achilles' reaction to those events: crucially at 24.525ff. and 19.270ff.; Zeus' prophecies at 8.473ff. and 15.59ff. also bear on the question.

[21] The question is not asked with sufficient rigour: cf. the vague and unhelpful comments of Otis, 249.

[22] As I show in the text, Jupiter is revealed by one scene to be enthusiastic for the destruction of Troy. At *Iliad* 15.69ff. Zeus suddenly prophesies in terms which might suggest either his desire or his intention to destroy Troy—but, as I say in the text, this is entirely untypical.

[23] A striking scene, not least because the gods are seen to intervene with unparalleled concreteness: cf. Boyancé, 24f.

Here, where you see the scattered masses and rocks torn from rocks, and smoke mixed with dust in eddies, Neptune shakes the walls and foundations, dislodging them with his great trident, and overthrows the city from its seat. Here most savage Juno is in the van, holds the Scaean gates, and, girt with iron, frenziedly summons her allied army from the ships. Turn, look: Tritonian Pallas is settled on the topmost citadel, flashing with storm-cloud and savage with Gorgon. The Father himself gives the Greeks courage and auspicious strength, himself rouses the gods against Dardan arms.

There, duly, is Neptune attacking the foundations of the walls; Juno holding the gates and summoning the Greeks; Pallas Athena on the citadel, shining and savage; *but also Jupiter ('The Father') himself inspiring the Greeks and inciting the gods against Troy.* So (it seems) Jupiter's plan does not just rise out of the destruction of Troy. It seems to encompass it: Troy's destruction seems part of his plan; otherwise his action is inexplicable. But why should Jupiter want or need the destruction of Troy? Because of Paris, and his insult to hospitality? Because of his adultery? The chorus in Aeschylus' *Agamemnon* imply that Zeus is hostile to Troy on the grounds of hospitality—without, it must be said, totally convincing some audiences or indeed themselves.[24] But no resentment against Troy on the grounds of either hospitality or adultery is attributed to or voiced by Zeus/Jupiter of the *Iliad* or the *Aeneid*. On the contrary, Zeus expresses his pre-eminent love for Troy and his regret at its imminent destruction (*Iliad* 4.31ff.); and in the *Aeneid*, Venus says specifically that the destruction of Troy is *not* due to the actions of Helen and Paris (her emphasis is particularly on their adultery),[25] but to what she terms the mercilessness of the gods. She prefaces the passage quoted above thus (2.601ff.)

> non tibi Tyndaridis facies inuisa Lacaenae
> culpatusue Paris, diuum inclementia, diuum
> has euertit opes sternitque a culmine Troiam.
> aspice . . .

---

[24] See *Agam.* 60ff., noting the slight change of tack in 62, and see then 228–30, 448–51, 799f. What is the audience to make of the issues? See the succinct and suggestive discussion of W. I. Winnington-Ingram, *Studies in Aeschylus* (Cambridge, 1983), 78ff., esp. 85–8, 93–100.
[25] The emphasis is contributed by 'culpatus' (602): see Austin ad loc.

It is not the hated beauty of Laconian Helen, nor the wickedness of Paris, but the mercilessness of the gods, the gods I say, that overthrows this wealth and flattens Troy from its pinnacle. Behold . . .

So the reason why Jupiter is hostile to Troy, or, to put it more precisely, the reason why his plan for a Roman future should so vigorously involve him in the *destruction* of Troy, is not clear. Venus can only talk of divine 'inclementia'. Jupiter's plan therefore has mysterious and troubling aspects. In this connection the phrases 'fato profugus' ['by fate an exile'] (1.2) and 'errabant acti fatis' ['they wandered driven by fate'] (1.32) deserve reconsideration—and reward it with enigma. Jupiter as a god has some of the inscrutability of Zeus. So Vergil's invention insinuates. If Book 1 suggests a comfortably Stoical Jupiter, a further voice complicates this picture.

Other information must be assessed and absorbed. For example, at 1.223–5, when Venus approaches Jupiter to supplicate him (above, p. 64), we are provided with the surprising information that all that chaos on earth—the illicit storm, the suffering of the 'Aeneidae'—had happened unseen by the almighty ('omnipotens', 1.60 etc.) provident Jupiter. His gaze had been averted. Only now, in 224f., he turns his eyes to Libya; only now is he anxious for the protagonists of Fate. Again we are reminded of Zeus rather than the Stoics' Providence: it is Zeus who, in lordly and serene manner, averts his eyes or directs his gaze according to his pleasure.[26] Is this Zeus-like trait (like the inscrutability referred to above) just a vestige, left over from Vergil's source and unassimilated in the new text? Or are we starting to build up a picture of a Jupiter who is certainly not just a copy of Homer's Zeus, but is not merely the embodiment of Fate either? A complex Vergilian creation, the product of many insinuating voices? If we consider now the question of Jupiter's Will and the war in Italy, we shall find further information that will push us to adjust our picture.

First consider the simple implications of Jupiter's statement in the divine 'concilium' that he had forbidden a war between Italy and the Trojans (10.8f.):

[26] Cf. Griffin, *Homer*, 179ff., esp. 197f.

Gods and men

> abnueram bello Italiam concurrere Teucris.
> quae contra uetitum discordia?

I forbade Italy to clash in war with the Trojans. What discord is this, contrary to my command?

With this we should couple the statement of the epic voice that the war was indeed contrary to Fate and the divine Will (7.583f.):

> ilicet infandum cuncti contra omina bellum,
> contra fata deum peruerso numine poscunt.

Straightway all, against the omens, against the Will of gods, overturning divine sanction, demand accursed war.

If what Jupiter forbids happens, it means (simply) that Fateful Jupiter, Jupiter 'omnipotens', has in fact *incomplete* power over the other gods, in particular Juno, even in such a grave matter as peace and war. Jupiter himself acknowledges this in another passage: in 12.804 he says to Juno that she had the ability to 'kindle an accursed war':

> terris agitare uel undis
> Troianos potuisti, *infandum accendere bellum* . . .

You were able to hound the Trojans by land and sea, to kindle an accursed war . . .

Jupiter has incomplete power over the other gods: a simple but significant point. Again we are reminded of the Iliadic Zeus: Jupiter 'omnipotens' reminds us of the Zeus 'the highest and best of the gods' and 'the mightiest of all'[27] who issues stern prohibitions against divine interference in the Trojan war only to find those prohibitions neglected and himself craftily circumvented.[28] Jupiter's Will may therefore be identifiable with Fate, but Fate—his Will—is less in control, less pervasive than we might have expected; and the plot, and the god, is correspondingly more interesting.

Next we should recall two lines in Jupiter's great prophecy to Venus in Book 1. Lines 263f. read:

[27] *Iliad* 19.258, 8.17.
[28] *Iliad* 8.5ff., 350ff., 13.1ff., 14.153ff.

> bellum ingens geret Italia populosque ferocis
> contundet moresque uiris et moenia ponet . . .

[Aeneas] will wage a mighty war in Italy; he will crush fierce peoples, and set up city walls and civilized institutions for men . . .

Would not this naturally imply and would not Venus take it to imply that it was part of Jupiter's plan that Aeneas should fight a war in Italy? But, as we subsequently learn (in Book 10), it was not. Why, therefore, does Jupiter speak so misleadingly? The problem must be tackled. (I would stress that there is too much evidence like this to render plausible the view that the difficulty here is due to, for example, the incomplete state of the poem. I find it difficult in any case to believe that such an important part of the poem as Jupiter's prophecy and the divine 'concilium' would have been kept inconsistent for very long by the author. The situation is simply that Vergil's invention is unexpected—and has implications.[29])

Not only does Jupiter prophesy as though the war were part of his plan; his allusion to the war ('bellum ingens . . .') makes it sound like a clean, imperial war, one with clear-cut, right and wrong issues. To borrow Anchises' phraseology, Jupiter rather implies that Aeneas will have simply to 'war down the proud' ('debellare superbos', 6.853; cf. 'populosque ferocis contundet') in order 'to impose civilization on top of peace' ('pacique imponere morem', 6.852; cf. 'mores uiris . . . ponet'). The addition of 'mores' and so on is presumably intended or hoped to be the eventual effect of the Trojans (cf. below, p. 82). But the war immediately facing Aeneas will be far from so clear-cut and clean in its issues or result as this description implies. Juno provokes a war that is tragic in its nature, agonizingly confused in its issues, more of a civil war than a clean imperial exercise. So why (again) does Jupiter speak misleadingly?

While our attention is focused on Jupiter's prophecy, let us consider another of his phrases: his expansive statement (1.279) 'imperium sine fine dedi' ['I have granted [to the Romans] empire without boundary']. From the vantage point of Vergil's time, this might seem to have been proved true. But

---

[29] Heinze, 297 n. 1, sees the discrepancy between prophecy and 'concilium' in this respect as simply a contradiction in the text. Surprisingly, Highet, 289, is inclined to view it similarly.

Gods and men

is it not expansive—bland, facile, conveniently omitting to mention the vast amount of blood, sweat, and tears the human recipients of his gift will have to expend (not to mention its enemies)? Convenient, facile: this is a 'well-packaged' prophecy! Herein, I think, lies the key to this and the other anomalies I have identified. What Jupiter is doing in this prophecy is adapting the facts to suit his immediate needs. He is prophesying *rhetorically*. Faced with his tearful, distraught daughter, he is revealing his knowledge of the future, or part of it, in a manner designed to afford her the maximum of comfort. It sounds better if he phrases the war in such clear-cut terms and implies it to be part of his plan. And so he does so. Similarly with 'imperium sine fine dedi': it sounds better than prophesying centuries of toil and struggle. This is not utterly honest behaviour on Jupiter's part perhaps, but it may be seen as kind. Jupiter possesses a Will that is identifiable with Fate, but he is still a god, a god with feelings, affections, emotions, intentions besides his 'grand intention'. And his intention in 1.256ff. is primarily to comfort Venus, to soothe his querulous daughter; so he chooses from his knowledge, bends the facts a little: 'packages' his revelation and so reassures her. Zeus and Hera at *Iliad* 15.47ff. in fact underlie the scene. Zeus can be warm towards his fellow gods, 'human' in his disposition. So can Jupiter—if we do not resist the implications of Vergil's invention.

Jupiter 'packages' not a revelation, but terms of reconciliation, in his deal with Juno at the end of the poem. It is convenient to mention the point here, though my main treatment of the 'reconciliation' will come below (pp. 94–8). Juno demands the demise of the Trojan language, name, and so on. Jupiter answers (12.833–7):

> do quod uis . . .
> sermonem Ausonii patrium moresque tenebunt,
> utque est nomen erit; commixti corpore tantum
> subsident Teucri. morem ritusque sacrorum
> adiciam . . .

I grant what you wish . . . The Italians will maintain their ancestral speech and customs (*mores*), and their name will remain as it is. Mingling in stock only, the Trojans will sink. I shall add civilized custom (*morem*) [or 'the manner'] and rites of religion . . .

There seems to be some equivocation in Jupiter's use of the word 'mos', 'mores' in 834 and (in particular) 836. The word can mean both 'civilized custom' and more generally 'way of life'; and it can mean simply 'manner' or 'mode'. What does Jupiter mean by 'morem' in 836? The question is, of course, complicated by his use of 'mores' in 834. Perhaps he means merely 'morem . . . sacrorum', the 'manner of religion', i.e. 'morem' amplifies 'ritus'. Or does he mean something substantial and separate, namely that a civilized quality ('mos') as well as religion will be added to Italian life from without? Or what? I think that Juno, reassured by 834, 'moresque tenebunt', may well be meant to infer the first of these alternatives. But what Jupiter is likely to be thinking of, ultimately anyway, is the second, the external addition of civilized customs. He is indeed equivocating: he is 'packaging'. This can be seen more clearly when we include for examination an equivocation definitely visible in the word 'adiciam', ['*I* shall add']: 'ritusque sacrorum adiciam'. Throughout the poem it has been an insistent theme of both narrator and characters that *the Trojans* will contribute religion (i.e. 'ritus sacrorum') to the Italians; and moreover (though less insistently) that they will contribute 'civilized custom' ['mos']. At 1.6 we were told that Aeneas' fated mission was 'to bring gods into Latium'. Hector's ghost told Aeneas in 2.293 that Troy entrusted her religion, 'sacra', and 'penates' to him and that he was to find them 'great walls' across the sea; and Hector 'handed' to him Vesta and the eternal flame (296) (cf. 320, 717). Aeneas then heads into exile with the 'penates and great gods' (3.12), the very same gods which will eventually grace his illustrious descendant Augustus (8.679). And at 12.192 Aeneas' magnanimous terms include the provision 'sacra deosque dabo' ['I shall give religion and gods']; he knew what was fated and what was his duty. Back in 1.264 Jupiter prophesied that Aeneas would impose 'civilized customs' ['mores'] on the Italians. That, of course, was a piece of 'packaging': Aeneas is not likely to be so lucky, not so cleanly lucky anyway, in the immediate present (above, p. 80). But we are, I think, supposed to infer that Jupiter plans the eventual effect of the Trojan contribution to be 'civilizing'; compare Anchises' instruction to Aeneas (as well as the Romans): 'pacique imponere morem' ['impose civilized custom on top of peace'] (6.852).

Gods and men

And are we not to suppose that the Trojans added both civilization and religion to the ruder Italians? What sacred fire (for example) was attended at Rome by Vestal Virgins? And what of the penates? What, therefore, is Jupiter up to, equivocating with Juno on the question of 'civilized custom', and suggesting that religion (and 'civilized custom', should 'morem' be taken that way) will not be a Trojan addition but—somehow, from somewhere—his? He is glossing the truth, packaging a fact that will be unpalatable to Juno. Juno is going to get a great deal of what she wants, but not all she wants. The Trojans will make vital contributions to the new race besides their stock: religion and civilization. Better to package that: 'I', Jupiter says vaguely, 'will add religion and "morem".'[30]

We might remind ourselves at this point that other gods, Homeric and Vergilian, are prepared to bend facts to induce an appropriate frame of mind in mortals who concern them. For example, at *Aeneid* 8.40f. the river god Tiberinus pronounces the following comforting statement:

> neu belli terrere minis; tumor omnis et irae
> concessere deum.

Neither be terrified by threats of war; all the turmoil and wrath of the gods has given way.

This is of course, if we reflect on what Juno has been up to in Book 7, patently not true, and presumably Tiberinus himself knows as much—indeed in 8.60f. he feels bound earnestly to recommend Aeneas to propitiate her. But his blandly general utterance is encouraging (and who knows? maybe the propitiation will work), and encouragement is what our anxious hero sorely needs at present.[31] Somewhat similar is the behaviour of Athena in *Odyssey* 1. In a speech to Telemachus at lines 179ff. she supplies him with the graceful falsehood that it is 'fierce men' not the glamorous Calypso who are detaining Odysseus on

---

[30] R. D. Williams (7–12) on 12.835f. 'commixti . . . Teucri' writes 'Jupiter here perhaps somewhat overstates the case in order to placate Juno'; on 836f., 'morem . . . adiciam', he writes 'i.e. Jupiter here takes responsibility for the mingling with the original Italian religion of the Trojan worship which was a vital aspect of Aeneas' mission'. These are over-cautious comments, but more perceptive than other scholars'.

[31] Servius *auctus* ad loc.: 'nondum concesserunt, sed utiliter dissimulat'. Servius cites other solutions to the 'problem'.

a sea-girt island. The truth might have confused the impressionable adolescent, dampening his ardour to preserve his mother against the day of his moral father's return.[32]

But to return to Jupiter: the trend of my argument has been that not only do Juno, Venus, and other gods retain much of their Homeric colour—they are devious, passionate, partisan—the 'father of gods and men' retains some too. He too displays affection, inscrutability, a willingness to bend facts, and other 'Homeric' qualities. And all this is in addition to, and not necessarily overshadowed by, his mighty Will; and (it is worth adding) some might think that that Will was pretty partisan. Anyway, Jupiter is *interesting*: a real god, living, moving, having his being; formidable, and, as I shall argue, able to be cruel, heartless, and unfair—like most gods in the ancient world.

Consider the question of morality. Death is the great divider between men and gods in the *Aeneid*, not much less so than it is in the *Iliad*;[33] but the question of morality, in particular the question of the consequences of actions, defines the difference almost as acutely, as I shall demonstrate. I shall consider in particular men and Jupiter, the most august of gods.

First, a small and general point. Within limits, certainly not limits set by men, gods can do what they like. Let a man emulate such divine 'morality' and he may be destroyed. Consider the question of deceit. In a sense Jupiter was deceiving Venus in Book 1; and I shall show him more vigorously deceitful shortly. But there are no *consequences*: it signifies nothing. Then we think of men: the cities of Troy and Oechalia were destroyed by Hercules, for perjury (8.291); the deceitful Mettus was torn asunder (8.642).

More crucially, let us think of Aeneas and his agonizing moral dilemma at Carthage; and of the guilt, suffering, and suicide of Dido. They both paid terribly for their 'immoral' love, called to order by a peremptory moral message from Jupiter reminding Aeneas of Fate, his duty, and so on. Agonized, Aeneas left; distraught, Dido committed suicide. It is interesting to glance back to Jupiter. The first point to notice is that his attention had actually been distracted, his eyes averted

---

[32] Cf. Griffin, *Homer*, 64.
[33] Cf. Griffin, *Homer*, esp. 187f., 191.

once more, in characteristic Zeus-like fashion (4.219ff.; cf. above, p. 78). His attention had to be drawn to the disgraceful goings-on in Carthage, which were threatening his Will.[34] This is odd behaviour on the part of the fateful 'Omnipotens'. It might have been a lot better for all concerned if he had been more alert earlier. We infer that he is not only a fateful 'Omnipotens'; he has his whims and distractions. But I pass to a more substantial point. Who drew Jupiter's attention to the disgraceful goings-on in Carthage? It was the jealous Iarbas—born of a nymph who had been raped by Jupiter himself—as we are told only twenty-two lines earlier (198). The irony is only too clear, and so cruel: Vergil's invention and 'dispositio' produces implications that we must not resist. Jupiter may indulge a violent *amour* and there are no consequences for him at all; it signifies nothing. But if a mortal loves, and that love conflicts with Jupiter's divine Will, it signifies everything: the consequences are crushing. The collocation in Carthage, 'immoral' Jupiter calling Aeneas back to morality, makes the point acutely: a further voice exploiting invention and arrangement comments on the difference between man and god.[35] For man, life is earnest, moral, desperately serious, beset by consequences. A god, even—perhaps especially—Jupiter, may permit himself immorality and frivolity. Again we are reminded of Zeus, of that frightening divine *Unernst* that even Zeus displays.

Stirred to this kind of thought, we might look forward to the end of the poem, to Book 12. It shows the difference between

---

[34] I hope it is evident that I see a function for this 'Homeric' motif in Vergil's text. Contrast Coleman, 163, who considers it one of those anthropomorphic vestiges that undermine Vergil's serious theodicy. Contrast too the way the motif strikes Klingner, 394f. (talking of 1.225f.): 'Über Elend, Wirrsal und Ungewissheit der ersten Szenen tut sich hoch . . . die Weite des Blicks und der Gedanken des höchsten Gottes auf und damit die allumfassende Ordnung der Welt . . .'.

[35] Contrast this comment by Boyancé, 28f.: 'S'il n'est plus guère question des amours de Jupiter, de ses nymphes séduites et de ses Ganymèdes, c'est évidemment pour la même raison [viz. that Vergil has responded to Plato's criticism of the Homeric gods]. L'Olympe virgilien est un Olympe moralisé . . .'. That 'guère' is pretty breathtaking. Critics find a very different Jupiter from mine in Vergil's text: cf. e.g. n. 34, or Pöschl, 17 'In ihm versinnbildlicht sich am grössten die göttliche Macht . . . die *"serenitas"*, jene Grundkraft der Latinität, in der sich Klarheit des Geistes, Heiterkeit der Seele und das Licht des südlichen Himmels zu einem unübersetzbaren Begriff verschmelzen . . . Der Jupiter Virgils ist das Symbol dessen, was Rom als Idee verkörpert.' Splendid stuff! But this august god eludes my reading of Vergil.

man and God in the matter of morals, and in the matter of what we might call generous feelings. At this point in the poem Jupiter finally reconciles, or appears to reconcile, Juno to his Will, securing the end of her enmity towards the Trojans. Here therefore, we could say, we have the great Jupiter before us whose Will is Fate, Jupiter who oversees the grand Roman future, Jupiter the provident. And so we have. But, in saying that, we should not blind ourselves to the fact that we also have before us a Jupiter who towards mere humans, *qua* individual humans, displays indifference—indifference, moreover, while all the protagonists, even those that serve him, are locked in dilemma or despair. But those words 'dilemma' and 'despair' reflect the mortal perspective. Jupiter, we might say, shows his difference from mortals in that indifference of his.

I proceed to detail. At the end of the poem, Aeneas, Jupiter's agent, is faced with an acute dilemma. It is a dilemma entailing dreadful consequences. Aeneas has to decide whether or not he should kill the suppliant Turnus. He kills. His action has repercussions that will range beyond the end of the poem and into history (when will there be reconciliation, 'foedus', between Italians and Trojans? What kind of 'foedus'?). It also has acute repercussions within the framework of the poem: human grief. We think of the sorrowful speeches of Amata and Latinus at the beginning of Book 12, in fear of Turnus' death. We think in particular of Juturna. Grief at the death of Turnus is proleptically expressed by her at 12.872ff. And hers is actually a very special grief, a unique grief, for she will lament for ever. Originally a mortal and still possessed of mortal sensibility (she is the *Aeneid's* Thetis figure),[36] she has been granted the 'gift' of immortality, a gift she would now do anything to be rid of. Meanwhile, above all this grief, the far-seeing gods. Jupiter smiles ('subridens', 829) in agreement with Juno—he has, it seems, what he wants. What a suggestive collocation, the smiling Jupiter and the grieving mortals! The epic voice tells of reconciliation in heaven; a further voice is I think, by this piece of arrangement, commenting on the callousness of gods.

---

[36] On Thetis see Griffin, *Homer*, 190f.

Not just Jupiter's absence of generous feeling, but also his morality is again commented upon. The dilemma that faces Aeneas, Jupiter's agent, at the end of Book 12 is his greatest moral dilemma since Carthage. And, as at Carthage, that dilemma occurs because of the demands of Jupiter's Will. We remember, however, that at Carthage Iarbas had revealed, by revealing Jupiter's casual immorality, what a different thing it is to be a god: Jupiter imposes a morality and an earnestness upon men which he does not dream of imposing upon himself. In Book 12, Juturna performs Iarbas' function. As Aeneas approaches the deadly earnest, moral decision that he must make in the matter of Turnus' life, Juturna reminds us (in her proleptic lament, 12.872 ff.) that it was Jupiter who, permitting himself an indulgence which men might call immorality, had taken her virginity. Again the difference between the hero, beset by consequences, and the god who orders him and is beset by none, is made cruelly clear—by Vergil's organization of scenes. Ironies compound our sense of unfairness. As a consolation prize for her virginity, Jupiter gave Juturna that catastrophic δῶρον ἄδωρον: he gave her the immortality that now makes her sorrow illimitable—as Juturna poignantly says (12.878–80). And the sorrow Jupiter renders illimitable is caused by his agent.

So the end of the poem leaves Aeneas bound up in the human consequences of his actions; it leaves Amata and Turnus dead, Latinus lamenting, and Juturna enslaved to eternal tears. Suffering and responsibility, these are inescapable human conditions. And Jupiter? Jupiter exhibits, it may be argued, national and historic benevolence in his Will (Fate). But towards individuals he shows indifference at best, and at worst he callously uses them, for his pleasure or whatever. Irresponsibility and selfishness characterize his attitude towards humans, just as much as any other god's. Implications like these emerge from Vergil's invention and arrangement, a further voice.

I now take up the question of Jupiter's and the other gods' participation in the war in Italy. Here Jupiter displays Zeus-like inscrutability, and qualities that deserve harsher labels. I begin with an item in Book 10. At this point of the narrative Turnus has been lured from the field of battle by a phantom of Aeneas constructed by Juno. Then, we are told (10.689):

> at Iouis interea monitis Mezentius ardens
> succedit pugnae . . .

But, in the meantime, on the advice of Jupiter, Mezentius comes in passion up to battle . . .

Why does Jupiter thus advise a formidable enemy of the Trojans to enter battle? Interpretations differ. Coleman and T. E. Page think it is to expedite the punishment of 'one who scorns the gods', a 'contemptor diuum'. R. D. Williams thinks Jupiter 'intervenes to balance the situation after Juno's removal of Turnus', in other words, that it is a pro-Italian move. There are, I think, factors which suggest Jupiter's motive was the latter.[37] But why? Why does Jupiter give advice which aids the Italians? *Trojan* victory is surely vital to Jupiter's plan. And has he not already in a sense done a favour to Juno and the Italians by permitting the removal of Turnus? And is not Jupiter supposed to be totally impartial at this stage? That is what he seemed to say in the council of gods at the beginning of Book 10. His words there should be scrutinized, for it is an important issue.

Jupiter opens by saying that he had forbidden the war in Italy (above, p. 78), and asks why it was happening nonetheless. Then, after listening to the arguments—tendentious and dishonest[38]—of the rival goddesses, Juno and Venus, he delivers his judgement as follows (10.104ff.):

> 'accipite ergo animis atque haec mea figite dicta.
> quandoquidem Ausonios coniungi foedere Teucris
> haud licitum, nec uestra capit discordia finem,
> quae cuique est fortuna hodie, quam quisque secat spem,
> Tros Rutulusne fuat, nullo discrimine habebo,
> seu fatis Italum castra obsidione tenentur
> siue errore malo Troiae monitisque sinistris.

---

[37] Coleman, 159; T. E. Page and R. D. Williams (7–12) ad loc. Factors suggesting it is a pro-Italian move: behind 10.689 lies *Iliad* 15.593f. where Zeus urges on the Trojans specifically to aid them, if only for a while; and the 'Iouis monita' at 4.331 are definitely to aid their recipient.

[38] See Highet, 65–72, a fine discussion.

>   nec Rutulos soluo. sua cuique exorsa laborem
>   fortunamque ferent. rex Iuppiter omnibus idem.
>   fata uiam inuenient.'

So take these words of mine to heart and fix them there. Since it could not be that Italians and Trojans join in alliance, nor does your discord admit an end, whatever the fortune of each today, whatever hope each may pursue, I shall make no distinction whether he be Trojan or Rutulian; whether it is by reason of the Italians' fate that the camp is besieged, or a bad mistake on the part of Troy and unfavourable counsels. Nor do I exempt the Rutulians. Each man's own endeavours will bring him his toil and his luck. King Jupiter is impartial. The fates will find their way.'

And he supports his decision with that most binding of divine oaths: 'Stygii per flumina' ['by the rivers of Styx'].

This speech is, if we accept the implications of Vergil's invention, a combination of teasing opacity, disingenuousness, and, I think, mendacity.[39] The opaque I pass by. But 'seu fatis Italum . . .', 'whether it is by reason of the Italians' fate that the camp is besieged, or a bad mistake on the part of Troy and unfavourable counsels', sounds a fair if rather obscurely expressed summary of the possibilities of the situation. In fact Jupiter is being disingenuous. I take 'fata' here to be in its 'passive' sense (see above, p. 73, i.e. 'what is willed'); and Jupiter, since he wills Fate *and* can prophesy, must know whether the siege of the Trojan camp is part of what is allocated, 'uttered', for the Italians or not. He chooses not to say so. He prefers to sound impartial. 'Fata uiam inuenient' also sounds fair and impartial; but since we are perfectly well aware that the 'fata', Fate, *is* Jupiter's Will, we again see his disingenuousness.[40] And as for 'rex Iuppiter omnibus idem', Jupiter's professed neutrality, what of his intervention apparently (mystifyingly) on the Italian side in 10.689? What of his permission to Juno to give Turnus breathing space (10.613 ff.)? But much more importantly, what of Jupiter's decisive intervention in 12.843 ff.?—which I turn to consider next. Jupiter in

---

[39] Klingner, 568, talks of Jupiter's 'Majesty' in this scene, of how it is filled 'mit dem tiefsten Ernst', and so on. Again a contrast.

[40] Jupiter's use of the phrase 'fata uiam inuenient' is one of the passages which convinced La Penna (above, n. 16) that 'fatum' and Jupiter are distinct. I think that the other evidence I cite suggests we should interpret it my way.

fact is not, and presumably does not intend to be, 'omnibus idem', neutral. Like Zeus in Homer, like other gods in Homer and other gods in the *Aeneid*, Jupiter deceives.

Various deities or their protégés in fact intervene in the battle after the council of Book 10 (Juno, Diana and Opis, Juno and Juturna, Venus), but none so effectively as Jupiter himself in Book 12. These other partisan gods tinker, unable or unwilling to affect the final course of events. The professed neutralist acts crushingly, delivering Aeneas victory. This makes sense for Jupiter's great plan. But it reveals emphatically that his solemnly sworn statement in Book 10 was mendacious—unless we are to suppose that he intended then to lean on the letter of the word 'hodie' (10.107).[41] In that case, he is revealed to be maliciously sophistical. Given the vagueness of the word 'hodie',[42] none of the gods would have deduced that he was promising neutrality merely for the next twenty-four hours. Mendacious or sophistical, he is certainly not neutral. And the means he employs, while exhibiting logic and symmetry, are perhaps disturbing.[43]

Juno started the war in Book 7 by summoning up the evil Fury Allecto from the Underworld. In 12.843ff., after a colloquy with Juno which I shall consider shortly, Jupiter decides to make his conclusive intervention: specifically, according to the epic voice, he decides to remove Juturna, who is assisting Turnus, and to this end he too deploys a Fury. We learn that of the three Furies 'born of timeless Night', two, who, since they are specifically said not to be Megaera, must be Tisiphone and Allecto herself,[44] 'show up'[45] to serve certain defined purposes when Jupiter requires them. Here is the passage in full (12.843-52):

---

[41] So apparently Knauer, in a surprisingly unsatisfactory reference to the passage (294f.).

[42] See, conveniently, *OLD* s.v.

[43] The symmetry is observed by Buchheit, 142, but nothing is made of it; cf. too Pöschl, 220. Greatly overstated but suggestive are the comments of Johnson, 14, 127ff.

[44] Cf. 7.324, 6.555, 10.761.

[45] Cf. *OLD* s.v. *appareo* 4. How and whence they 'show up' is not here specified, but there is no inconsistency with Allecto's underworld location at 7.324ff., 561ff.

Gods and men

> his actis aliud genitor secum ipse uolutat
> Iuturnamque parat fratris dimittere ab armis.
> dicuntur geminae pestes cognomine Dirae,
> quas et Tartaream Nox intempesta Megaeram
> uno eodemque tulit partu, paribusque reuinxit
> serpentum spiris uentosasque addidit alas.
> hae Iouis ad solium saeuique in limine regis
> apparent acuuntque metum mortalibus aegris,
> si quando letum horrificum morbosque deum rex
> molitur, meritas aut bello territat urbes.

When these things had been accomplished, the Father turns over something else in his heart. He prepares to dismiss Juturna from her brother's side. There are twin pestilences called by name the Dread Ones whom timeless Night bore in one and the same birth as Tartarean Megaera, and wreathed them with the same snaky coils and added to them wings of wind. These show up at the throne of Zeus, at the threshold of the savage king, and whet fear for sick mortals,[46] if ever the king of the gods is engineering terrifying death and diseases, or is frightening cities who deserve it with war.

In lines 856ff. we are told that Jupiter dispatches one of these two Furies from the 'aether', commanding it 'to be an omen' to Juturna; the Fury flies down, metamorphoses itself into an owl and proceeds thus (865–8):

> hanc uersa in faciem Turni se pestis ob ora
> fertque refertque sonans clipeumque euerberat alis.
> illi membra nouus soluit formidine torpor,
> arrectaeque horrore comae et uox faucibus haesit.

Changed into this form [i.e. the owl], the pestilence flew and flew again against the face of Turnus, hooting, flapping and beating his shield with its wings. Strange numbness loosens Turnus' limbs because of fear, and his hair stands on end in horror, his voice sticks in his throat.

And then Juturna recognizes the bird for what it is, laments, and abandons her brother and protégé.[47]

Two points need to be stressed. First, Jupiter's action not only has the effect of removing Juturna; the mode the Fury

---

[46] The phrase 'mortalibus aegris' also at *Georg.* 1.237, *Aen.* 2.268, 10.274. I find the epithet in this context hard to assess. The phrase is Lucretius' (6.1; perhaps originally Ennius'), a rendering of Homer's δειλοῖσι βροτοῖσιν. But it seems less compassionate. Contrast Vergil's 'miseris mortalibus' at 11.182.

[47] Cf. Apollo's fateful departure at *Iliad* 22.213.

employs has a crushing effect on Turnus himself.[48] This is presumably foreseen by Jupiter; it certainly could have been stopped. The Fury is his agent, and under his control—as was Juno's Fury under her control. And the crushing effect on Turnus is emphasized. As well as the lines I have just quoted, note how Turnus reacts to the taunting speech of Aeneas that ensues on the departure of Juturna (894f.):[49]

> ille caput quassans: 'non me tua feruida terrent
> dicta, ferox; di me terrent et Iuppiter hostis.'

He, shaking his head, says: 'Your fiery words do not scare me, fierce one; the gods scare me and the hostility of Jupiter.'

And Turnus' physical strength, though still heroic, is revealed to be crucially impaired. He tries to cast a stone at Aeneas, Diomedes-fashion (see p. 134), with this result (896ff.):

> nec plura effatus saxum circumspicit ingens,
> saxum antiquum ingens, campo quod forte iacebat,
> limes agro positus . . .
> uix illum lecti bis sex ceruice subirent,
> qualia nunc hominum producit corpora tellus;
> ille manu raptum trepida torquebat in hostem
> altior insurgens et cursu concitus heros.
> sed neque currentem se nec cognoscit euntem
> tollentemue manu saxumue immane mouentem;
> genua labant, gelidus concreuit frigore sanguis.
> tum lapis ipse uiri uacuum per inane uolutus
> nec spatium euasit totum neque pertulit ictum.
> ac uelut in somnis . . .
> sic Turno quacumque uiam uirtute petiuit, (913)
> successum dea dira negat.

With no more words he looks around and sees a huge rock, a huge ancient rock which by chance lay on the plain, placed there as a boundary mark . . . twice six chosen men would scarcely lift it, men with such physique as earth now produces. But Turnus with hasty grasp seized and hurled it against his enemy, rising high up and speeding along in all his heroic stature. But he knows himself not as he runs nor as he moves, as he raises it with his hands, as he hurls the

[48] Pöschl, 165, aptly compares Apollo and Patroclus, *Iliad* 16.791 ff.
[49] Does Turnus hear what Juturna utters at 12.872 ff. and learn from that? Or is Juturna's speech a monologue, and does Turnus simply draw his own—correct—conclusions from his own condition? Quinn, 336, argues for the latter; so does A. Barchiesi in a suggestive paper, *MD* 1 (1978), 99–121.

giant stone. His knees totter, his blood freezes in chill. The stone itself whirled through the empty void, did not cover the whole distance nor carry its blow home. And, just as in dreams . . . so with whatever valour he sought his way, the dread goddess denies fulfilment.

We note that the Fury (the 'dread goddess') is still there, continuing to act against him ('successum dea dira negat'). Therefore Jupiter is not by any means neutral, 'omnibus idem'. Arguably, he makes a more decisive, concrete, and partisan intervention in the affairs of men at this point than either he or any other god does in the rest of the poem—and, incidentally, a more concrete intervention than ever Zeus makes in the *Iliad*.[50] So our Fateful Jupiter is, in the final count, as partisan and deceitful as any other god—but better at it: more powerful, more efficacious. The evidence is there: we must not resist the implications.

The second point I wish to stress is this. The fact that Jupiter uses the same instrument of terror in ending the conflict as Juno used in starting it (a Fury, perhaps even the same Fury, Allecto) may suggest a certain artistic symmetry and possess a kind of logic; but it is also worrying. Allecto we remember, as described in 7.324 ff., was unequivocally evil; and Jupiter's Furies, as described in 12.845 ff., are far from unequivocally the agents of justice. Do the 'sick' mortals deserve the fear that is whetted for them? Who receives the horrifying death, the diseases? Does 'meritas' define retrospectively, or is it limited to the noun and clause that grammatically claim it? The answers to these questions are not clear. Jupiter employs ambiguous agents; and how, why, and when he would employ them on other occasions is not at all evident.

Much evidence therefore requires us to reassess our initial picture of Jupiter. In Book 1 he may seem perspicuously provident; this is, I think, the picture that the epic voice encourages. Further voices, exploiting invention and arrangement, suggest that we adjust it. Jupiter *is* provident: nothing quite gainsays the revelations of Book 1. But his Will has its enigmatic aspects, sometimes uncomfortably reminding one of Zeus' *boulē*; and its realization involves actions and suffering glossed over in the rosy package presented to Venus. And the power

---

[50] Cf. *Iliad* 15.594, 694, 16.120; also Griffin, *Homer*, 170.

that he wields: this too has its ambiguous, enigmatic aspects. Add then Jupiter's willingness to deceive, his immorality, the indifference to human feeling—and the provident Jupiter of Vergil's invention begins more and more to resemble the frightening deities of the *Iliad* or Euripidean drama.

One more characteristic confirms a traditional and disturbing side to the provident, Fateful Jupiter. He acknowledges the importance of divine status—and divine pride. One passage in the poem demonstrates this spectacularly. I have in mind the 'reconciliation' of Juno in 12.791 ff.[51] To put this scene in its proper context, we must recall Juno's original grievance, the reason why she has to be reconciled. This was explained at the beginning of Book 1 (cf. above, p. 63): her love for Carthage and hatred of the Trojans. It should now be noted that when Vergil explains Juno's hatred of the Trojans, he presents to us a particularly chilling goddess, perhaps a more chilling one than had been traditionally presented. Ennius' Juno had hated the Trojans (and then the Romans), and we may infer important things about Ennius' and therefore the traditional explanation of her hatred from Horace *Odes* 3.3. In this ode Horace stages Juno uttering a speech of 'reconciliation' in regard to Romulus and the Romans. It has clear affinities with the speech of 'reconciliation' that Vergil gives Juno in *Aeneid* 12; it is argued, in fact, that both are broadly based on Ennius.[52] At 18 ff. Horace imputes Juno's hostility to *moral* outrage: outrage at

---

[51] Johnson's discussion of this scene, 124–7, is his common mixture of the very wrong and the very suggestive. Feeney's account, 'Reconciliations', esp. 182 f., which concentrates on another aspect, should be read in conjunction with mine.

[52] See Feeney, 'Reconciliations', esp. 186 f., 190 f., with full bibliography. He argues that Vergil's and Horace's conciliatory Junos have a common source in Enn. *Ann.* 1. He maintains that at the same time as Ennius' Juno agreed to the apotheosis of Romulus in *Ann.* 1 (51 ff. Sk.), she was *partially* reconciled, on certain conditions (the obliteration of Troy, etc.), to the Roman State, making a speech as in Horace and Vergil; her *complete* reconciliation then came during the Second Punic War. Feeney's thesis seems to me highly probable. (He does not, however, perceive and evaluate the difference in Juno's motive for hostility in Horace and Vergil.) Buchheit, 145 ff., does not believe in an early, partial reconciliation in Ennius, and thinks Horace conflates the apotheosis 'concilium' of *Ann.* 1 with Juno's eventual, complete reconciliation (during the Second Punic War) in *Ann.* 8 (VIII. xvi Sk.). At that stage, of course, Juno could no longer have harped on the obliteration of Troy etc., and this supposition does not therefore explain Vergil's and Horace's joint use of the motif in the neat way that Feeney's argument does. We would have to suppose that one was supplying the other.

the inchastity of Paris, and at Laomedon's deceitful behaviour towards gods. I would point out that moral outrage, in particular adultery, is a most natural and obvious cause of offence for the goddess of marriage (Juno); so that Horace rather than Vergil is likely to be the closer reflection of Ennius and therefore of tradition in this particular respect. Anyway, the difference between the two is striking, and affords an instructive contrast. For Vergil's Juno is unconcerned on the topic of Paris' adultery (cf. Venus' comment, above, p. 77) and Laomedon's perjury, the *moral* questions, but is concerned with questions of her *status*: with Paris' insult to her honour (as she sees it), and with other such slights. That is indeed more chilling. A morally outraged goddess is awesome but has reacted predictably and in a sense fairly; and time and good behaviour may expiate the sin. A goddess who feels hugely offended because of slights to her beauty, sexuality, and, as she sees it, honour is by comparison unfair, arbitrary, and unpredictable. What next may offend her? And how to appease her? Aeneas tries and tries again in the *Aeneid*, without success.

There is a factor exacerbating Juno's anger: basically, it is status again, her pre-eminent status as wife and sister of Jupiter. As a consequence of her anger Juno wants to avenge herself on the Trojans; but *although* she is 'the wife and sister of Jupiter', she cannot (yet) get satisfaction. Juno herself puts the point thus in Book 1, contrasting her experience—dishonestly[53]—with the lowlier Athene's (1.39ff.):

> Pallasne exurere classem
> Argiuum . . . potuit . . . ?
>
> ast ego, quae diuum incedo regina Iouisque   (46)
> et soror et coniunx, una cum gente tot annos
> bella gero. et quisquam numen Iunonis adorat
> praeterea aut supplex aris imponet honorem?

Was Pallas able to burn up the Argive fleet . . . ? But I, who move as queen of gods, and sister and wife of Jupiter, wage war for so many years with one people! Is anyone still going to worship the deity of Juno or in supplication lay honouring offerings on her altars?

Juno's lofty position as wife and sister of Jupiter is important to

---

[53] Athena had a more substantial grievance against the Argives in the form of the rape of Cassandra, than Juno had against the Trojans (p. 63).

her—as was Hera's to her.[54] And because she, the wife and sister of Jupiter, is angered and unsatisfied, she harries the Trojans to the end of the poem: until Jupiter reconciles her.

Jupiter makes his move in the famous scene that interrupts Turnus' and Aeneas' final duel (12.791 ff.). His speech combines affection ('desine iam tandem precibus . . .' ['Cease now and be persuaded by my entreaties, that such great grief may not consume you in silence, nor may bitter cares so often return to me from your sweet lips'], 800–2) with authority ('ulterius temptare ueto' ['to attempt anything further I forbid you'], 806). Juno's reply combines apparent submission ('summisso . . . uultu . . . "ista quidem quia nota mihi tua, magne, uoluntas . . ."' ['with downcast mien, she says . . . "Because your will is known to me, great one, I have unwillingly left Turnus and Earth . . ."'], 807 ff.) with submerged anger and residual defiance ('nec tu me . . .' ['else would you not see me here now alone, enduring fair and foul . . .'], 810 ff.). And she claims a very large 'quid pro reconciliatione': she demands that, though the Trojans are to be victorious, the Trojans' name, language, and dress should be buried, replaced by their Italian and Roman counterparts. This is an audacious and defiant request. For it would be natural—and just by ancient custom—for the victors, the Trojans, to impose *their* name, language, and so on on conquered peoples, not vice versa.[55] It is particularly audacious when we recall the comparatively trivial reason for Juno's original hatred. There might be some sense in, and justification for, a morally outraged Juno demanding the effective demise of a morally outrageous nation, in spite of its victory. To demand its demise—in spite of its victory—because of her own personal pique is megalomania of an ambitious order.

How does Jupiter react? As follows (829 ff.):

> olli subridens hominum rerumque repertor:
> 'es germana Iouis Saturnique altera proles,
> irarum tantos uoluis sub pectore fluctus.
> uerum age et inceptum frustra summitte furorem.
> do quod uis, et me uictusque uolensque remitto . . .

[54] Cf. *Iliad* 4.58 ff.
[55] Sall. *Jug.* 18.12; Serv. *Aen.* 1.6; Buchheit, 143.

Gods and men

Smiling at her, the originator of men and gods says: 'Verily you are the sister of Jupiter and Saturn's other child, such waves of anger do you roll beneath your breast. But come now, subdue your wrath vainly begun. I grant you what you wish, and yield myself conquered and content . . .

The logic of the scene must be scrutinized and its implications accepted.[56] What Jupiter is doing here is (I submit) recognizing the vast anger ('tantos uoluis . . .') that *still* mightily moves Juno, underlying her apparent submissiveness ('summisso . . . uultu'), and expressing itself in this last audacious request. And he responds to it first with affection: with a smile ('olli subridens'); his sister and wife, he perceives, is still acting in character, wrathful—a leopard which has not changed its spots. He also responds with what must be respect.[57] That vast anger is proof to him of her pre-eminent status as his sister: 'es germana Iouis'; it is the deduction which he draws from her anger; and because of that anger, because of her status which in consequence of her anger he is minded to recall, Jupiter grants what she asks for. It may, in fact, seem that he grants more than she asks for[58] while, comparatively gently, repeating his injunction to her to set aside her rage. God acknowledges and respects god, and reacts accordingly. This, it seems to me, is the logic of the scene; and it is rather chilling. If we do not resist the implications of Vergil's invention, his divine system is far from reassuring.

The poem in fact accomplishes a circle, disturbingly. The 'germana Iouis' who, at the beginning of the poem, felt that her status as 'germana Iouis' was being dishonoured, at the end of the poem gains from Jupiter more than she could then reason-

---

[56] It has been understood in a variety of wrong ways: see Buchheit, 141. Servius ad loc. is more acute than most: 'soror Iouis es, id est Saturni filia: unde non mirum est tantam te iracundiam retinere sub pectore. nam scimus unumquemque pro generis qualitate iram moueri. . . .' Cf. Feeney, op. cit., 183, concentrating on another and, I think, valid point.

[57] Cf. how Zeus will respond to Hera with something approaching respect: *Iliad* 15.47ff. (and remember Hera's expectation of respect, 4.58ff.). Cf. the scene at *Aeneid* 10.607ff. There Jupiter allows himself to be more ironically patronizing of his 'germana atque eadem coniunx', and Juno appears humbler; but again she gets a portion of what she wants.

[58] R. D. Williams (7–12) on 12.834 comments: 'This concedes more than Juno had asked in 825; 'mores' ("way of life") is the fullest concession that could be made . . .'. But Jupiter probably has a card up his sleeve: above, pp. 81–3.

ably expect, precisely because of that status. Jupiter may embody Fate in his Will, and plan and oversee the inception of a Roman Empire; but the gods, Jupiter among them, are still to a greater or lesser extent also the old gods: proud, wilful, partial, deceitful, immoral, insensitive, cruel—and, when divinity meets divinity of equivalent or greater stature, respectful of that stature. This last characteristic is as alarming as all the others we have identified. Questions occur, prompted by Vergil's invention: further voices. What next may Jupiter's consort request? What next may Jupiter concede? How genuine or lasting is her reconciliation, and what of her love for Carthage? Readers of Naevius and Ennius could provide alarming answers to these queries; so indeed could anyone who knew his history.[59] The reconciliation of Juno to Jupiter and Fate in Book 12 sounds and is portentous but at bottom it is based on a divine balance of power, divine mutual respect, divine concessions, a deal; and that could be and indeed was precarious.

And the *smiling* Jupiter deserves a final comment: Jupiter 'subridens'. Affectionately amused by Venus' querulously maternal tears in Book 1, he is in the same way affectionately amused by Juno's mighty anger, that had led countless mortals into suffering and death and was in the next minutes to entail the death of Turnus. Now there is a god for you, a god who could indeed be easily accommodated within the frightening and plausible religion of the *Iliad*. The tears of his divine daughter weigh, the *amour propre* of his consort weighs, and also of course his own plan weighs. But since he is a god, viewing life on earth from a divine perspective, with divine priorities, individual human suffering emphatically counts as little. The evidence is there for us to assess, implications generated by Vergil's invention and arrangement; and we must not resist the implications.

There is a final point to be gathered. *No* god in the *Aeneid* has what can be called a definitely moral reason for opposing

---

[59] Cf. Buchheit, 54ff.; Feeney 'Reconciliations'; Feeney (see esp. 183) sees the dubious and partial nature of Juno's 'reconciliation' in Book 12 in more specific terms than I do, and our accounts are, I think, interestingly complementary. Klingner accepts the implications of Juno's continuing 'historical' hostility towards Rome in connection with the debate in Book 10 (570), but not in connection with the 'reconciliation' scene of 12 (595).

Troy. The only candidate I suppose is Neptune, angered (5.811) by 'periura Troia'. But whereas the anger of Horace's Juno at Laomedon's fraud and perjury may and indeed must be moral (*Odes* 3.3), Neptune's motive is complicated by materialism and self-interest: for Laomedon's fraud had cheated him personally of his 'merces'.

3

Allusion

Aeneas, Odysseus, and Achilles: new odyssey and new Trojan War; Ajax again; Lavinia and Menelaus; Aeneas and Apollo the plague-bringer; Aeneas, Medea, and Dido; Turnus, Diomedes, and the last two lines of the poem; Aeneas and Diomedes; Juturna and Procne.

1. Introduction

Underlying the *Aeneid* are the Homeric poems and other texts: Vergil made extensive use of the *Iliad*, the *Odyssey*, Apollonius' *Argonautica*, other epic poems, tragedies, and so on. All this is known and demonstrable. But to what extent does Vergil allude to, as well as borrow from, these sources? To what extent are the underlying texts part of the new, the Vergilian, fabrication? And with what effect? These are difficult questions, to which far from unanimous answers are available. The general concept of allusion in ancient literature has been tackled, but still awaits completely satisfactory treatment. Meanwhile, individual authors' practices must be assessed by their own interpreters. Vergil is, I think, the poet potentially most amenable to generalization, and Vergilian allusion is the subject of this chapter.[1] My intention first of all is simply to advance certain wide-ranging theses, and then to proceed to examples. I am aware that these theses are phrased with

---

[1] G. Pasquali, 'Arte allusiva', *Stravaganze quarte e supreme* (Venice, 1951), 11–20 = *Pagine stravaganti* (Florence, 1968) 2.275–83 is a famous essay and still worth reading. The most stimulating and bracingly methodological study of allusion in Latin literature in general is Conte, *Memoria dei poeti*, esp. 30ff.; see too the 'author's introduction' to the English translation of Conte's works, which supplies abundant additional bibliography. On Homer and Vergil see Conte, *Il genere*, 147ff.; Wigodsky, *Vergil and Early Latin Poetry*, 8ff. (Wigodsky considers the question of allusion to Ennius side by side with that of allusion to Homer; cf. below, n. 23); Clausen 75f. W. S. Anderson's 'Vergil's Second *Iliad*' is perhaps the

uncomfortable inexactness, and are far from completely confirmed by the ensuing examples. Exactness of phrasing and completeness of proof must—assuming they are available and desirable—be sought at a future date.

Let us recall the examples of allusion floated in Chapter 1. Two of these are rather special, and can be set to one side. First, the 'farmers' of 12.453 (p. 7). I argued that in this vicinity Vergil exploits significance attending 'agricolae' and so on that he himself had established in the *Georgics*: in other words, he alludes in this instance not to a distinct passage but to many passages, a whole poem—and his own poem at that. I have cited other examples of this phenomenon, and do not wish to take it further at this point. Secondly, in 'ductor Rhoeteius' at 12.456 (p. 10) Vergil alludes to an association supplied not by a specific source passage, nor even by a specific text, but more generally by literary and historical tradition. I shall supply an example comparable with this at the end of the chapter. A more definable and concrete type of allusion occurred at 12.451 ff. (p. 10) and 8.408 ff. (p. 43). Vergil adapts a specific

most suggestive piece to date on the topic. Knauer's *Die Aeneis und Homer* is indispensable to the study of Vergil's Homeric allusion, though more as a source book than anything else. He himself (53) is disinclined to see allusion in Vergil's detailed borrowings, *Detailimitationen*: 'bis auf bestimmte, wohl begründete Ausnahmen lässt sich nicht unbedingt eine innere Beziehung zwischen dem homerischen und vergilischen Zusammenhang erkennen.' He allows exceptions: he argues most acutely (162), for example, that Vergil's modelling of 1.415–17 on *Od*. 8.362–6 imports an irony. It does indeed: this is a humorous allusive touch like that in the matter of Aeneas' horses, mentioned below. Knauer thinks that the Homeric text is systematically significant only at the level of scene and structure; but when he interprets the relationship (for much of the book he has in fact little *interpretative* comment to make), he does so in the unsatisfactory terms of 'Typology' (352 ff., e.g. 'Der Sinn der Homernachfolge Vergils scheint also in der ... Überwindung, dem Sieg Trojas über Griechenland zu liegen'): for acute criticism of typological interpretation, see J. Griffin, *Latin Poets and Roman Life*, Ch. 9. With Knauer's judgement on allusion in *Detailimitationen*, cf. this comment of Camps (in Gigante, 25): 'È chiaro inoltre che spesso, quando una reminiscenza omerica viene identificata, questa non aggiunge niente per il lettore alla qualità poetica della versione virgiliana: come nel caso della patetica esclamazione di Enea nella tempesta *o terque quaterque beati* ...'. On 'o terque quaterque beati' see below, p. 104. The problem of when to consider a borrowing or imitation a purposed allusion is, of course, not confined to Latin studies: cf. e.g. R. Lonsdale, 'Gray and "Allusion": The Poet as Debtor', in: *Studies in the 18th Century*, IV (Canberra, 1979), ed. R. F. Brissenden, 31–55. Lonsdale concludes (54): 'I suspect that modern critical interest in coping with poetic borrowings by the facile assumption that they are all purposeful allusions ultimately derives from Eliot's *The Waste Land*': food for thought.

passage, a simile, from, respectively, Homer and Apollonius of Rhodes, and, as I argued, alludes to those passages as he does so: the context of the original simile, the person and circumstances to which it was originally attached, are relevant to the new composition. Likewise with the provenance of Aeneas' words at 12.435: Vergil alludes to the tragic Ajax. This type of allusion I wish to take up now. First, my theses.

(*A*) When use of a source is extensive, and affects features such as plot and structure (as, for example, use of the *Odyssey* affects the 'Odyssean *Aeneid*'), allusion is certainly operative. The reader is supposed to know the source material and the significance it had in its own setting, and bring that knowledge to bear when he reads the new construction.

(*B*) The effect of such allusion is to provide the reader with a constant invitation to 'compare and contrast'. Character X, let us say, or situation X is modelled on character Y or situation Y. We find ourselves constantly invited to compare and contrast X with Y, the present poem with the text we sense in the background. And then, often, we find ourselves stirred to ask whether it is right or appropriate that X should thus be like or unlike Y.[2]

(*C*) The comparisons and questions which we are stirred to make and ask provoke responses and answers. These may prove disturbing, out of harmony with the ostensible signifi-

[2] This is baldly stated, but my discussion will show that I have in mind something more complex and interesting than, say, the relationship between character and model envisaged by the typologists: they see the new character as simply, so to speak, outstripping and replacing the old. Cf. Knauer cited in n. 1. Contrast the wiser formulations of Griffin, *Latin Poets and Roman Life*, Ch. 9. I quote a couple of sentences (from pp. 189f. and 197): 'All this is different from . . . typology because it does not imply that the later figure of each pair outstrips and replaces the former . . . We do not simply enjoy the pleasure of recognition of a source, but we are guided in our emotional response by Virgil's use of that recognition.' (I would emphasize 'guided': we have to compare and contrast.) Cf. further Wigodsky, *Vergil and Early Latin Poetry*, 9ff., and G. Williams, 83f.; and cf. how 'intertextualists' (see n. 4) see the allusive relationship: Barchiesi, 12: 'I due testi si propongono al lettore come in una continuità immediata, che lascia apparire più evidente il sistema delle differenze' (cf. 18f.); Conte, *Memoria dei poeti*, 14: 'Quello stesso iato che si produce per il linguaggio figurato tra la lettera e il senso, si produce tra la cosa detta—come appare *prima specie*—e il pensiero evocato per allusività.' Aware of such 'differences', such a 'hiatus', we are forced (I would say) to ask questions: to compare and contrast.

cance of the action and the message of the epic voice. Allusion in short is a mechanism for further voices.

(*D*) I propose here an extreme position, possibly an Aunt Sally, but possibly too a working hypothesis. Allusion is operative not only when plot and structure and other prominent features of the poem are supplied by a source text. It extends systematically, where Homer and Apollonius are concerned (I go no further for the moment), to detail: to lines, phrases, words.[3] Vergil's almost constant use of Homer thus always involves allusion. In a borrowed simile we are supposed to remember the original simile, its context, its significance in context, and its wording, and to apply that knowledge to the new poem before us, noticing similarities and dissimilarities ('comparing and contrasting'). Likewise with Apollonian material, and I think much more. Source texts are *part* of the new text, constantly and in detail, continually inviting the process of comparing and contrasting, offering scope for a further voice. The situation is what we might call one of designed intertextuality.[4] To read the *Aeneid* is to be constantly aware of other texts in and behind the new creation.

(*E*) Proposition *D* sounds like a recipe for very hard work on the reader's part. It is. But in one way Vergil helps us. He likes to assist us in the perception of unobtrusive and/or important allusions by means of various 'signals'. For example, I argue below for unobtrusive but important allusions to Homeric 'Diomedes' material in Books 7 and 12. Aeneas' initial, explicit, and spectacular apostrophe to Diomedes and the explicit presence of Diomedes in the poem helps us to pick up such underlying material: explicit appearances by Diomedes 'signal' Diomedes allusions.[5] Likewise the striking verbal similarity of

---

[3] I do therefore think that Vergil alludes in *Detailimitationen* (above, n. 1). The situation with early Latin poetry is, I think, different: cf. Wigodsky, *Vergil and Early Latin Poetry*, 5ff., and below, n. 23.

[4] On the concept of intertextuality see the refreshingly lucid remarks of Conte, *Il genere*, 146. When I discuss allusion I find it wrong to exclude ideas of intention and design: hence my heretical hybrid, 'designed intertextuality'.

[5] Cf. how Jupiter's explicit reference to Sarpedon at 10.471 may 'signal' allusive Sarpedon material in this context (cf. Knauer, 299). (Jupiter's reference to Sarpedon is what Conte, *Memoria dei poeti*, 38–45, would call 'allusione riflessiva'. For a penetrating discussion of this allusion see Barchiesi, 16ff.)

Aeneas' opening situation to Odysseus' in *Od.* 5: it signals the presence of Odysseus behind the figure of Aeneas—inviting us to compare and contrast, and to ask questions.[6]

2. Aeneas, Odysseus, and Achilles; new Odyssey and new Trojan War: cf. theses *A, B, C* and *E*

To illustrate what I hope is not too contentious a thesis I choose fairly familiar material. I am impelled to tackle more challenging stuff in section 3.

If we view *Aeneid* 1–6 as based on the *Odyssey* (the 'Odyssean *Aeneid*'), and 7–12 as based on the *Iliad* (the 'Iliadic *Aeneid*'), we shall be maintaining a position which does some violence to the subtlety and evasiveness of Vergil's structuring,[7] but is sufficiently true to be useful. First, I consider the 'Odyssean *Aeneid*'.

Aeneas' opening scene, when the hero is caught despairing in a storm at sea, closely recalls one of Odysseus' early and striking scenes. The recall is so striking that we must, I think, assume Vergil wishes us to remember (he is 'signalling') his Homeric source and see the parallel. Aeneas is described thus (1.92ff.):

> extemplo Aeneae soluuntur frigore membra;
> ingemit et duplicis tendens ad sidera palmas
> talia uoce refert: 'o terque quaterque beati,
> quis ante ora patrum Troiae sub moenibus altis
> contigit oppetere! o Danaum fortissime gentis
> Tydide! mene Iliacis occumbere campis
> non potuisse tuaque animam hanc effundere dextra . . .!'

---

[6] Cf. Knauer's discussion of Vergil's use of the 'Zitat'. He argues that Vergil helps us to 'think of' source scenes by quoting a citation from them (a 'wörtliches Zitat'): Knauer, 119, 146, esp. 152, 310f., 335. Cf. Pasquali's use of the term 'motto' in reference to Horatian practice: see Conte, *Memoria dei poeti*, 9. (The term 'motto' had been used by both Norden and R. Reitzenstein: E. Fraenkel, *Horace* (Oxford, 1957), 159 n. 2.)

[7] Some wise comments in this respect in Camps, 51ff. The persistence of *Odyssey* material in the 'Iliadic *Aeneid*' is something that Knauer well stresses. Note, e.g., the thought-provoking way in which Aeneas is modelled on Telemachus in 8: Knauer, 249ff.; note too the influence of the *Odyssey* on the end of the *Aeneid*: Knauer, 323ff., esp. 327.

Straightway Aeneas' limbs are loosened with chill; he groans and, stretching both his hands to the stars, cries thus aloud: 'Oh thrice and four times blessed were those whose chance it was to die before their fathers' eyes beneath the lofty walls of Troy! Oh son of Tydeus [Diomedes], bravest of the Danaan people, could I not have fallen on the Ilian plain and poured forth this spirit at your hand . . .!'

With this compare Odysseus, despairing in the storm of *Od.* 5, lines 297 ff.:

καὶ τότ' Ὀδυσσῆος λύτο γούνατα καὶ φίλον ἦτορ,
ὀχθήσας δ' ἄρα εἶπε πρὸς ὃν μεγαλήτορα θυμόν.
'Ὤ μοι ἐγὼ δειλός . . .

τρισμάκαρες Δαναοὶ καὶ τετράκις οἳ τότ' ὄλοντο
Τροίῃ ἐν εὐρείῃ, . . .
ὡς δὴ ἐγώ γ' ὄφελον θανέειν . . .'

And then were Odysseus' heart and knees loosened, and in indignation he spoke to his great-hearted spirit: 'Wretched am I . . . oh thrice and four times blessed were the Danaans who perished in broad Troy . . . oh that I had died then . . .'

Then, after this beginning, Odysseus' travels and travails continue to be Vergil's major and prominent source in the first six books. Since the reader knows Homer's poem, it is inevitable that the *Odyssey* and Odysseus will be in his mind as he reads Vergil's 'Odyssean' poem. He finds that Aeneas is appearing in the role of a new Odysseus. This prompts him to 'compare and contrast', to ask questions. In what precise ways is Aeneas like and unlike Odysseus? How appropriate for him are the similarities, or dissimilarities? Answers to such questions are, to a greater or lesser extent, available, illuminating Aeneas and his situation, clarifying the harsh individuality of his heroic role.[8]

I illustrate the point with some examples. Odysseus, we remember, was impelled to travel and suffer on land and sea; but he always had his home as his goal—a humanly 'happy-ending' was always conceivable for him. Aeneas? He travels his arduous odyssey away from all he knows and loves, with no

---

[8] I find the secondary material very unsatisfactory on this topic. Cf. e.g. Otis, 215ff., esp. 231f.; R. D. Williams, 'The Purpose of the *Aeneid*', 34ff.; Knauer, 148ff.; G. Williams, 118f. Clausen, 76, is more helpful than most.

prospect of a happy ending in human terms. That fact is focused: by allusion, the process of comparing and contrasting.

Again, Odysseus faces capricious, partial, and inscrutable gods, polytheistic gods acting not in concert. So does Aeneas (cf. Ch. 2). But unlike Odysseus, Aeneas is also saddled with the burden of Jupiter's Will, his fated duty to the future of a whole people: he is doubly tried by divinity. Allusion defines the point.

Odysseus at times despairs: notably when he faces drowning, the worst of deaths, in that scene in Book 5. So does Aeneas, in his parallel scene, quoted above. But what is appropriate and natural for Odysseus is natural but inappropriate for Aeneas. Allusion, the process of comparing and contrasting, underlines a very important difference. In fact, comparing and contrasting the two heroes in this instance identifies, at the beginning of the poem, a crucial *tension* in the life of Aeneas and the plot of the poem, a tension which is one of the poem's key sources of energy. The point is as follows.

Heroes like Odysseus may and do indulge the vast, passionate, and superb egoism which is their natural prerogative—and which forms part of their attraction to us, their temporizing spectators. Odysseus indulges despair, rage, and revenge. Achilles gives vent to implacable anger and impassioned violence, bowing before nothing and no one. And Aeneas? He too is by nature a hero of this stamp, as Book 2, for example, eminently demonstrates.[9] 'Arma amens capio' ['madly I take up arms'], he says (2.314), and dashes furiously into the battle seeking a heroic and egoistic death—'moriamur et in media arma rua-

---

[9] Book 2, that is to say, as Vergil has chosen to make it. It could have been otherwise. Sophocles had Aeneas leave Troy before its sack, warned by the Laocoon episode. Vergil preferred to work with the tradition of Timaeus and Hellanicus, in which Aeneas stayed until the last. In this way he could construct his heroic Aeneas, necessary to his plans. On Vergil's choice of sources in Book 2 see conveniently R. G. Austin, *P. Vergili Maronis Aeneidos Liber Secundus* (Oxford, 1964), xiii; Klingner, 413. The 'heroic' (i.e. Homeric-heroic) character of Aeneas is underestimated by major Vergilian critics, e.g. Clausen, 77, 80f. 'we have the sense of a man rather like ourselves—moody, hesitant, reflective—thrust into a situation that seems to call for heroic action' (that is almost the reverse of the truth), 83; La Penna, lviiff.; Wlosok, 'Der Held', e.g. 14f.; this error is identified and corrected by Stahl.

mus' ['let us die, rushing into the midst of conflict'] (2.353; cf. below). He too is inclined to subordinate emotion and heroic impulse to nothing and no one, despair included. As we have seen, in desperate straits, in the storm of Book 1, he despairs and gives vent to that egoistic emotion. But he—and here is the crucial difference—minded to subordinate his emotional impulses to nothing and no one, *must* subordinate them: to Fate and Jupiter's Will. In desperate straits like Odysseus, facing drowning (the worst of deaths) like Odysseus, he is not in the same situation as Odysseus, having a duty not just to himself but to a nation and history. He must therefore, here and subsequently, suffer and grieve like Odysseus, but not allow scope for grief as a hero like Odysseus naturally would; he must suffer desperately and yet consider despair a culpable indulgence. Compare the situation in Book 2. Aeneas the hero in pursuit of a heroic death had actually been told to flee: 'Alas, flee, oh goddess's son!' ['heu fuge nate dea'] Hector's dream-apparition had said (2.289): an impossible order to a hero but one which nonetheless eventually had to be obeyed.[10] In all things Aeneas has in fact to display 'pietas': that 'piety' which involves devotion, loyalty, self-abnegation, and, crucially, *subordination*,[11] to a greater good or cause; a quality which came quite naturally to historical Romans ('non sibi sed patriae natus'[12]), but which was manifestly ill-suited to the intensely individual, egoistical hero. Aeneas has to learn to become someone dutiful and subordinate, the 'heros pius', a paradoxical and unblessed role. And he does so of course at great cost, and far from consistently.[13] How could it be otherwise? Such is the character and situation of Aeneas, potentially defined even in his first scene, with the assistance of allusion, the process of comparing and contrasting: a hero in a role shot through with paradox and pain.

I now briefly consider Aeneas and allusion in the 'Iliadic *Aeneid*'. Here the situation is in a sense simpler but also

[10] Cf. Ch. 4 s. 10.
[11] On 'pietas' see Austin on 1.10 with extensive bibliography; Wlosok 'Der Held', 10f.; Cic. *Inv.* 2.66, 161, *Rep.* 6.16.
[12] Cf. Cic. *Mur.* 83, *Sest.* 138, *Phil.* 14.32, *Fin.* 2.45.
[13] See below, Ch. 4 pp. 182–3, 185–8.

subtler. At 6.86ff. the Sybil makes the following announcement to Aeneas:

> bella, horrida bella,
> et Thybrim multo spumantem sanguine cerno.
> non Simois tibi nec Xanthus nec Dorica castra
> defuerint; alius Latio iam partus Achilles,
> natus et ipse dea.

Wars, harsh wars I see and the Tiber foaming with much blood. You will not lack a Simois, nor a Xanthus, nor a Doric camp; another Achilles has already been brought forth in Latium, he too the offspring of a goddess.

This speech creates the expectation of, it 'signals', an 'Iliadic *Aeneid*', which in fact ensues. The second portion of the poem is based to a large extent on the *Iliad*. Scene after scene recalls an Iliadic model: the 'catalogue of forces' (Book 7; cf. *Il.* 2); 'divine arms for the hero' (8; cf. *Il.* 18); the 'absence of the hero' (8 and 9; cf. *Il.* 1ff.); the 'night expedition' (9; cf. 10); the slaying of the hero's friend and lieutenant by the foremost of the foe (10; cf. 16); the vengeance the hero extracts from the enemy in general (10; cf. 21), and, in a duel, from the opposing hero in particular (12; cf. 22); and so on. Parallels could be multiplied indefinitely. The reader senses the *Iliad* behind *Aeneid* 7–12, he knows the poem, and it becomes part of the new text. The process of comparing and contrasting is prompted, and with it questions: and this time more troubling, disharmonious questions, suggesting troubling further voices. And Vergil's mode of allusion here exploits an idea not generally exploited in the 'Odyssean *Aeneid*'. I illustrate the point.

In the 'Iliadic *Aeneid*' we find that characters themselves have views about the roles being played. It is clear, for example, that in the Sybil's view Turnus is to play the role of a new Achilles. This is Turnus' own view, contained in his vaunt over the doomed Pandarus (9.742):

> hic etiam inuentum Priamo narrabis Achillem.

You will tell Priam [in the Underworld] that you have found an Achilles here too.

The Trojans, it would therefore seem, are doomed to refight the war at Troy, with the Italians playing the role of the

Achaeans of old. Amata reinforces this impression, suggesting that Aeneas is potentially a new Paris (7.363f.):

> at non sic Phrygius penetrat Lacedaemona pastor,
> Ledaeamque Helenam Troianas uexit ad urbes?

Did not the Phrygian shepherd penetrate Sparta in this way, and carry off Ledean Helen to the city of Troy?

Juno made the same point with characteristic unpleasantness (7.319ff.):

> nec face tantum
> Cisseis praegnas ignis enixa iugalis.
> quin idem Veneri partus suus et Paris alter . . .

It was not only the daughter of Cisseus [Hecuba] who was pregnant with, and gave birth to, a torch of marriage. Nay, Venus too has the like in her offspring, a second Paris . . .

Juno, I say, makes the point unpleasantly. But it was in fact a way of viewing the facts that was neither indefensible nor unreasonable; and Turnus, his allies, and others insistently and repeatedly do so view them.[14]

So characters have views about the roles being played. In a sense, therefore, they as well as the author allude. Turnus sees himself as a new Achilles, Amata sees Aeneas as Paris; and they allude to that effect. And Turnus' view, like Amata's, was not unreasonable. But as *Vergil's* allusion develops we find that in terms of that allusion Turnus' view is substantially incorrect.[15] So is Amata's. In fact a growing, increasingly consistent irony emerges in the text, an irony which puts Italian efforts in an almost tragic light, Trojan efforts in a brightening light of optimism. For, as is evident enough from the list of parallel scenes cited above, it is *not* the Italians who, in terms of the main Iliadic sources, play the part of Greeks. In terms of the *Iliad* and the author's allusion it is the Trojans who emerge, once the catalogue is over, ever more clearly as the new

[14] The Sybil in the speech referred to above implies (6.93f.) that Lavinia is a second Helen and Aeneas a second Paris (cf. Knauer, 144); cf. Iarbas in the 'Odyssean *Aeneid*' at 4.215, 'et nunc ille Paris . . .'. At 9.138ff. Turnus compares himself to Menelaus, and presents Lavinia as Helen and the Italians as in a sense super-Greeks; cf. too his comparison of himself to Diomedes, below, p. 134.
[15] Cf. the excellent article of W. S. Anderson, 'Vergil's Second *Iliad*'; but Anderson does not see that Vergil's pattern of allusion raises disturbing questions.

Greeks—and Aeneas as the new Achilles. And upon Turnus descends the mantle of Hector.[16] Let me draw attention to two episodes in particular—as I say, scene upon scene underscores the point.[17] The death of Pallas (10.474ff.) provokes Aeneas to an 'aristeia' of merciless vengeance (10.510ff.) involving the killing of defeated and suppliant victims which is practically identical to that performed by Achilles in *Iliad* 21, stirred to wrath and grief by the killing of Patroclus. And in *Aeneid* 12, when Amata and Latinus plead with Turnus not to fight Aeneas, and Turnus turns nevertheless to confront Aeneas—with increasing lack of confidence—we recall, we feel at work in the text, *Iliad* 22: Hecuba and Priam pleading with Hector, and Hector confronting Achilles without confidence in his fatal duel.[18]

Allusion has therefore insinuated a productive irony in the text, one that, as I say, presents Trojan efforts in a brightening light of optimism. But here, as in the 'Odyssean *Aeneid*', allusion prompts the process of comparing and contrasting, and suggests questions. Aeneas, once the new Odysseus, is now the new Achilles. But, we must ask: in what sense, to what extent, is Aeneas like and unlike that great Homeric hero? What of the circumstances of the two? Is it *right* that he should be like Achilles, if and when he is like Achilles? And these questions, provoked by allusion, prove more crucial, more disturbing in their implications than those prompted in the 'Odyssean *Aeneid*'. Further voices are audible.

---

[16] Not, however, exclusively. At the beginning of 12 Vergil makes sure that Turnus receives the mantle of Paris too: Knauer, 291.

[17] Turnus' claim to be an Achilles in fact comes at an ironic moment. He makes his boast (9.742) when inside the Trojan camp. The camp had been opened and the walls defended by Pandarus and Bitias (9.672ff.), characters based on the Greeks Polypoetes and Leonteus, defenders of the Achaean walls at *Il.* 12.127ff.: *Il.* 12.127ff. underlie *Aen.* 9.672ff. Other scenes which suggest that the Trojans are the new 'Greeks' and the Italians the 'Trojans': the Italian debate in 11 aligns Italians with Trojans, as do other events in this book (Knauer, 283ff.); the Catalogue of Etruscans in 10 corresponds to the Catalogue of Myrmidons in *Il.* 16, occurring at a corresponding point of crisis (Knauer, 297); and see further Knauer and Anderson, op. cit. Some episodes are productively ambiguous. Thus, as Anderson says (25), Nisus and Euryalus, predominantly recalling the Greek night expedition, suffer the fate of Dolon; while Pallas, who in the final count emerges as the *Aeneid*'s Patroclus, for a while plays the role of Sarpedon: Knauer, 298ff. (a summary, 306; Patroclus also supplies material for Camilla: Knauer, 310ff.).

[18] Anderson, op. cit., 29.

Allusion

I consider in this respect simply the two scenes singled out above. As the 'Iliadic *Aeneid*' unfolds and the allocation of roles clarifies, it early becomes evident that Aeneas, as the new Achilles, will win. The *victorious* Aeneas is like the *victorious* Achilles, and in that respect the likeness is obviously good and satisfying. But what of the episodes in Book 10 and at the end of the poem? We recall the sources, the allusion, follow the process of comparing and contrasting. Achilles was roused to scenes of pitiless killing in *Iliad* 21 by feelings of love and revenge in response to the death of Patroclus. His 'right' to do so is, at the time, hardly questionable. Aeneas acts in the same way in Book 10, in response to the death of Pallas. But is this right for him, in his circumstances? Should he thus act the Achilles? The question is focused by allusion. Our answer must start thus. Roman sentiment could accommodate vengeance as a virtue; the Emperor Augustus, avenger of the divine Julius, offers a conspicuous illustration of the fact, erecting a temple to Mars Ultor.[19] Aeneas in his Achillean role of relentless avenger may therefore seem laudable. But there is, of course, a complication. Anchises, in his great exposition of Roman imperial duty, which he uttered in the first place for Aeneas' benefit (6.847-853: above p. 4), had chosen to emphasize *other* martial ideals, equally applauded by Romans:[20] war there must be, to 'war down the proud', but *peace* should be the goal of armed action and clemency vouchsafed to those who submit. Anchises thus gives other ideals; and are not these *greater* ideals? Aeneas' Achillean actions in Book 10, provoked by a passionate desire for personal vengeance and not peace, seem, in this light, Anchises' light, different. Aeneas the vengeful

---

[19] Cf. Cic. *Cat.* 4.12 (a most interesting passage, too long to quote), *Inv.* 2.66. Ov. *Fast.* 5.569ff. and Suet. *Aug.* 29.2 tell us that Octavian vowed the temple of Mars Ultor on the field of Philippi 'pro ultione paterna': cf. R. Syme, *History in Ovid*, 192f.; the story is disbelieved by Weinstock, 128ff., but a temple to Mars Ultor was at any rate built, and (the most important fact for my purpose) Ovid's story was presumably what people in Augustan Rome wanted or were prepared to hear. Doublethink presumably allowed Augustus to boast both vengeance and clemency: on Caesarian 'clementia' see Weinstock, 233-43. (One must, of course, be wary of regarding Roman sentiment as monolithic in this respect: note the very interesting disagreement of Cicero and M. Brutus: *Epp. ad Brutum*, 5.5, 6.2, 23.10 (Shackleton Bailey), and see the text.)

[20] Cf. 'Vergil and the Politics of War', 188ff.

Achilles is, in this light, disturbing.[21] At the very least, his Achillean actions in his circumstances provoke questions which Achilles' actions in his circumstances did not. Allusion provokes questions, and nudges us towards answers: allusion supplies a further voice.

With the death of Lausus in Book 10, Aeneas' passion dissolves. As he proceeds towards and into his final duel in Book 12, there are again ways in which he is patently like Achilles, cast by allusion in the role of Achilles. Achilles in *Iliad* 22 is bent on his final revenge and achieves it, or most of it, in his showdown with Hector. Similarly Aeneas: he achieves his showdown with Turnus. But allusion, the process of comparing and contrasting, defines him as vitally dissimilar as well. Achilles entered his duel bent on revenge: revenge was his *purpose*. Aeneas approaches his duel in a mind to establish peace, as is evident from, among other evidence, his speech in 12.176ff. (cf. above, p. 4: it is, I said, as if Anchises' words are loud in his ears). When the first attempt at a duel is thwarted and the second is set up only after frustration and difficulty, Aeneas the new Achilles is still dissimilar to the old in this vital respect: his aim is still, fundamentally, to 'war down the proud', the proud Turnus, and to establish peace. And he wins; he incapacitates Turnus with a wound. Turnus submits, unequivocally and unconditionally; he supplicates. But, clad in the belt of Pallas, he reminds Aeneas of Pallas, stirs Aeneas loyally to avenge the dead and dishonoured Pallas, and pays with his blood. Now therefore, the dissimilarity to Achilles fades: in the last seconds of the poem the new Achilles is again virtually identical in action and motivation to the old Achilles, in particular to the Achilles of *Iliad* 22.[22] But is this appropriate? What of Anchises' words? The circumstances of the two heroes *are* different. For Aeneas another goal besides vengeance has been proposed. And has not the proud been

---

[21] La Penna, lxiii, attempts unsuccessfully to explain away Aeneas' actions.

[22] To be fair to Homer and to Achilles, we must not forget that the *Iliad* does not end with 22. Book 24 teaches Achilles, and us, a lot about the futility of vengeful killing. Note esp. 24.540ff. It is of course notable and suggestive that no such grand scene of humanity concludes the *Aeneid*.

rendered subject, a candidate for clemency? And would not clemency be more conducive to peace than killing? Questions are provoked, troubling questions; Aeneas, focused at the end of the poem in the role of Achilles, disturbs. The poem closes ambiguously. The imperial hero has been presented, and some of the troubling complexities, dilemmas, and tragedies of his position adumbrated. And no little part in this adumbration has been played by allusion, by the presence of the Iliadic text in our own, and the process it encourages of comparing and contrasting. Constantly we have asked: in what sense and with what implications is Aeneas like Achilles? Is it *right* that he should in this or that way repeat Achilles? And there are answers available for the questions. A further voice exploiting allusion insinuates.

Ajax again

There is one striking scene in which Vergil, appearing to agree with Turnus' assessment of the 'new Trojan War', puts him in the role of a prominent Greek. After Turnus' boasting claim to be an Achilles at 9.742, Vergil concludes that book (9.806–14) by modelling Turnus on Ajax, in one of Ajax's famous scenes.[23] But the identification is brief—and impressively ironic: the self-styled victorious Achilles of 9.742 finds himself in the role of the retreating Ajax of *Iliad* 16.102–11.

Vergil's allusion to Ajax fits into a larger picture, containing another and different irony. As we have seen, Vergil transfers the Achilles role claimed by Turnus to Aeneas (above, p. 110); he also hands over to Aeneas the Ajax role which he himself had—in this back-handed way—bestowed on Turnus. Aeneas' receipt of the role of Achilles at least allows us to feel optimism, before we start asking questions. His receipt of the role of Ajax does not even allow us that: for the role he

---

[23] Ennius too imitated the scene (391–8 Sk.). Vergil's behaviour with his available sources here follows a well-paralleled pattern. He exploits Ennius for diction, but draws on the original Homeric source for its contextual significance: it is Ajax, not Ennius' tribune, who contributes to our context. Cf. above, n. 3, and Wigodsky, *Vergil and Early Latin Poetry*, 61 ff. as well as 5 ff.; cf. too Quinn, 368 f., Klingner, 375 f.

receives is that of the tragic not the Homeric Ajax, quite a different matter (above, pp. 9–12). Vergilian irony greets the aspirations of the heroic Turnus; gloomier voices utter in the background of his Roman hero.

3. More challenging examples

Compare *A*, *B*, *D* and *E* above. The examples of allusion that I shall now consider are much less obvious than those in the previous section. Indeed some of the passages that I discuss have been regarded as problematic or even baffling; I think an understanding of allusion explains them. I have chosen such challenging examples, eschewing more available ones, for a purpose. If I can convince readers that allusion is operative where no allusion has been proved or even sensed before, it should make my extreme proposition—that Vergil's use of Homer, Apollonius etc. constantly involves allusion (*D* above)—more plausible, less of an Aunt Sally.

Lavinia and Menelaus

At the beginning of Book 12 Turnus has decided to fight Aeneas in single combat.[24] Amata begs him not to. Lavinia is listening. Her response to Amata's speech is to weep and blush (12.64 ff.):

>accepit uocem lacrimis Lauinia matris
flagrantis perfusa genas, cui plurimus ignem
subiecit rubor et calefacta per ora cucurrit.
Indum sanguineo ueluti uiolauerit ostro
si quis ebur, aut mixta rubent ubi lilia multa
alba rosa, talis uirgo dabat ore colores.
illum [sc. Turnum] turbat amor . . .

Lavinia heard her mother's words, her burning cheeks drenched with tears; a great blush kindled fire in her and ran through her heated face. As when someone stains [more exactly, 'defiles'] Indian ivory with blood-red dye, or when white lilies blush with many a rose: such colours did the maiden's face display. Love throws Turnus into turmoil . . .

Several questions arise. What do the similes contribute, in

[24] A fuller version of this section appears in *GR* 30 (1983), 55–64.

particular the stained-ivory simile? Why are they there? More basically: why does Lavinia weep? And why does she blush?

Most scholars believe that Vergil does not develop Lavinia as a character with feelings and emotions.[25] For them Lavinia's own state of mind obviously cannot supply answers to these questions. But some scholars do sense a real character—in particular, in these lines. Some scholars even sense that Lavinia is in love. That would be interesting. With whom? Most naturally it would be Turnus, her most eminent and eligible suitor (see below).

I must say that if Lavinia were characterized enough to be in love I would find this welcome. The *Aeneid*'s Helen should not be a mere cipher. If, however, there was any suggestion that she was in love with, specifically, Turnus, it would be troubling. It would seriously complicate our emotional if not our moral response to the rapidly approaching denouement. But that would not be implausible. Our responses are pretty complex already (cf. e.g. above, p. 112 and below, pp. 186–8). And the suggestion is in fact there. Lavinia comes alive in these lines. A further voice makes itself heard, via allusion. Vergil does indeed suggest that Lavinia is in love: with Turnus. It is not only suggested: the fact attracts comment.

We should not, of course, expect such a disturbing revelation to be a floodlit part of the unfolding drama, broadcast by the epic voice. The future wife of the founder of the Roman people cannot too explicitly have loved another man; it ill suits a proto-Roman 'uirgo' to have such emotions at all. On the other hand, a suggestion to this effect does not fly completely in the face of the dramatic facts. Why should not the nubile Lavinia, 'plenis nubilis annis' (7.53), have set her heart on Turnus, her most beautiful and outstanding suitor (7.55) and a 'youth excelling in spirit' in the opinion of an admirable judge (12.19)? But I must pick up the text at 12.54. At this point, Amata, hearing Turnus' decision to face Aeneas in single combat, begs

---

[25] I quote a range of opinions in *GR* 30 (1983), 61f. Cf. too D. C. Woodworth, 'Lavinia: an Interpretation', *TAPA* 61 (1930), 175–94, who sees in the heroine a mixture of paragon and cipher, and explicitly denies her being in love (186). Warde Fowler, *The Death of Turnus*, 40, and J. Perret, *REL* 45 (1967), 347, on the other hand believe that Lavinia loves Turnus, but do not substantiate their belief.

him not to—and provokes the reaction in Lavinia already quoted.

Amata begs him, passionately, devotedly, in tears (54ff.):

> at regina noua pugnae conterrita sorte
> flebat et ardentem generum moritura tenebat: (55)
> 'Turne, per has ego te lacrimas, per si quis Amatae
> tangit honos animum: spes tu nunc una, senectae
> tu requies miserae, decus imperiumque Latini
> te penes, in te omnis domus inclinata recumbit.
> unum oro: desiste manum committere Teucris.
> qui te cumque manent isto certamine casus (61)
> et me, Turne, manent; simul haec inuisa relinquam
> lumina nec generum Aenean captiua uidebo.'
> accepit uocem . . .

But the queen, terrified by the new turn in the battle, wept and, doomed to die, held her fiery son-in-law (55): 'Turnus, by these my tears, by whatever esteem for Amata may touch your spirit—you are now my one hope, you the peace for my wretched old age, in your hands are the honour and sovereignty of Latinus, in you rests all our sinking house—one thing I beg: forbear to fight the Trojans. Whatsoever perils await you in that contest (61) await me, too, Turnus; I shall straightway quit this hateful light and shall not as a captive behold Aeneas as my son-in-law.' Lavinia heard . . .

Amata's speech does indeed attest deep devotion; her feelings for Turnus appear to be rather more than is normal for a possible future mother-in-law. In the light of our analysis of Allecto's assault on her (Ch. 1 s. 2), we can define them: they are—in part—erotic. And the parallels to be adduced for items in this speech themselves confirm if not independently suggest the same conclusion. Note Amata's words at 61f., a promise to die on the same day as Turnus. This is a protestation suited to a lover (cf. e.g. Propertius 2.20.18). And once more Amata recalls and exhibits the passion of, in particular, Dido.[26] She recalls the 'moritura' Dido ('determined, doomed to die') beseeching her parting lover Aeneas. With 55f. and 61f., com-

---

[26] For Amata recalling Dido, see La Penna, lxxiif.; he does not, however, pin any significance to the fact. See too Putnam, 161f., 176–9.

Allusion

pare 4.307 ff., 'nec moritura tenet crudeli funere Dido? . . . per ego has lacrimas . . . oro . . . cui me moribundam deseris . . . ?'[27] ['Does not Dido, doomed to die by a cruel death, detain you . . . By these my tears I beg you . . . to whom do you abandon me on the point of death?']. Amata is an interesting creation. As I have said, I think there is something of a Phaedra in her—upon which Allecto works. Certainly she utters sentiments here that are redolent of passionate devotion. And that, for my immediate purpose, is all I need to establish. For my concern now is with Lavinia. As Amata utters her devotedly passionate appeal, Lavinia is listening. And she responds. Her tears and blush follow directly upon Amata's appeal. Why?

It seems that Lavinia's sense of propriety, or Vergil's sense of propriety, forbids Lavinia herself to speak. But Amata's words seem in some way to have spoken for her. For she reacts to Amata's words; more particularly, I would stress, she reacts *in line* with them. She weeps—'accepit uocem lacrimis'—like, and with, the weeping Amata. Why? A great many possible reasons suggest themselves. But one not to be excluded is the obvious one. She weeps for the same general reason as Amata. She weeps in similar response to the same crisis: a person who arouses passionate emotion in her is meditating leaving on a dangerous enterprise. It is a natural interpretation. It is also a natural interpretation that she is weeping for the same person (i.e. Turnus) as Amata, with whom she weeps. Even the dra-

---

[27] There are no other examples of an appeal 'per has lacrimas' in Vergil. The feminine 'moritura' is used in the *Aeneid* only of Dido (4.308, 415, 519, 604) and Amata (12.55, 602).

With 'moritura' at 12.55 Vergil conveys Amata's own sense that she was doomed, and the fact that she was doomed (in the terminology of Ch. 6 'moritura' conveys the feelings of a character and reports the opinion of the epic voice, enjoying an ambiguity). And Amata *was* indeed doomed, and had cause to intuit as much: passion for Turnus, long since fierce within her (Ch. 1 s. 2), was going to drive her to death: 12.602. In the light of these observations, it is interesting to read Housman's reaction to 12.55. In connection specifically with 'moritura' he had this to say (in a letter to Mackail, *Selected Letters*, ed. H. Maas (London, 1971), 423): 'Virgil's besetting sin is the use of words too forcible for his thoughts, and the 'moritura' of Aen. XII 55 makes me blush for him whenever I think of it . . .'. But the 'thought', the substance to justify 'moritura', is there, and the word is not too forcible. Housman was resisting the implications of Vergil's invention (and had he forgotten 12.602?). So was Ribbeck, who emended to 'monitura'.

matic action, the epic voice, seems to suggest she is in love. Harder evidence follows.

Lavinia blushes as well as weeps: 'flagrantis ... genas ... rubor ... calefacta per ora'. Why? Let us try following our interpretation of her weeping and see if it all fits. It does, and a pleasant parallel offers itself. Passion for Turnus has been uttered (by Amata); Lavinia reveals her heartfelt sympathy with that utterance (in weeping). So she reveals her love. That is what she might think. In consequence she is embarrassed, guilty even: 'conscia'. And therefore she blushes—as modest girls are wont to do when caught in such a position, revealing that they are in love. Compare the girl in Catullus 65.19–24:

> ut missum sponsi furtiuo munere malum
>   procurrit casto uirginis e gremio,
> quod miserae oblitae molli sub ueste locatum,
>   dum aduentu matris prosilit, excutitur,
> atque illud prono praeceps agitur decursu,
>   huic manat tristi conscius ore rubor.

just as an apple, sent as a stealthy gift by her betrothed, rolls out from a maiden's chaste bosom—it had been placed beneath her soft gown, but she forgot, poor thing; she starts forward as her mother arrives, and the apple is jolted out and tumbles headlong down, while over her sad face spreads a guilty blush.

The girl jumps forward; the apple, a love-token, falls from her bosom, giving her away; so she blushes—just as, so I infer, Lavinia's tears have given her away, at least in her own opinion, and so she blushes. The parallel seems to me a most suggestive one. And from Hellenistic times on, of course, 'eros' has often provoked a maidenly blush—for example, in Apollonius' Medea (3.297f.) and Hypsipyle (1.790f.).

Let us now concentrate on the phrasing of the blush: 'flagrantis genas', 'ignem subiecit rubor', 'calefacta ora'. It seems a tremendous amount of *fire* to attribute to a blush. But that is what the text seems to say: 'in whom a great blush kindled fire'—and produced, presumably, the 'burning cheeks' and 'heated face' as well as the 'fire'. Of course Vergil helps to explain the amount of heat by stressing the huge size of the blush ('plurimus' ['great']). But it is not sufficient explanation. I think that the odd and striking concentration of *fire* terms hints

Allusion

at an image. Fire, as we shall soon recall, is a very significant and familiar image of love in the *Aeneid*. By describing Lavinia's blush in the symptoms and terminology of fire, Vergil suggests, he insinuates, its erotic cause. For Lavinia, with 'flagrantes genae', with (in particular) 'ignis' kindled in her, with 'calefacta ora', is, we could say, 'on fire'; and the implications of that sort of statement about a girl in a Vergilian text are, I think, unmistakable. The text is suggestive, containing a hint of imagery. This is something distinct from the dramatic action: a further voice speaking to us in a way with which we are familiar. And the voice becomes more insistent.

Now come the similes. The source of the first, the stained-ivory simile, is well known: the simile describing Menelaus' wound in *Iliad* 4.141 ff., as blood spills on his thigh:

ὡς δ' ὅτε τίς τ' ἐλέφαντα γυνὴ φοίνικι μιήνῃ
Μῃονὶς ἠὲ Κάειρα . . .

As when a woman stains ivory with scarlet, some woman of Maeonia or Caria . . .

No one can deny that Vergil's choice of simile here is quite surprising, its literary purpose unobvious.[28] Of course Vergil is shortly to base a whole scene (the breaking of the truce) on precisely this section of the *Iliad*; and some might maintain that he uses the simile simply because it is present to his mind and attractively decorative. On the other hand, Vergil usually displays profounder artistic principles than convenience, and seeks more in his similes than extrinsic ornament. We have learnt to expect multi-correspondence,[29] and so on. What is going on here?

The very unexpectedness of the simile prompts us to consider the source, and the context of the source; it acts as a 'signal', taking us back to *Iliad* 4 and Menelaus. But what is the significance of the allusion, if such it be? What has Menelaus to do with Lavinia? Personally, and on the face of it, nothing. But there is a connection, a very significant connection.

Two details of vocabulary in comparison with Homer are

---
[28] For a spirited attempt to interpret the simile see Putnam, 158–60. Wigodsky, *Vergil and Early Latin Poetry*, 11, tries, unconvincingly to me, to explain the allusion to Homer.
[29] D. West, *JRS* 59 (1969), 40–9. Cf. below, n. 67.

noteworthy. (*1*) 'sanguineus', 'blood-red'. This epithet is an addition to the Homeric source. (*2*) 'uiolo', 'stains'. The word that Homer uses for the staining of the ivory is μιαίνω. Now this in fact has moral connotations ('sully'). But Vergil's 'uiolo' has a stronger moral connotation ('defile'). And 'uiolo' is used of physical injury in a way that μιαίνω is not. In four out of its eight other uses in the *Aeneid* (all Vergil's examples occur in the *Aeneid*) it makes up a formula 'uiolauit uulnere', *vel sim*.[30] We could say that, especially for Vergil, 'uiolo' was a 'wound' word. This nuance obviously works with 'sanguineus'. They cooperate to suggest 'wound'. Thus, paradoxically, these variations from Homer assist the recall of Homer (they 'signal'): they remind us that the simile originally applied to a wound (Menelaus' wound). And they also focus our attention upon what in the original context is relevant to our own: it is the *wound*. In Homer the simile pictured a wound. That is what contributes to the present context.

The simile, in the first place decoratively illustrating Lavinia's blush, suggests by allusion, by the recall of the Homeric source (the recall is assisted and the suggestion reinforced by the words 'sanguineus' and 'uiolo'), that Lavinia is *wounded*. So, too, by a concatenation of emotions including love, is Turnus: 'Poenorum qualis in aruis / saucius ille' (12.4f.); he is like a wounded lion. So, pre-eminently, was Dido. Wound, and fire, were the dominant and striking images for Dido's love in Book 4: 'at regina graui iamdudum saucia cura / uulnus alit uenis et caeco carpitur igni' (4.1f.) ['the queen, now long since *wounded* by grievous care, nurtures a *wound* in her veins and is consumed by hidden *fire*']—and so on; the images recur at salient intervals in the book.[31] Wound and fire: the passionate, loving Dido's images. But also Lavinia's: 'flagrantis', 'calefacta', 'ignis' (fire); and allusion assisted

[30] 11.277, 591, 848, 12.797.

[31] See Otis, 70ff., Pöschl, 103ff. These sequences of fire and wound images are fine examples of 'linked imagery': see Ch. 4 s. 12. They introduce among other things a sense of tragic inevitability. Dido's love wound is converted remorselessly and seemingly inevitably in the maintained imagery into the wound of her suicide; and the fire of her love is converted with similar but less sympathetic inevitability into the fires of her curse.

Allusion

by the words 'sanguineo uiolauerit'[32] introduces the notion of wound. Discreetly but insistently further voices reinforce the suggestion that Lavinia, like Dido, is in love: she is in love with, it must be, Turnus.

Further voices thus suggest to us, by allusion and imagery, more than the immediate burden of the epic voice. We can also detect here Vergilian feelings about that additional information. Opinions are implicit in the types of image chosen, wound and fire (my comments here have significance for *Aeneid* 4). Wound imagery easily suggests sympathy. Wounds involve suffering, which we pity: remember how Dido's 'tacitum uulnus' was amplified into the pitiable picture of the wounded hind, and finally realized in the frightful 'uulnus stridens' of her suicide (4.67, 69ff., 689). With wound imagery Vergil points us to sympathize with Dido. Likewise with Lavinia. Fire imagery is less sympathetic, potentially aggressive, and destructive: we remember how Dido's 'ignis' switched fluently to the 'atri ignes' of her curse (4.384).[33] Vergil implies an antipathetic as well as a sympathetic aspect to Dido's violently passionate love. We perceive the same ambiguity in his delicate adumbration of Lavinia's more delicate passion: wound and fire. But in the final count, however sympathetic with its victims, Vergil tends to condemn passionate love itself—he has done so (arguably consistently) since *Eclogue* 2: note especially *Georgics* 3.209ff. And Vergilian disapprobation of love, his distaste, is evident here in the Lavinia context, in the moral connotation of 'uiolauerit'. The dye *defiled* the ivory. The blush produced by love defiled Lavinia.

I summarize the points just made, in the terminology that I favour. The epic voice tells us that Lavinia blushes in an exotic way, and perhaps begins to suggest she was in love. A further voice confirms she was in love, with Turnus, and suggests that this was a troublingly ambiguous fact. (And, we might note,

---

[32] We can if we like see 'sanguineus' and 'uiolo' as extreme examples of 'transfusion of terms' (to use West's phrase, op. cit, 48) or of 'tenor' terms intruding into the 'vehicle' (to use the terminology favoured by M. S. Silk, *Interaction in Poetic Imagery* (Cambridge, 1974), 138–42). Instead of being told that Lavinia is 'wounded' and then finding metaphorical 'wound' language in the simile to illustrate that 'wound', we find such language *only* in the illustrative simile.

[33] These 'ignes' are richly polysemic: see the excellent discussion of Pöschl, 113f.

Lavinia's love was in its effect troubling: 'illum turbat amor';
Turnus' recognition of it sends him into turmoil.[34])

There is of course still a simile to come: 'aut mixta rubent ubi
lilia . . .', Vergil's comparison of the blushing Lavinia to lilies
and roses. I comment in brief.[35] This sort of imagery, 'two-
flowers' imagery,[36] belongs in an erotic context. It reminds one
of a lover describing his beloved; Propertius describes Cynthia
in such terms (2.3.10ff.). And one should also be put in mind of
Catullus' epithalamium. At 61.185ff. the amorous bride is
described to the bridegroom thus:

> uxor in thalamo tibi est,
> ore floridulo nitens,
> alba parthenice uelut
>   luteumue papauer.

Your wife is in the bridal chamber, bright with a blooming complexion, like the white camomile or the orange[37] poppy.

The type of imagery was arguably conventional in epitha-
lamia.[38] Some more parallels could be adduced, but these are
sufficient, and guide the simile's interpretation. It seems a
simile appropriately uttered *by* someone in love about their
beloved, and it seems a simile appropriately uttered *of*
someone in love, by an onlooker. Subtleties of interpretation
are possible, but I shall content myself here with saying that the
erotic connotations of the simile are certain. Vergil corrobor-
ates the suggestion that Lavinia is in love; in love with, it must
be, Turnus, at whom all this emotion (weeping, blushing) is
directed. And this time Vergil seems to present the fact as
something innocent and pretty rather than not—we remember
in particular the parallel with the engaging bride in Catullus.
The comment is thus quite different from that contained in
'uiolauerit'. But to suggest options in interpretation, even
opposed options—that is not unexpected, given the evasiveness
of Vergil and his further voices.

[34] On 'illum turbat amor' see further *GR* 30 (1983), 60.
[35] More fully in *GR* 30 (1983), 59f.
[36] Cf. Fordyce on Catull. 61.187.
[37] On the colour 'luteus' see Fordyce on Catull. 61.10.
[38] See *GR* 30 (1983), 60.

Aeneas and Apollo the plague-bringer[39]

At 1.657ff. Venus decides to put Cupid to work, to inflame Dido. The scene is based on Aphrodite's employment of Eros in Apollonius Rhodius 3.111–66 and 275ff., the story of Medea.[40] It is Vergil's first clear signal that Dido's story will have elements of that ominous and disastrous tale: Dido is destined to remind us of (to be compared and contrasted with) other heroines besides Nausicaa[41] or Arete, or even Circe and Calypso. And Aeneas is destined to remind us of other heroes besides Odysseus.

In 4.143ff. Aeneas is compared to Apollo:

> qualis ubi hibernam Lyciam Xanthique fluenta
> deserit ac Delum maternam inuisit Apollo
> instauratque choros, mixtique altaria circum
> Cretesque Dryopesque fremunt pictique Agathyrsi;
> ipse iugis Cynthi graditur mollique fluentem
> fronde premit crinem fingens atque implicat auro,
> tela sonant umeris . . .

As when Apollo abandons Lycia, his winter home, and the streams of Xanthus, and visits his mother's Delos, renewing the dances, and Cretans, Dryopians, and painted Agathyrsians mingle round his altars and raise their voices; he himself ranges the ridges of Cynthus and with soft leafage shapes and confines his flowing hair, and entwines it with gold; his arrows clash on his shoulders . . .

The primary source of this is also in Apollonius, a simile applied to Jason (1.307–10). In Apollonius the main function of the simile is to suggest the beauty and splendour of Jason. The superficial function in Vergil is to illustrate similar qualities in Aeneas. But of course, if we sense an allusion to Apollonius,

---

[39] I am particularly indebted in this section to Andrew Crompton and Matthew Taylor.

[40] Cf. Knauer, 155.

[41] The invitation to compare and contrast Dido with the charming and innocent character of Nausicaa is single and fleeting, but it is memorable, occurring at the moment of Dido's entry (cf. Knauer, 155, esp. n. 3, but Knauer makes nothing of it, seeing no invitation): Dido's Diana simile at 1.498ff. recalls Nausicaa's (*Od.* 6.102–8). Dido's entry is thus marked by a breath of happiness and innocence as well as much else. Vergil then links Dido's Diana simile to Aeneas' Apollo simile in 4.143–9 (quoted above), to much effect: cf. the admirable remarks of Pöschl, 84ff.; other points can be inferred from my discussion above. Dido's simile is the one that attracted the imperceptive criticism of Valerius Probus: Gell. 9.9.12–17. For further discussion and bibliography see Rieks, 1035 and below, Ch. 4 pp. 194–6.

there is a disturbing association for our hero: Aeneas as a Jason figure. In what sense? A further voice intrudes a troubling question. This is not the only time such an association is suggested.

But Aeneas' Apollo simile has other sources besides Apollonius, and many functions in the text.[42] I select one source and one function, another allusive function, that has escaped scholarly notice. I have in mind that final item, Apollo's arrows 'clashing on his shoulders' ['tela sonant umeris']. Now we should expect a concluding detail like this to be important. We may make a simple inference and assume a simple correspondence: Aeneas is armed like Apollo, armed for the hunt. But Apollo in arms is surely too significant and ominous a figure to perform merely this function: poets introduce him in warlike as opposed to peaceful guise with deliberation, and for awesome purposes.[43] Added to which, the arms here in question are particularly sinister arms, for this is Apollo from a most sinister source. A highly disturbing allusion is in fact operating. 'Tela sonant umeris' is a translation of Hom. *Il.* 1.46. And *Il.* 1.46 describes *Apollo the plague-bringer*, describes, to be precise, the very means by which Apollo delivered plague. In *Iliad* 1 Apollo came down from Olympus to punish the Achaeans with plague, and 'his arrows', the instruments of that plague, 'clashed on his shoulders' as he descended—a striking, ominous, and memorable moment: ἔκλαγξαν δ' ἄρ' ὀϊστοὶ ἐπ' ὤμων, 'tela sonant umeris'. Vergil's simile therefore culminates in a recall of this most memorable moment, the advent of the divine plague-bringer. So the allusion (assuming it to be such) intimates the suggestion: *Aeneas the plague-bringer*. Aeneas a plague-bringer? It seems an anomaly, ludicrous even, until consideration of the *Aeneid*'s context and the process of com-

---

[42] See, e.g., n. 41.
[43] Since Apollo has both peaceful and violent roles, the poets distinguish and define the Apollo that is relevant to their needs. Cf. Verg. *Aen.* 8.704f., Prop. 4.6.39f.: Apollo in arms, on an august occasion. Contrast the expressly peaceful Apollo of Hor. *Odes* 1.2.31f., Prop. 4.6.69f., likewise deliberately deployed. At *Carm. Saec.* 61, Horace for a special purpose invokes Apollo in both his guises. All these passages reinforce the point that Apollo, armed, peaceful or whatever, is not lightly or formulaically adduced.

paring and contrasting reveals not dissimilarity but disturbing similarity. Consider 1.712, 'pesti deuota futurae', Dido 'doomed to a plague to come' and 4.90, 'tali persensit peste teneri' where Dido 'feels herself in the grip of such a plague'. 'Plague' is one of the images used to depict Dido's fatal and tragic love;[44] and the second example quoted occurs just 53 lines before the Apollo simile and its allusive comment on Aeneas. So allusion, a further voice speaking in the background of the text, casts Aeneas' part in the disastrous love-affair in less attractive a light than does the epic voice, which gives us only the barest clues. It casts Aeneas as the bringer of Dido's plague. This is not the only time that a further voice has disturbing things to say about Aeneas' role at Carthage.[45]

Aeneas, Medea, and Dido*

Allusion in Lavinia's blush was discreet in the way it supplied material, and in the way it commented on it; but what it supplied was potentially dynamite. Allusion, we could say (to change our metaphor for a moment), functioned like a device to encode material that could not be broadcast in explicit language. The situation is similar at 8.18 ff., where Aeneas' anxious thoughts are compared to beams of light reflected from a vessel of water. And here, as well as the encoding of material, we shall find (once more) allusion to Apollonius of Rhodes; we shall find, too, a passage which having defeated all commentators,[46] now, given an understanding of allusion, submits to interpretation.

Aeneas sits on the bank of the Tiber, anxious and temporarily sleepless. He is described thus (8.18 ff.):

> talia per Latium. quae Laomedontius heros
> cuncta uidens *magno curarum fluctuat aestu*,
> atque animum nunc huc celerem nunc diuidit illuc
> in partisque rapit uarias perque omnia uersat,

---

[44] The 'disease' of love is a commonplace: cf. Barrett on Eur. *Hipp.* 476 f., Norden on *Aen.* 6.442, Lyne on *Ciris* 182 and 248 f. This fact shows that the sense 'plague', 'pestilence' is the one that *pestis* is contributing (*OLD* s.v. 2).
[45] Cf. Ch. 4 s. 12.
* My special thanks are due in this section to Helen Quinn.
[46] They exhibit defeat, if they do not admit it. Cf. e.g. Pöschl, 178, Johnson, 85–7 (a spectacular failure). The simile has attracted both praise and blame: cf. Eden ad loc.

> sicut aquae tremulum labris ubi lumen aenis
> sole repercussum aut radiantis imagine lunae
> omnia peruolitat late loca, iamque sub auras
> erigitur summique ferit laquearia tecti.
> *nox erat et* terras animalia fessa per omnis
> alituum pecudumque genus sopor altus habebat,
> cum pater in ripa gelidique sub aetheris axe
> Aeneas, *tristi* turbatus pectora *bello*,
> procubuit seramque dedit per membra quietem.

Such were the events throughout Latium. Perceiving it all, the hero of Laomedon's line *tosses on a great surge of troubles* and directs his thoughts now hither, now thither, casting them into different areas, turning them to every aspect: like flickering light from the sun or shining moon's semblance which is reflected from water in brazen vessels and darts everywhere, now rising skywards and striking the panelled ceiling of the lofty house. *It was night, and* over all lands deep sleep held wearied creatures, both birds and beasts, when father Aeneas, his breast disturbed by *woeful war*, lay down on the bank beneath the vault of the chill heavens, and let sleep come tardily upon him.

Aeneas, anxious and wakeful on the banks of Tiber, is given a simile taken from Apollonius Rhodius, 3.755 ff., a simile in which dancing rays of sunlight reflected from a cauldron or pail of water image in somewhat artificial fashion the fretful throbbing of Medea's amorous heart. If the simile is artificial and unobvious in Apollonius, it is even more unobvious in Vergil—and, arguably, less appropriate. Flashing rays of sunlight may be thought a better illustration of an involuntary action like the throbbing of Medea's heart than of the apparently purposive movements of Aeneas' anxious thoughts. It is a puzzle—but one thing that Vergil does *not* seem to be aiming at is a clear illustration of what thought-processes are like. Something else is going on. Something allusive, something sensitive: a most interesting further voice. The oddity of the simile is again a 'signal'. We must look at the Apollonian source more carefully.

When we do so, we find that not just the simile but the whole striking passage that I have quoted from Book 8 (the anxious, temporarily sleepless Aeneas) is based on Apollonius (the amorous, fretful, sleepless Medea); in particular, Vergil's use of the 'nox erat . . .' topic is also directly based on Apollonius. Vergil has simply reversed the Apollonian order so that *It was*

Allusion

night ... everything was sleeping ... except *wakeful, anxious Medea* + simile becomes, in the *Aeneid, wakeful, anxious Aeneas* + simile ... *It was night ... Everything was sleeping.* But I now quote the Apollonian passage in full (3.744 ff.):

> Νὺξ μὲν ἔπειτ' ἐπὶ γαῖαν ἄγεν κνέφας· οἱ δ' ἐνὶ πόντῳ
> ναῦται εἰς Ἑλίκην τε καὶ ἀστέρας Ὠρίωνος
> ἔδρακον ἐκ νηῶν· ὕπνοιο δὲ καί τις ὁδίτης
> ἤδη καὶ πυλαωρὸς ἐέλδετο· καί τινα παίδων
> μητέρα τεθνεώτων ἀδινὸν περὶ κῶμ' ἐκάλυπτεν·
> οὐδὲ κυνῶν ὑλακὴ ἔτ' ἀνὰ πτόλιν, οὐ θρόος ἦεν
> ἠχήεις· σιγὴ δὲ μελαινομένην ἔχεν ὄρφνην.
> ἀλλὰ μάλ' οὐ Μήδειαν ἐπὶ γλυκερὸς λάβεν ὕπνος.
> πολλὰ γὰρ Αἰσονίδαο πόθῳ μελεδήματ' ἔγειρεν
> δειδυῖαν ταύρων κρατερὸν μένος, οἷσιν ἔμελλεν
> φθίσθαι ἀεικελίῃ μοίρῃ κατὰ νειὸν Ἄρηος.
> πυκνὰ δέ οἱ κραδίη στηθέων ἔντοσθεν ἔθυιεν,
> ἠελίου ὥς τίς τε δόμοις ἐνιπάλλεται αἴγλη
> ὕδατος ἐξανιοῦσα, τὸ δὴ νέον ἠὲ λέβητι
> ἠέ που ἐν γαυλῷ κέχυται· ἡ δ' ἔνθα καὶ ἔνθα
> ὠκείῃ στροφάλιγγι τινάσσεται ἀίσσουσα·
> ὣς δὲ καὶ ἐν στήθεσσι κέαρ ἐλελίζετο κούρης.

Night then drew darkness over the earth. Sailors on the sea looked from their ships towards the Bear and the stars of Orion; wayfarer and gatekeeper longed for sleep, and deep slumber covered a mother whose children were dead; there was no longer any barking of dogs throughout the city, nor sounding voices: silence held the blackening gloom. But sweet sleep did not take hold of Medea. In her love for Jason many cares kept her wakeful, for she feared the mighty strength of the bulls by whose agency he was likely to die in an unseemly fate in the field of Ares. Fast did her heart throb in her breast, as a sunbeam in a house quivers, reflected from water, water that has just been poured in a cauldron or pail; and hither and thither does it dart and shake on the eddy; even so the girl's heart quivered in her breast.

Vergil's debt to Apollonius here, the allusion (if such it be), is thus very extensive, more extensive than the commentaries tend to suggest. Something must be going on. But what? In what way is Aeneas like or unlike Medea, besides being awake and anxious? And with what implications? There seems, in fact, to be no very plausible or profitable way in which Aeneas can be compared or for that matter contrasted with Medea.

128   *Allusion*

However, the apparent irrelevance of Medea to Aeneas might remind one of the apparent irrelevance of Menelaus to Lavinia; and we might, therefore, be chary of finding no meaning in the comparison.

The key to the solution lies earlier in Vergil's poem. Our passage of Apollonius, in particular the 'Night, peace, and an individual's wakefulness' section, directly underlies not one but two vivid scenes in the *Aeneid*: it is the source not just of the anxious Aeneas in 8, but of the anxious, sleepless Dido of 4.522 ff.:

> *nox erat et* placidum carpebant fessa soporem
> corpora per terras, siluaeque et saeua quierant
> aequora, cum medio uoluuntur sidera lapsu,
> cum tacet omnis ager, pecudes pictaeque uolucres,
> quaeque lacus late liquidos quaeque aspera dumis
> rura tenent, somno positae sub nocte silenti.
> at non infelix animi Phoenissa, neque umquam
> soluitur in somnos oculisue aut pectore noctem
> accipit: ingeminant curae rursusque resurgens
> saeuit amor *magnoque irarum fluctuat aestu.*

It was night, and over the earth wearied creatures were enjoying peaceful slumber; the woods and wild oceans had sunk to rest; it was the time when stars roll midway in their gliding course, when every field is silent, and silent the beasts and painted birds, those that inhabit the clear expanse of lakes and those that dwell in the shrubs of the countryside, stretched out in sleep beneath the silent night. But not so the Phoenician [Dido] ill-starred in her heart: she never relaxes into sleep nor draws the night to herself in eyes or heart. Doubled is her anguish and love once more swells up fiercely and *tosses on a great surge of anger.*

Now this passage (4.522 ff.) may readily be seen as a direct allusion to Apollonius 3.744 ff.; and to compare and contrast the passionate and desolated Dido with the amorous and eventually betrayed Medea is plausible and productive. But the most important point to be grasped is the *connection* effected between the two passages of the *Aeneid*: between Dido in Book 4 and Aeneas in Book 8. What happens is this: the strange simile in Book 8 'signals' us to the text of Apollonius—a striking signal to a fairly strange text. We ask: in what way can we usefully compare and contrast Aeneas and Medea? We cannot: not directly. However, once signalled to the Apollonian text, we find that the allusion is more extensive: the 'nox erat' section is also based on Apollonius; and we are then prompted to recall that another passage in the *Aeneid* is supplied by this same Apollonian material. So *two* passages, we discover, allude to the one passage of Apollonius, and are connected by this shared allusion (connection through allusion is in fact a well-paralleled phenomenon):[47] Dido sleepless and anxious in Carthage is connected to Aeneas anxious and temporarily sleepless on the bank of the Tiber. This connection is then reinforced by (among other things) a shared use of Catullus: Catullus' Ariadne imagery (64.62): Dido's love 'magnoque irarum fluctuat aestu' and Aeneas 'magno curarum fluctuat aestu'.[48]

A connection is therefore made. But what is the significance? I would argue as follows. Allusion in Book 8 initially suggests that we might compare and contrast Aeneas and Medea. That seems inappropriate and puzzling. We look for something else, and turn to the text which shares the same allusion: 4.522 ff. Allusion here suggests that we should compare and contrast Dido and Medea. That seems more promising. The situation therefore is that allusion *first* shows Dido *plausibly* in a Medea-like turmoil, *then* shows Aeneas more *surprisingly* in the same condition. Strikingly, therefore, history is shown to repeat itself, in different characters: first Dido, fretting, anxious, and compared *naturally* by allusion to Medea, and second Aeneas fretting, anxious, and *oddly* compared by allusion to Medea. Here in fact is the basic function of Aeneas' allusive compari-

---

[47] Juno's monologues in 1 and 7 are connected by the fact that both are based on Poseidon's in *Od.* 5: see Knauer, 152, who refers to more such examples. Add that the landing at Carthage in 1 (note esp. lines 159–69) and the landing at Tiber in 7 (note esp. lines 30–4) are connected by a joint allusion to *Od.* 13.96 ff.: cf. Buchheit, 183–7. Connection between 8 and 4 is strengthened by the fact that 8.20 f. repeat 4.285 f. See Eden on 8.20 f., Austin and Pease on 4.285 f; some have doubted the genuineness of the lines in 4.

[48] Note too 'laquearia' at 8.25. Vergil uses the word one other time in the *Aeneid*: of Dido's palace at 1.726.

son to Medea: to underline the fact that he is acting *like Dido* who was like Medea. To put that another way: Vergil shows us very pointedly that Aeneas repeats Dido's turmoil by giving him not only similar language and motifs but Dido's own allusive persona. So it is obviously very important to Vergil that we perceive Aeneas to be repeating Dido's turmoil. That much should now be clear. But why is it so important?

A further voice suggests thereby a measure of poetic justice—or what some might feel was poetic justice. For some might feel that it is *right* that Aeneas should pointedly repeat Dido's suffering in this way, that he should suffer some of what she had suffered, that he should, as it were, pay her out and get a little of his own medicine. Certainly Dido might think thus: for her indeed there might be a particular pleasure—and here we get to the very nub of the issue. For in fact, for Dido, this scene could in a way seem an answer to her prayers—and that Vergil should in this way insinuate into the narrative such an answer to her prayers must, I think, be indicative of his own sympathies. The point is as follows.

Dido's rage, mentioned in the description of her Medea-like anxiety ('irarum', 4.532), expands into a terrible curse (607ff.). Its first items are as follows:

> si tangere portus
> infandum caput ac terris adnare necesse est,
> et sic fata Iouis poscunt, hic terminus haeret,
> at *bello* audacis populi *uexatus* et armis,
> finibus extorris, *complexu auulsus Iuli*
> *auxilium imploret* uideatque indigna suorum
> funera . . .

If that accursed being must needs reach harbour and glide to shore, and if Jupiter's fates thus demand and this is a boundary that is fixed, let him nonetheless be *harried by warfare* from a bold people, let him be an exile far from home, let him be *torn from the embrace of Iulus and beg for aid*, and see his own people perish in shame . . .

Dido's Medea-like anxiety expands thus into a hate-filled prayer that Aeneas may be harassed by war, separated from his son, and forced to beg for aid from foreigners. The scene in 8.18ff. shows Aeneas not only very pointedly repeating a Dido-like anxiety but repeating it *almost exactly in respect of what*

Dido herself had called down upon him. He is anxious about war ('bellum'), and he must imminently sue for aid ('auxilium') from a foreign people (the Arcadians), leaving his son behind him. It is in a sense a kind of answer to Dido's prayers: Aeneas in a turmoil of Dido-like anxiety in response, it might seem, to a Dido-uttered curse. There is some consolation here for Dido, some *Schadenfreude* for her ghost. And it should not escape us that the ghost of Dido is in a sense there, in Aeneas' simile: in the moon, an addition of Vergil's to his Apollonian source: 'sole ... aut ... imagine lunae' ['from the sun *or moon's semblance*']. The moon, palely reflecting Dido's earlier moon-and-Diana imagery, palely reflects Dido;[49] and the 'imago' of the moon recalls her 'imago', her shade (4.654, 'et nunc magna mei sub terras ibit imago', Dido had said, 'and now a great semblance of me will go beneath the earth'). There is, I say, some consolation here for Dido—but only some. The intercession of Tiberinus and other factors make Aeneas' 'bellum', his need to sue for aid and so on, a great deal easier than Dido wished or prayed—and Aeneas in his scene does eventually sleep. Events do not always turn out quite so fairly and symmetrically as some might wish them. But Dido's curse contained other items ... .[50]

A further voice thus supplies much sensitive material at this point, exploiting allusion most subtly. And there is one further striking detail underlining the connection between the two passages, and underlining the impression that Dido is in a sense being vindicated—and hinting once more, I think, at Vergil's own sympathies. In her sleepless soliloquy (4.534ff.) Dido remarks (541):

> nescis heu, perdita, necdum
> Laomedonteae sentis periuria gentis?

Alas, hopeless woman, do you not yet know, do you not yet understand the perjuries of Laomedon's race?

(which echoes a thought that had preoccupied Vergil at the end

---

[49] Pöschl, 185–9, aptly associates the 'luna' of 6.454 with Dido's Diana simile of 1.498ff., but does not of course see the connection between these two and 8.23. He also ties in Iopas' song, the 'errantem lunam solisque labores' (1.742), in a way which I find increasingly plausible.

[50] On Dido's curse and its fulfilment, see Buchheit, 76; Heinze, 136 n. 2; R. D. Williams (1–6) on 4.615f.; Quinn, 321f.

of *Georgics* 1). Now Vergil, who concocts manifold periphrases for his hero (always significant in their variation), connects Aeneas with his illustrious and perjurous ancestor just once: 8.18. So Aeneas as 'Laomedontius heros' frets Dido-fashion about the difficulties that Dido, betrayed (as she saw it) by the 'Laomedontia gens', had prayed for. To some this mode of expression might seem particularly fitting and satisfying.

A last point. Given that our thoughts are directed towards Apollonius at 8.18ff., we should not miss the fact that Aeneas' journey up the Tiber, which almost immediately ensues (86ff.), echoes the departure of Jason for Colchis (*Arg.* 1.544ff.)[51]—a suggestive and perhaps invidious comparison for Aeneas, given that memories of Dido-Medea have just been revived. Compare the recall of *Arg.* 1.307–10 at 4.143ff. (above, p. 123).

4. Turnus, Diomedes, and the last two lines of the poem; Aeneas and Diomedes

In my discussion of Aeneas and Achilles in the 'Iliadic *Aeneid*' (above, s. 2), I pointed out that the process of allusion was rendered subtler by the fact that characters as well as author allude. Turnus saw himself as a new Achilles; authorial allusion designated him rather as a Hector. Something comparable happens with the figure of Diomedes; and Diomedes serves Vergil's allusive technique in other ways.

First we should remind ourselves of the identity of Diomedes, and recall his explicit role in the *Aeneid*. In the *Iliad* Diomedes had been a very special and implacable enemy of Troy and the Trojans. He had been the one to revive the dispirited Agamemnon in *Iliad* 9.32–49 (and cf. 697–709); he had even declared his intention to remain and take Troy with one companion alone, if needs be. In the 'Diomedeia' (*Iliad* 5) he very nearly kills Aeneas himself; he was also the hero who in the same book did not even balk at attacking Aphrodite (Venus). In the *Aeneid* we learn that he has done his share of wanderings after the Trojan War and finally settled at Arpi in Italy (11.242ff.). To him the Italians send an embassy, seeking his assistance (8.9ff.). In the 'concilium deorum' Venus makes much capital out of his expected resurgence (10.28–30), and

---

[51] See Briggs, 975.

Allusion

recalls the fact that he had attacked her (29f.). However, the implacable Diomedes reveals (11.252–93) that he is converted, and refuses to join in against the Trojans, whom he praises fulsomely—Aeneas in particular; he advises the Italians to make peace; he also regrets his attack on Venus. His new attitude signals, among other things, that the tide of history has turned.

I focus now on that scene in which Diomedes nearly kills Aeneas: *Iliad* 5.302 ff. Diomedes casts a giant stone at Aeneas, a stone 'which two mortals as they are today' could not lift, strikes him devastatingly, and brings him to his knees. Only the intercession of Aphrodite, protecting Aeneas with her 'peplos', saves him from death. Now if one thinks about it, this sore discomfiture of Aeneas was a potentially embarrassing scene for the poet of the *Aeneid*. Vergil might well have drawn a discreet veil over it. On the contrary, however, he decided to confront it head on. And what happens is that in the *Aeneid* Diomedes' victory in *Iliad* 5 is so to speak reversed, paid for, avenged. Diomedes, as we have seen, now explicitly defers to Aeneas and the Trojans. But the defeat is also reversed in another way: by allusion.[52]

Vergil chooses to make Aeneas refer to his encounter with Diomedes in his very first speech, his speech of despair at sea quoted above (1.94ff.). There Aeneas apostrophizes Diomedes, declaring that he wishes Diomedes had in fact killed him in their encounter. Such is the measure of his despair, that inappropriate despair that I talked of (p. 107). The reader must hope that this despair will pass. He may well hope too that in some way Aeneas will get his own back on Diomedes. And he does, *allusively*—as well as through that stated deference of Diomedes in Book 11.

Turnus knows of Aeneas' tangle with Diomedes. He refers slightly to Venus' rescuing him from it (12.52f.):[53]

---

[52] See Knauer, 318ff., for the material. Knauer comments usefully, but does not bring out the point that Aeneas *allusively reverses* his defeat at Diomedes' hands by defeating Diomedes' self-styled heir.

[53] Turnus or Vergil (cf. 10.82f.) apparently conflates Aphrodite's action (using her 'peplos' and her arms) with Apollo's subsequent use of a cloud (*Iliad* 5.311ff. and 344f.). But cf. Knauer, 318 n. 1, who thinks Vergil is referring simultaneously, at both 12.52f. and 10.82f., to Aphrodite's rescue of Aeneas in *Il.* 5 and to her rescue of Paris at 3.380f.—and to other rescues as well.

> longe illi dea mater erit, quae nube fugacem
> feminea tegat et uanis sese occulat umbris.

His goddess mother will not be at his side, far from it, to protect the runaway in a woman-contrived cloud and to conceal herself in empty shadows.

Besides belittling Venus, these lines show that Turnus is thinking of himself in a particular way. In fact, just as at 9.742 Turnus saw himself as an Achilles, so here he suggests he is another Diomedes; more particularly, a potentially efficacious and unthwarted Diomedes. And this time Vergil appears to agree with and to confirm the identification. For by his own subsequent allusion Vergil puts Turnus in that role. Turnus picks up a stone 'which twelve mortals of the sort that earth now produces would scarcely support' and casts it at Aeneas; and the lines describing the event (12.896ff.: quoted above, p. 92) are based predominantly on, and allude to, those lines in *Iliad* 5 (302ff.) in which Diomedes made his original cast. So Vergil puts Turnus in the role of Diomedes, casting a lethal stone like Diomedes. But the issue is different. Unexpectedly (such stone-casts are usually effective in the *Iliad*) Turnus fails. He cannot even make the stone carry (12.896ff.). In fact, compared with the episode in the *Iliad*, the result is pointedly reversed. In the *Iliad* Aeneas was forced to support himself on hand and knee. In the *Aeneid* Turnus, the thrower of the stone, finds his knees giving way—and we are mere moments away from Aeneas' victory. So while Turnus sees himself as a potentially successful Diomedes, Vergil presents him as a discomfited and defeated Diomedes (all this while the Aeneas–Achilles/Turnus–Hector allusions progress), and the process of comparing and contrasting is done for us. Turnus, it transpires, is not quite the great and successful hero he thinks he is. And the defeat of the aspiring Diomedes may seem in a way to even the score, repaying the original Diomedes for his success in the fifth book of the *Iliad*. Along with that, Aeneas' inappropriate despair in Book 1 (his wish to have died at the hands of Diomedes) is triumphantly and welcomely overcome.

Vergil effects this last turnabout most pointedly. Defeatist despair involving Diomedes is turned into victory involving 'Diomedes'. A verbal repetition presses the point home. Vergil turns a phrase which had described Aeneas at his lowest moment—wishing he had died at the hands of Diomedes—to mark his highest point: he uses it to describe Aeneas' victory over Diomedes' self-styled heir. When, defeated and desperate, Aeneas utters his wish that Diomedes had killed him, it is said that 'his limbs loosen with chill', the chill of fear.[54] When in Book 12 he dispatches his prime enemy the aspiring Diomedes to defeat and death, Vergil describes the latter's 'limbs' as 'loosening with chill'—the chill of death: 'soluuntur frigore membra' (1.92, 12.951). Vergil uses the same phrase on both occasions—and nowhere else. The irony marks Aeneas' victory. The poem has, we could say, moved full circle.[55]

But 'soluuntur frigore membra' is not the last line of the poem, and before I make one further comment on the allusive role of Diomedes, I should like to consider the last line. What I have written above may suggest that the poem ends in facile triumph. That is, of course, not the case. Vergil complicates the conclusion in innumerable ways. One of them is his choice of last line. Further voices exploiting allusion and repetition insinuate loss as well as triumph.

In the last *two* lines of the poem Turnus dies:

> ast illi soluuntur frigore membra
> uitaque cum gemitu fugit indignata sub umbras.

But his limbs loosen in chill, and with a moan his life fled indignant to the shades.

The penultimate line, a dense line, takes us back to Aeneas' first scene and suggests the point that Aeneas has triumphantly reversed despair. As such it resonates victory. The last line is even denser, and different in direction.[56] In the first place it alludes to Homer. It is based on and thus recalls the line in the

[54] This chill is supplied by Livius Andronicus' translation of *Od.* 5.297: 'igitur demum Ulixi cor frixit prae pauore' (fr. 16, Morel).
[55] Cf. Knauer, 320f. But Knauer does not see the full significance of the repetition of 'soluuntur frigore membra', nor how it fits into the Diomedes material. For another attempt to interpret the repetition see Putnam, 200f.
[56] Knauer, 309f., sees the significance of the last line differently from the way I do.

Iliad used to describe the deaths of both Hector and Patroclus (16.857, 22.363). The sadder aspect of Aeneas' victory, as opposed to its triumph, is thereby enhanced. Turnus dies beloved by many, in death recalling by allusion those most sympathetic heroes, each the most sympathetic hero on his respective side: Hector and Patroclus. The allusion underlines the fact that Turnus dies beloved by many. But the last line also *repeats* the line assigned to the death of Camilla (11.831), its only other occurrence in the poem: *both* the last two lines are thus repetitions of lines occurring only *once* elsewhere in the poem, and likely therefore to be significantly repeated. The last line repeats the death of Camilla: and Camilla entails Dido. A mass of parallels links these two heroines, female, redoubtable, but ultimately vulnerable and tragic;[57] and recall of Dido has

[57] Camilla is 'Amazonian'; one of her functions in the *Aeneid* is to be Vergil's version of Penthesilea, the heroine of Arctinus' *Aethiopis* (cf. E. Fraenkel, *JRS* 35 (1945), 11 = *Kleine Beiträge zur klassischen Philologie*, 2 (Rome, 1964), 165). She is compared to—in fact in strict textual terms she is identified as—an Amazon at 11.648f. 'at medias inter caedes exsultat Amazon / unum exserta latus pugnae, pharetrata Camilla' ['but in the midst of the slaughter exults the Amazon, one breast bared for battle, quivered Camilla']. Her companions are compared in more orthodox fashion to Amazons, 'columns with their crescent shields', at 11.659ff.; and in that simile Camilla is figured explicitly as Penthesilea or Hippolyte. She is beloved of Diana (11.532ff.) and bears Diana's weapons (652): 'aureus ex umero sonat arcus et arma Dianae' ['a golden bow and the arms of Diana clash on her shoulder']. Her father had been an enforced *émigré* from his city, and had brought Camilla up dedicated to Diana; and she lived her young life in the wilds, a huntress and committed virgin (11.539ff.). She fights like a man (she is introduced at 7.805 as 'bellatrix'), and rules as a man more normally would: she is queen, 'regina', of the Volscians (11.498f., 801).

Dido is an enforced *émigrée* (1.340ff.). In her migration she displayed a masculine authority (1.364, 'dux femina facti') which she continued to display as 'regina' (1.340, 'imperium Dido Tyria regit urbe profecta', 594, 'reginam', etc.) until her catastrophic love. Having been married she cannot of course be committed to virginity; but, widowed, she has committed herself to a viriginal existence (4.15ff.). Her first simile (1.498ff.) suggests an affinity between her and Diana, more particularly Diana the huntress, who bears her quiver on her shoulder (1.500). And by describing Penthesilea (who 'leads her columns with their crescent shields . . . one breast bared, a warrior-maiden ('bellatrix')' in the lines immediately preceding Dido's entry (1.490ff.) Vergil suggests some sort of affinity between the Carthaginian queen and the Amazon (Penthesilea functions as a 'modello d'interpretazione' for Dido; Conte, *Il genere*, 103, 107).

Camilla is a character who realizes, intensifies, unequivocally exhibits qualities of leadership, originality, and toughness more insecurely present in Dido, more hesitantly attributed to her by the poet. She picks up Dido's baton, and she too dies.

Allusion

already been prepared for by numerous echoes of Book 4 in the last scenes of Book 12.[58] The effect of the repetition is therefore to bring to mind two key figures who have suffered and been lost in the process of Trojan advancement, two other figures besides Turnus himself: the tragic heroines Camilla, the 'Iliadic *Aeneid*'s' Dido, and through her, Dido herself. Allusion enhances the pathos of Turnus' loss, repetition recalls the loss of others, the heroines. Much is therefore gathered up in this last line, much which tells of loss. The penultimate line may resonate triumph, victory, a circle full turned. The ultimate line is a dense expression of counterbalancing cost. This is a pattern which, of course, runs through the entire *Aeneid*.

To return to Diomedes. There are a couple of other ways in which the *Aeneid* allusively reverses, corrects, makes amends for Aeneas' rather inglorious adventure in *Iliad* 5. I refer to one of them, which is by no means obvious but it is most pleasing. Here we find a further voice that is piquant, entertaining, almost humorous.

In the 'Diomedeia', Sthenelus, on the instructions of Diomedes, captures and bears off the horses of the defeated and humbled Aeneas (5.259ff., 319ff.). They are very special horses, described thus (265–72):

> τῆς γάρ τοι γενεῆς, ἧς Τρωΐ περ εὐρύοπα Ζεὺς
> δῶχ' υἷος ποινὴν Γανυμήδεος, οὕνεκ' ἄριστοι
> ἵππων, ὅσσοι ἔασιν ὑπ' ἠῶ τ' ἠέλιόν τε,
> τῆς γενεῆς ἔκλεψεν ἄναξ ἀνδρῶν Ἀγχίσης,
> λάθρῃ Λαομέδοντος ὑποσχὼν θήλεας ἵππους·
> τῶν οἱ ἓξ ἐγένοντο ἐνὶ μεγάροισι γενέθλη.
> τοὺς μὲν τέσσαρας αὐτὸς ἔχων ἀτίταλλ' ἐπὶ φάτνῃ,
> τὼ δὲ δύ' Αἰνείᾳ δῶκεν, μήστωρε φόβοιο.

They are of that strain which far-sounding Zeus once gave to Tros as a recompense for his son Ganymede; wherefore are they the best of horses beneath dawn and sun. Anchises, lord of men, stole from that strain, putting mares beneath them without the knowledge of Laomedon. From these, a stock of six were bred in his halls. Four he kept and nurtured himself in his manger. But these two he gave to Aeneas, two horses, authors of fear.

Aeneas thus loses his very fancy horses to his conqueror Dio-

---
[58] See R. D. Williams (7–12) on 12.843f.

medes. The event was inglorious—and uncomfortably memorable; it is directly recalled on two other occasions in the *Iliad*: in Book 8, when Diomedes uses these horses to rescue Nestor, and in Book 23, when he wins the chariot race with them (8.105ff., esp. 106–8, 23.290 and subsequently, esp. 290f.). The episode was not, one would have thought, a topic to be aired in the *Aeneid*. But it is. Vergil confronts this as he confronted the other episodes of Aeneas' defeat in the 'Diomedeia'.

The question of Diomedes and horses very soon surfaces in Vergil's poem. On the temple of Juno at Carthage, Aeneas sees depicted the fate of Rhesus, whose horses were also driven off by Diomedes (1.469ff.). One wonders whether this reminded Aeneas of his own tangle with Diomedes and the fate of his own horses. If he was not reminded then, he must surely have been by Dido's precise and embarrassing question at 1.752: 'rogitans . . . nunc quales Diomedis equi' ['asking . . . of what sort were the horses of Diomedes']. Was Aeneas reminded? Perhaps the question is inappropriate. But what is certain is that a reader of Vergil, familiar with the 'Diomedeia', would be so reminded: would remember Diomedes' capture of Aeneas' fancy horses and would be alert to any further reference or allusion. Vergil is jogging our memories, wanting us to recall that inglorious and memorable event, putting us on the alert for any further reference.

It comes in *Aeneid* 7: an allusion. In Book 7 Latinus gives presents to the Trojan embassy. Presents in the *Aeneid* generally carry significance, symbolic or otherwise:[59] so we attend with care. The present for Aeneas comprises a chariot and horses, described thus (7.280–3):

> absenti Aeneae currum geminosque iugalis
> semine ab aetherio spirantis naribus ignem,
> illorum de gente patri quos daedala Circe
> supposita de matre nothos furata creauit.

---

[59] Cf. my remarks on Aeneas' gifts to Dido, Ch. 1 pp. 22–3. See the excellent comments of Quinn, 345f., on the significance of Dido's gifts at 11.72–5, not missing his surely true perception, 346 n. 1. Cf. too Buchheit, 161f., Pöschl, 180.

For the absent Aeneas [he chooses] a chariot and twin horses of heavenly seed, breathing fire from their nostrils, sprung from the stock of those whom cunning Circe, stealing them from her father, bred as bastards from the mare she mated.

These horses, with their strange history (derived from divinity by deceit), clearly recall Aeneas' own original horses that were driven off on Diomedes' instructions in *Iliad* 5: *Aeneid* 7.280 ff. in fact allude to *Iliad* 5.265 ff. If the allusion seems not so immediately clear, we must remember those references to the topic of Diomedes and horses which Vergil inserted in the text. They were designed to help us. They act as a 'signal' that the story of Diomedes and horses, one of the stories of Diomedes and horses, is going to participate in our text. And here is the moment: in 7.280 ff. And the effect of the allusion? The process of comparing and contrasting suggests similarity, even identity. Behind Latinus' gift we sense Aeneas' own original horses. So, Aeneas is not just getting *any* fancy horses. In terms of the text to which *Aeneid* 7.280–3 alludes, he is getting back his *own* horses. A wrong is as it were righted: such is the slightly piquant, even amusing suggestion offered by a further voice, speaking through allusion.

5. Juturna and Procne

In 'ductor Rhoeteius', 12.456 (above, p. 10), Vergil alluded to an association supplied not by a specific source but by literary and historical tradition in general. Poets as artistically conscious and literate as, say, Vergil and Horace are always aware of 'cultural' associations, often presuppose similar awareness in their readers, and, to a greater or lesser extent, exploit this common pool of knowledge in the making of their dense and allusive poetry. A frequent phenomenon is 'implicit myth'. Poets can and do assume great familiarity in their readers with myths and fables; and they often expect readers to sense a myth or fable behind a text with the aid of minimal explicit reference ('signal') or indeed with none at all. Some examples. At *Odes* 3.11.13 ff. Horace needs us to think of the myth of Orpheus, at 3.1.17 ff. of the story of Damocles and Dionysius, at 2.5.21 ff. of Achilles on Scyros. At *Georg.* 3.258–63 Vergil wishes us to think of Hero and Leander, at 4.511 of Philomela, at 1.511 ff.

of Phaethon,[60] at *Aen.* 7.698 ff. of Cycnus;[61] and the practice is prevalent in others too.[62] On occasion the myths assumed to be known in this way are very important to the context: they function like texts introduced by allusion, providing further voices. *Georg.* 1.511 ff. is, I think, one such example—and a fine instance of a disturbing further voice in the *Georgics*.[63] *Aen.* 12.473 ff. is another example. Here a myth is implicit, indeed alluded to by means of a perceptible signal. And the allusion provides scope once more for a Vergilian further voice.

At this stage in the story Juturna is disguised as Turnus' charioteer. She parades him before the enemy, veering this way and that across the plain, but keeps him out of Aeneas' and harm's way. She is given a simile which runs as follows:

> nigra uelut magnas domini cum diuitis aedes
> peruolat et pennis alta atria lustrat hirundo
> pabula parua legens nidisque loquacibus escas,
> et nunc porticibus uacuis, nunc umida circum
> stagna sonat . . .

As when a black swallow flies through a rich lord's great house and crosses lofty halls seeking small crumbs and scraps of food for her chattering nestlings, and now in the empty porticoes and now around the water ponds cries . . .

This is R. D. Williams's comment (7–12, ad loc.):

> The point of resemblance in this simile is the darting circular flight of the swift with the rapid swerving course of Juturna driving Turnus' chariot. There is an unusually large proportion of non-similar elements in the simile, the palace, the seeking of food for the baby birds, the noise of the swift . . . As far as we can tell the simile is original . . .

In having no very obvious source, the simile is quite possibly unique in Vergil; but whether the simile was in fact as original

---

[60] A suggestion of Andrew Crompton—who, however, was not as confident about it as I am.

[61] See O. Berthold, *Die Unverwundbarkeit in Sage und Aberglauben der Griechen* (Giessen, 1911), 47.

[62] Cf. W. R. Smyth on Propertius, in *CQ* 43 (1949), 119, 123 f.

[63] At *Georg.* 1.463 ff. the sun, 'Sol', is associated with Julius Caesar (cf. Lyne in *Quality and Pleasure in Latin Poetry*, ed. T. Woodman and D. West (Cambridge, 1974), 51 f.). In the impotent 'auriga' of 514 there is a whisper of the Sun's son Phaethon, figuring the 'son' of the dictator, as yet ineffective in managing the chariot of State.

Allusion

as it seems we cannot, of course, tell.[64] Williams like Warde Fowler[65] identifies the 'hirundo' as a swift. It may be that the term 'hirundo' covered birds related to the swallow, such as swifts, but there is no justification for making that precise identification here, and I shall retain the conventional translation. It also seems obvious to me that the details of the swallow's seeking food for its nestlings is not in fact 'non-similar': it images the protective, quasi-motherly care that Juturna at this moment accords Turnus.[66] But what else does the simile contribute? As yet it still seems, for a Vergilian simile, fairly unproductive and unintegrated.[67] Something is being neglected. Let us rather say (reminding ourselves of a point made earlier): something optional is being neglected. The drama may proceed unencumbered if that is what we choose. On the other hand, we may choose to pause and attend to a voice additional to the epic voice; for it is there.

What is being neglected is, I maintain, a myth: in the background of the simile and the object of Vergil's allusion is the myth of Procne and Itys. The essentials of that story can be summed up as follows.[68] Procne was married to Tereus. Tereus raped her sister Philomela, and cut out her tongue to keep her quiet. But Procne became apprised of the facts, and took her revenge by killing their son Itys and serving him up for dinner to Tereus. Then all three, Procne, Philomela, and Tereus, were changed into birds. Now according to the main Greek version of the myth, Procne the mother was changed into the nightingale. The appropriateness of this is obvious. Procne was supposed to have become appalled at her killing of her son, and to have lamented his death for ever. The nightingale's song was conventionally interpreted as a lament: the bird was thus naturally seen as the perpetually lamenting Procne. Meanwhile, in the main Greek version, the tongueless Philomela was

[64] But cf. Achilles' simile at Hom. *Il.* 9.323f.
[65] *The Death of Turnus*, 95, following a communication by J. Sargeaunt.
[66] Cf. Otis, 378, Giancotti in Gigante, 473.
[67] On Vergil's similes, see D. West (above, n. 29); Pöschl, 86f., who has this unequivocal comment '[weil] bei Homer oft, bei Virgil immer der *ganze* Vergleich ... der Verdeutlichung und Erhöhung des Geschehens dient', discussing 1.494ff., and citing bibliography. Cf. further Pöschl, 132.
[68] See Coleman on *Ecl.* 6.78, Bömer on Ov. *Met.* 6.669, Kiessling-Heinze on Hor. *Odes* 4.12.5.

changed, also appropriately, into the twittering swallow; and Tereus was changed into a hawk or hoopoe and perpetually pursued both of them.

In the Vergilian simile we have a swallow: the tongueless, twittering Philomela. If we apply that in context, if we assume that that is what Vergil is alluding to, it may not seem to make much sense.[69] Let us try another tack. A certain amount of confusion enters the tradition about which sister was changed into what bird; but another firm version emerges (which seems characteristically Roman) in which the *mother* of Itys (not always named as Procne) was changed into the 'hirundo', the swallow; as early as Hesiod (*Erga* 568) in fact, the song of the swallow had been interpreted not as senseless twittering but as a lament. Compare, for example, Vergil himself at *Georg.* 4.15, where the swallow is described as 'manibus Procne pectus signata cruentis' ['Procne whose breast is stained by bloody hands']; Ovid, *Ars* 2.383f. 'altera dira parens haec est, quam cernis, hirundo: / aspice, signatum sanguine pectus habet' ['another dread parent [sc. besides Medea] is this swallow that you behold: look, her breast is stained with blood']; and a conveniently full, though slightly post-*Aeneid* example is Horace, *Odes* 4.12.5ff., an announcement of spring:

> nidum ponit Ityn flebiliter gemens
> infelix auis et Cecropiae domus
> aeternum opprobrium, quod male barbaras
>   regum est ulta libidines.

Now builds its nest she who tearfully laments Itys, the bird ill-starred, the eternal shame of the house of Cecrops, in that evilly she punished the barbarous lust of kings.

This is the version that I think Vergil particularly has in mind in 12.473ff.—the swallow as the lamenting mother of Itys; this is the version that he most certainly wants us to sense behind his text.

---

[69] Actually, I think it does, and I think Vergil means us to have this line of interpretation open to us as an option. Did not someone behave towards Juturna as Tereus behaved towards Philomela? It is a thought eminently worth pursuing.

There is confirmation that we should hear this myth (in this version) behind the simile; there is even, we might say, a signal towards it.[70] Look how the simile ends: 'nunc umida circum stagna sonat': the *song* or *cry* of the swallow. That is a very curious detail to emphasize in a swallow simile illustrating *movement*, 'the rapid swerving course of Juturna', as Williams saw it; it is a curious detail to emphasize in a swallow simile illustrating Juturna's 'protective, quasi-motherly care', which was my initial formulation. It is indeed completely redundant in the simile in both those functions—and redundant in a way which does not strike me as in Vergil's manner. But it is, of course, exactly the feature one would and did highlight if one was alluding *through* the swallow to Procne, as Horace shows: for the bird's characteristic song, interpreted as lament, was the key element in that story. The emphasis on 'sonat' is in fact a signal: it indicates that not just a swallow but Procne is under reference. We should find that Procne and, in particular, her cry are relevant to our narrative.

And they are. The myth and the detail 'sonat' contribute superbly. At first reading the simile strikes one as an image of Juturna's movement, more importantly as an image for Juturna the solicitous protector. That is how the simile superficially works; that is the message of the epic voice. But underneath that surface, behind that solicitous mother swallow, we may sense the tragic mythical mother who murdered her son and then lamented him for ever. This further voice foreshadows the end that is now imminent, the tragic death of Turnus and the sorrow of Juturna the immortal—Juturna who is shortly to bemoan precisely this fact, that she will lament for ever: 12.872ff. Of course (it may be said) Juturna does not actually destroy Turnus, as Procne did Itys. On the most literal level that is clearly true. On the other hand there is this to think about: if Juturna had not thwarted the first duel (at the beginning of Book 12) when Aeneas was not passionately angry, if

---

[70] There may be another one, besides that mentioned in the text. 'Nigra' is an epithet perhaps oddly gloomy in signification for a swallow; less so for the lamenting Procne. See Warde Fowler, *The Death of Turnus*, 94, on the colour of swallows/ swifts and how it is registered in Latin. 'Nigra' caught the eye of Tiberius Claudius Donatus, who for once is more acute than his successors. His comment ad loc. is: 'nigram hirundinem pro dolentis persona, etiam lugentis posuit'.

that duel had been allowed to reach its conclusion, Aeneas might not have been moved to slay Turnus in the moment of victory. Further observations along these lines could be made.[71] It is certainly possible to argue that Juturna's solicitousness over Turnus' life was fatal to him. This, like the imminence of Turnus' tragedy, is a line of thought encouraged by the further voice—a line of thought with dreadfully ironic implications for Juturna, and, too, more sinister implications for Juno, the naïve nymph's instigator.

Other details in the simile can be pressed into service, but I prefer to leave them to work in their own way. I recommend, for example, consideration of 'diuitis aedes'. And at least one other quite distinct line of interpretation is open.[72]

---

[71] See e.g. 12.481ff. and my remarks in Ch. 1 pp. 4–6.
[72] See above, n. 69. And there is suggestive discussion in Putnam, 172f., following a quite different idea.

4

The Hero and His Son

Invention, 'negative' invention, and arrangement;
linked imagery and motifs

1. Apparent lack of characterization: the 'cut-off' technique

In my opening chapter I demonstrated that Vergil can and does characterize by both word and action. But sometimes he appears to decline the opportunity. A fact that particularly requires explanation is one noticed by Richard Heinze.[1] Conversation is well suited to the purposes of characterization, and Homer freely exploited it. Yet Vergil seems strictly to limit it. Why?

We should first remind ourselves of the role that conversation may play in characterization. It exhibits men in their relationships with one another, affording an author splendid opportunities to individualize and to differentiate his characters. Homer capitalized on its potential. In his poems we find scenes with extended sequences of conversation, and multiple participants. We have only to think of the quarrel scene in *Iliad* I or the embassy in Book 9 to realize what use he makes of conversation to illuminate character. Achilles' clash of personality with Agamemnon, his difference from Odysseus, Ajax, Phoenix (a wide spectrum) is *audible*.

Vergil does appear to pass up the chance. His normal practice (there are some exceptions)[2] is to restrict conversation to two characters, and on each occasion to permit no more than a speech, a reply, and then perhaps a further retort by the first speaker. Multiple participants and long, free, and frank exchanges are out. And this policy of restriction seems to be a

---

[1] Heinze, 404 ff.
[2] e.g. Venus and Aeneas in 1, Nisus, Aletes, Ascanius, Euryalus in 9, Jupiter, Venus, and Juno in 10; Heinze, 405.

conscious and deliberate one. For we find Vergil as it were *interrupting* when an extended chat seems imminent. For example, Helenus appears on the scene at 3.345 to divert Aeneas and Andromache. When Deiphobus ends his speech to Aeneas at 6.509ff. with interested questions and Aeneas is perhaps minded to reply, the Sibyl intervenes: 'nox ruit, Aenea' ['night rushes on, Aeneas'] (6.539). More tantalizingly, Dido breaks off her great speech 'nec tibi diua parens . . .' ['no goddess was your mother . . .'] (4.365ff.) and dashes out leaving Aeneas 'preparing to say many things' (4.390). Of course in each of these cases the interrupting characters (Helenus, the Sibyl, Dido herself) act not implausibly. But Vergil organizes these and other interruptions; it is his invention. To what purpose? We may call it his 'cut-off' technique.

Heinze explains these 'cut-offs' in a way which is not obviously despicable.[3] He refers us to Vergil's demonstrable desire to make all his material contribute positively to the advance of the plot. He then argues that what Aeneas might have said to Deiphobus and to Andromache *we* should know already: so that the plot would be unnecessarily retarded, not advanced, by such conversations. Hence the policy of interruption, the 'cut-off' technique: Heinze's Vergil will not delay the story for incidental characterization. Now there are probably elements of truth in this. Yet we must retort: are there not details in Aeneas' potential reply to Andromache that we do not exactly know? Might we not like to know? We certainly cannot be sure what Aeneas would have replied to Dido. And I for one would love to know.

I glance now at another scene referred to by Heinze,[4] the crisis point of the exit from Troy, 2.634ff. (my remarks are merely preliminary; the scene is an important one and I shall be returning to it). Here conversation is very strikingly limited. The crisis is caused by Anchises' refusal to leave Troy; and it affects three adults: Anchises himself, Aeneas, and Creusa. First Anchises announces and explains his refusal to leave; then Aeneas responds and announces his intention—if Anchises is staying—to return to battle; and this speech, which of course

[3] Heinze, 405f., 409f.
[4] Heinze, 410.

The Hero and His Son

introduces an entirely new crisis (what about his family?), leads to an appeal by Creusa to Aeneas. So a great deal is happening. But so far we have just these three speeches. And that, in fact, is the lot. Creusa's appeal, the last of the three, is introduced and phrased thus (673 ff.):

> ecce autem complexa pedes in limine coniunx
> haerebat, paruumque patri tendebat Iulum:
> 'si periturus abis, et nos rape in omnia tecum;
> sin aliquam expertus sumptis spem ponis in armis,
> hanc primum tutare domum. cui paruus Iulus,
> cui pater et coniunx quondam tua dicta relinquor?'

But then! my wife clasped my feet and clung to the threshold, and stretched out little Iulus to his father: 'If you are leaving to die, take us with you, into any eventuality. But if from your experience you place some hope in the arms you have taken up, protect this house first. To whom is little Iulus, to whom is your father, to whom am I, once called your wife, abandoned?'

It is a moving and affecting appeal, putting Aeneas, in human terms, right on the line. We wait for his reply. Among other things this reply would characterize him. It would or should characterize him as much as Hector's reply characterizes Hector when he is similarly put on the line by Andromache (*Iliad* 6.440ff.).[5] Hector replies—but for Aeneas' reply we wait in vain. The scene is then 'cut off'. An omen occurs (2.679f.):

> talia uociferans gemitu tectum omne replebat,
> cum subitum dictuque oritur mirabile monstrum.

Crying such things she filled the whole house with her moaning, when suddenly and marvellous to relate a portent arises.

The omen convinces Anchises to leave, and his decision solves

---

[5] Characterization is here enhanced by defeated expectations. The audience want to know: how will Hector reply to Andromache's lacerating appeal of 6.407ff.? I think the expectations must be that he will say something similar to his reply to Helen at 6.360ff.—which would (it is worth noticing) be the kindest thing that he could say in the circumstances; Homer programmes such expectations by organizing this previous interlocution with Helen (by invention and arrangement, 'encouraging us to views'; see Ch. 6). In fact Hector says something quite different. Put on the line by Andromache, he reveals his deepest motivations.

the second crisis, provoked by Aeneas' response to his initial refusal. The plot can move on.

We may make some observations. First, the restriction that is here set on conversation is very striking: the episode might most naturally have been one of extended speechifying (Creusa as well as Aeneas appealing to Anchises; then Anchises as well as Creusa reasoning with Aeneas; and finally—and in particular—Aeneas' reply to Creusa). Secondly, we can appreciate that pace is in this way given to the drama. There is indeed no diversion, no retardation: the action hurries excitingly on. Heinze's explanation may therefore be thought to have some validity. On the other hand, we do not know what Aeneas would have said to Creusa any more than we know for certain what he was preparing to say to Dido. And I at least would very much like to have heard a speech that might so vividly have characterized the hero. Is the desire to avoid retardation a sufficient explanation for its omission?

Heinze can provide another reason why Vergil should avoid conversation—or indeed any other device that would make for individual characterization. He simply does not want and is perhaps unable to draw psychologically complete and individual characters.[6] He is concerned (I am paraphrasing Heinze) with morality and passion: his characters are designed to embody a certain moral quality or a certain state of emotion on a given occasion. Subtleties and subsidiary shadings of character do not serve his grand plan—and are not, perhaps, within his ability.

It can, I think, be argued that the *Aeneid* is concerned with moral dilemmas first, with the people living and demonstrating those dilemmas second—in *consequence* of the fact that they demonstrate them; that the poem does not derive its primary strength from the interaction of people, the raw clash of personalities, in the way that many of us think that Greek tragedy does.[7] And other reasons can be advanced to explain

---

[6] Heinze, 279ff., 410ff.

[7] For this sort of view of the *Aeneid* cf. C. M. Bowra, *From Vergil to Milton* (London, 1945), 37 (Vergil's characters are 'types, examples, symbols' lacking the 'lineaments and idiosyncrasies, the personal appeal, and the intimate claims' of Homer's characters), and, in more up-to-date language, Conte, *Il genere*, 72ff.; see too Ch. 1 p. 44.

why characterization in the poem may not match everyone's expectations. For example, the sort of moral qualities that Aeneas is called upon to display are not the best material for the dramatic characterizer: subordination does not translate itself into theatre so well as vast, egoistic passions do. But the *Aeneid*, though it is not the *Iliad*, is not so very deficient in characterization. We remember Priam and Hecuba, the intense characterization of Dido, and for that matter the figures of Turnus, Mezentius, Lausus, even Amata and Lavinia, and Aeneas himself, particularly in Books 10 and 12.[8] When he wants to Vergil can, it seems, delineate subtleties in character, exploiting action and word; he can, more particularly, characterize people in their relationships with one another. And yet on some occasions he seems to pass up the chance, when none of the factors that might dissuade him seems to apply– I think in particular of Aeneas and Creusa, Aeneas and Dido. Why are these scenes 'cut off'? The matter needs further investigation.

2. Aeneas in his relationships: Creusa

I shall now attend particularly to the characterization of relationships. This seems to be the key area; for this, obviously, is what is most reduced by the cut-off technique.

When we study this topic, we should remember that relationships are often well characterized by action, or rather *interaction*, as well as speech: the sort of things people do together can be the best indicator of the type and quality of their relationship. Homer knew this, and put his knowledge to brilliant use. We have only to think of Achilles and Priam in *Iliad* 24, of Hector, Andromache, and Astyanax in *Iliad* 6, of Odysseus, Achilles, and Agamemnon in Book 19: crucial relationships in these scenes are characterized as much by what the figures do— or refuse to do—together as by what they say.

With this in mind we turn to the *Aeneid*. Again we find a curiously negative picture. While speech is 'cut off', interaction is minimal. But now we can be more precise. This epic centres

---

[8] See Ch. 1 pp. 13–15, 45–55; Ch. 3 pp. 106–7, 114–22. Note the fine characterization of Turnus by word, action, and description at 12.614–83. Pöschl, 122ff., has a stimulating discussion of Turnus.

very emphatically on Aeneas. It is Aeneas who comes or should come most interestingly and often into contact with other people. But it is his interaction with others that is minimal. In general it is Aeneas' relationships that Vergil appears to neglect. Vergil seems curiously disinclined to show Aeneas responding or relating to others. Much of the time the hero seems to stand and act alone, not always very appealingly.[9] But is this Vergil's neglect? Or is it his provoking *invention*? Are we to sense a further voice saying something unobvious?

Let us recall Aeneas and Creusa. In that fast-moving scene Aeneas does not, as we have seen, address direct speech to her. No actions help to define his relationship to her either. She clasps his feet and stretches out their son to him, to reinforce her desperately affecting appeal (673f.). He responds to the child, it seems (but the text is not very clear: 681).[10] But he does not respond to her: neither to her appeal, nor to the gesture she directs towards him—contrast Hector with Andromache (cf. above, p. 147), and for that matter Achilles with Priam.[11] The attention of all is, of course, soon distracted: by the omen. But—and this should be stressed—although Vergil does pretty swiftly 'cut off' the scene, he does not suggest that Aeneas had *no* chance to respond to Creusa's speech or gesture, either then or later. Nor, incidentally, does he suggest that Aeneas was brimming over with things—anything—to say. He has ways of making such a suggestion: in the cut-off scene with Dido, for example, we are told that Aeneas 'was preparing to say many things'.

Aeneas' lack of contact with Creusa, physical and, apparently, emotional, is maintained as the story continues. In the *third person* he informs her how she should leave the city; and he tells her that she is to follow 'at a distance' behind himself, Anchises, and Ascanius: 'longe seruet uestigia coniunx' ['let my wife follow at a distance'] (711).[12] Aeneas' policy here may

---

[9] D. Feeney has studied this side of the hero in his article 'The Taciturnity of Aeneas' and finds a much more sympathetic hero than I do. Similarly La Penna, lix, lxix, with bibliography. I recommend Feeney's stimulating and intelligent piece as a counterbalance to my chapter. Cf. too Johnson, 107; Quinn, 347.

[10] See Austin ad loc. But is his 'who bends to him' justified? I am inclined to think not.

[11] See esp. *Iliad* 24.508.

[12] I accept Austin's argument ad loc. that 'longe' need imply no great distance: cf. 2.725, 'pone subit coniunx'.

accord with Roman, dynastic, and practical priorities: 'pietas' is primarily owed to Anchises, whose leadership is in any case still needed; the future rests with the young Iulus; and Creusa is strictly, in these terms, third in importance. But his policy also facilitates, if not causes, Creusa's death. This point must not and will not be ducked. But, an interim conclusion: 'longe seruet uestigia coniunx' are the last words that Aeneas utters in connection with Creusa before her death. To all intents and purposes their relationship in life is at an end. Vergil seems therefore well concerned to achieve pace, drama, and so on during the episode; and Creusa's speech and action do something to characterize her in her relationship with Aeneas. But what Vergil seems disinclined to do is to characterize Aeneas' feelings for her.

Unless we are meant to ask: does Aeneas have them? If he has, can he express them? In short, is Vergil 'negatively' and disturbingly *inventing* rather than revealing lack of interest in such characterization?

3. Aeneas and Ascanius

It might be argued that Aeneas' relationship with Creusa is a special case. The scene is simply designed to accord with Roman sentiment: it ill befitted a hero of Roman and Stoical tradition to manifest feelings towards his wife. Actually, I do not think this explanation bears scrutiny, but let us consider another relationship: Aeneas and Ascanius. And for this let us gather a little comparative material. As an epic example of a father in his relationship with his little son, *Iliad* 6 offers us Hector and Astyanax, a scene which is tenderly moving as well as toughly heroic, and which characterizes by word and interaction.[13] Homer also offers us the extensively elaborated and characterized picture of Telemachus growing up and into his role as Odysseus' son.[14] And Roman tradition admired and recorded fathers who were attentive to and anxious for young sons. Plutarch shows us the Elder Cato occupied in teaching his son reading (he provided him with a copy of his own *History of Rome* which he had written out in big letters), law, swimming,

---

[13] See esp. *Iliad* 6.466–81: indeed both tenderly moving and toughly heroic.
[14] Cf. W. J. Woodhead, *The Composition of Homer's Odyssey* (Oxford, 1930), 212–14; A. Thornton, *People and Themes in Homer's Odyssey* (Dunedin/London, 1970), 66–77; Maurach, 362–4.

other athletics, and military skills.[15] Suetonius records that Augustus taught his adopted grandsons reading and (probably) swimming, 'and other basic training'; and Augustus liked to travel with the boys, and never dined in their presence unless they sat at his own couch.[16] A noble father might be moved and troubled by his son's danger. At the battle of Pydna, Plutarch records,[17] the consul Aemilius Paullus' teenage son (the later Scipio Aemilianus Africanus Numantinus) was swept off in hot but risky pursuit of the enemy: the consul felt no joy in the victory until his son had returned safely. Such weakness was not considered unpardonable. These examples suggest that there was nothing unepic nor unRoman about fathers exhibiting interest in and concern for their sons—on the contrary. And Vergil himself confirms this to be true. Consider Mezentius and Lausus in Book 10, Evander and Pallas in Books 8 and 11 (to which I shall return).

We might therefore be predisposed to expect a relationship between Aeneas and Ascanius to exist and to be characterized. Indeed we might feel that such an important relationship—important historically as well as humanly—*ought* to be characterized. And we can think of many possible scenes: Aeneas schooling his son for the spiritual and physical hardships awaiting him, Aeneas anxious for him particularly in the war and during their separation, Aeneas sharing moments of snatched leisure, and so on. There are indeed many obvious ways in which Aeneas might be shown relating to Ascanius, even the aspiring Stoic Aeneas in the fate-bound *Aeneid*. What in fact do we find?

Vergil makes Aeneas address direct speech to his son just once in the whole poem: in the last book, at 12.435ff. This is the speech that starts with those sombre, Ajax-like words already referred to (p. 8); the rest of it I shall discuss later. To this speech Ascanius, not very surprisingly I suppose, does not answer. Aeneas' words have much and varied significance, particularly for Aeneas himself. But one thing they do not do is open up a picture of Aeneas in a warm, human relationship with his son.

[15] Plutarch, *Cato* 20.3–5.
[16] Suetonius, *Aug.* 64.3. The reading 'natare' was changed by Lipsius to 'notare'.
[17] Plutarch, *Aemilius Paulus* 22.

The Hero and His Son

This same point in the poem sees one of the very few occasions when there is any significant inter*action* between father and son: only the second time that they touch, and the first and last time that Aeneas embraces Ascanius (the *genuine* Ascanius).[18] 12.433f.:

> Ascanium fusis circum complectitur armis
> summaque per galeam delibans oscula fatur . . .

He clasps Ascanius in an iron embrace, and, lightly kissing him through his helmet, he says . . .

What a touch, what an embrace! The one and only time that Aeneas embraces his son it is in armour, and the kiss is through the iron of his helmet. These lines are of course exceedingly striking, with a resonance and significance that must and will be defined (s. 11). But the point I wish to draw at the moment is again the simple one: embrace no more than speech affords much view of a human relationship between father and son.

When else does Vergil present Aeneas and Ascanius in a scene whose words and actions might seem to characterize their relationship? In the scene of exit from Troy, there is, besides 2.681 (above, p. 150), a momentary but vivid picture of father and little son at 2.723f. (this is the other time they are said to touch):

> dextrae se paruus Iulus
> implicuit sequiturque patrem non passibus aequis.

Little Iulus entwined his hand in mine [lit. my right hand] and followed his father with steps that did not match.

Here the action of 'implicuit' as well as that suggested in 'non passibus aequis' is expressive. But notice that it is Ascanius who initiates. That may prove a significant little detail. Then, when Aeneas is safely installed in Dido's palace, he shows love and concern for Ascanius (now older)—the sort of love and concern which in fact he did not (as I shall argue) show during the exit from Troy: 1.643ff.

---

[18] Contrast 1.715. Some irony here—which might be compared to the irony in Aeneas' *too late* reactions to Creusa and Dido (see below).

> Aeneas (neque enim patrius consistere mentem
> passus amor) rapidum ad nauis praemittit Achaten,
> Ascanio ferat haec ipsumque ad moenia ducat;
> omnis in Ascanio cari stat cura parentis.

Aeneas—for a father's love did not allow his mind to rest—sends Achates on in haste to the ships, to bear this news to him, and to bring him to the city; in Ascanius all his parent's care is centred.

And, returning to Book 12, we find Ascanius among those who assist and commiserate with the wounded Aeneas (12.385 and 399). There are too a couple of other moments in that book which will be mentioned later. But I would maintain that none of this characterizes father and son very much in their relationship together. In fact, no words or actions in the whole poem depict much of a relationship between the two: we are particularly disappointed if we search for an *affective* relationship.[19] There is nothing in the poem to suggest a bond like that between Hector and Astyanax, Odysseus and Telemachus, or Cato and Aemilius and their respective sons. This is a curious fact, I think. Do we infer disinclination, even inability, on Vergil's part to characterize Aeneas in an important relationship? Or should we assume 'negative' invention, and seek to interpret it? Is there a further voice?

The situation is even more curious than I have so far described it. For we can point out occasions when Vergil might well have coloured in an affective relationship between the two—ought to have, one is tempted to say—but does not.[20] For example, the 'lusus Troiae' in Book 5 might have led Aeneas to feel pride or pleasure in his son, and Vergil to let him express it. Nothing specific is recorded; the acclamation and pleasure is general (5.575ff.). Then, too, Ascanius' major and vital role in the crisis of the burning ships might well have been acknowledged (5.667ff.). Not so. Aeneas turns instead to his own vast cares (700ff.). Again, if Augustus could demonstrate affection at dinner, so might Aeneas. I think in particular of that pregnant moment at 7.116 when Ascanius' joking comment that 'they were eating their tables' marks the welcome fulfilment of

---

[19] J. C. B. Foster's comment (*LCM* 2 (1977), 118) is baffling to me: 'the sympathetic depiction of young Ascanius and his relationship with his father is an attractive feature of *1* and *4*'.

[20] Highet, 32, observes one or two such occasions, but makes nothing of them.

a prophecy. Vergil could have used that and other mealtimes to colour in a relationship. But not so. We may compare and contrast how Homer exploited the motif of eating to convey human relationships.[21] And perhaps most suggestive of all is this thought: how much concern is Aeneas made to display for Ascanius while he himself is absent at Pallanteum in Book 8? How much does he even expressly think of him? A party is dispatched to bear news at 8.550 (we hear nothing further of it). That is the only sign. It is an odd fact. After all, things do go badly wrong back at the camp, as is narrated in Book 9, and we might expect the absent Aeneas to express some anxiety—remember Aemilius Paulus. We might expect it not only on natural and psychological grounds, but on technical grounds too. For if Aeneas had expressed anxious forebodings during Book 8, it would have amounted to a *foreshadowing* of the events of Book 9. And Vergil is fond of the technique of foreshadowing—elsewhere.[22]

To Aeneas in his relationship with Ascanius I shall return. Here I would simply conclude that the relationship of father and son, particularly the feelings of father towards son, seem markedly uncharacterized, in a way that is not obviously explained by epic convention, by Roman sensibility, or indeed by Vergil's practice elsewhere (above, p. 152 and below, p. 160). Is this Vergil's lack of interest, or, by negative means, his provoking invention? By now it will be clear which way I think. But before I try to explain, the picture needs to be filled out.

4. Aeneas and Pallas

I pass on to consider another of Aeneas' relationships, that with Pallas. Again, it offers surprises.

The young son of Evander is an important figure for Aeneas, and for the plot of the poem. His death and dishonouring at the hands of Turnus prompt Aeneas to a sequence of merciless and disquieting killings in Book 10. In the final moments of the poem, it is the desire to avenge Pallas that is the crucial factor

---

[21] Cf. Griffin, *Homer*, 15–17.
[22] See G. E. Duckworth, *Foreshadowing and Suspense in the Epics of Homer, Apollonius, and Vergil* (Princeton, 1933), esp. 120ff. Homer is, of course, much fonder of the technique than Vergil.

in persuading Aeneas to abandon the piety of clemency and to slay his defeated enemy.

Why does Pallas' death have this effect on Aeneas? In terms of facts this is easy to explain. The young man whom Turnus kills and dishonours is not only young, brave, splendid, and so on: he has large claims on both Aeneas' affection and his sense of responsibility. At their very first encounter, Pallas had emphatically extended the hand of hospitality to him, 8.121–5:

> obstipuit tanto percussus nomine Pallas:
> 'egredere o quicumque es' ait 'coramque parentem
> adloquere ac nostris succede penatibus hospes.'
> excepitque manu dextramque amplexus inhaesit.

Pallas was smitten with amazement at so great a name [the Trojan name]: 'Whoever you are,' he said, 'come forth; address my father face to face and enter our home as a guest.' With a grasp of welcome he took and held his hand.

(Aeneas soon learns that this is the second time that the Arcadians had so greeted his family: the young Evander had entertained Anchises.) Then of course, at great cost to himself, Evander had offered Aeneas the service of his beloved son in war. In so doing, he used words that show he saw Aeneas as a kind of tutor, in a sense *in loco parentis* (8.514–17):

> hunc tibi praeterea, spes et solacia nostri,
> Pallanta adiungam; sub te tolerare magistro
> militiam et graue Martis opus, tua cernere facta
> adsuescat, primis et te miretur ab annis.

And besides I shall ally Pallas here to you, Pallas my hope and comfort; under your guidance let him become accustomed to endure warfare and the stern work of Mars, let him become accustomed to behold your deeds, and let him wonder at you from his early years.

There is therefore good reason why Aeneas should feel responsible for Pallas and affectionate towards him. That he does indeed hold him in affection is revealed by, among other things, the emotional terms in which he invokes him in the last lines of the poem. His allusion 'meorum' ['one of my people'] at 12.947 suggests he sees him as a relation.

These feelings of affection and responsibility lead Aeneas to his anguished, merciless actions. Since these actions are so

The Hero and His Son

climactic in the plot, we should expect the feelings that stimulate them to have some palpable effect on the plot beforehand. To put it another way, we should expect Aeneas to be characterized in his relationship with Pallas, if this relationship is to contribute so vitally to the outcome of the poem.

Literary tradition also encouraged characterization of a beloved and esteemed lieutenant. The main antecedent of Pallas is clearly Patroclus, and we remember how deftly and warmly Homer characterized Patroclus and Achilles, especially in *Iliad* 16.[23] The Euripidean development of Pylades is also relevant.[24] A famous fragment of Ennius (268 ff. Sk.)[25] also shows how developed and appropriate such a figure might become in the rugged Latin epic:

> haece locutus uocat quocum bene saepe libenter
> mensam sermonesque suos rerumque suarum
> consilium partit, magnam quom lassus diei
> partem triuisset de summis rebus regundis,
> consilio indu foro lato sanctoque senatu;
> quoi res audacter magnas paruasque iocumque
> eloqueretur . . .

So saying he called to the one with whom he very often shared his table, his conversations, and the advising of his own affairs, when, tired out, he had spent a great part of the day in guiding affairs of highest moment, with advice in the wide forum and sacred senate-house; to him he would often without anxiety speak out boldly matters great and small, jokes too . . .

The fact that Ennius may be describing himself here (see Skutsch ad loc.) does not affect the influence the character might have had on subsequent epic writing, nor the expectations it might have aroused in its readers. And it is not irrelevant, I think, to mention that loyal lieutenants were à la mode in Vergil's own contemporary history and literature:

---

[23] I find Achilles' choice of simile at 16.8–10 particularly expressive.
[24] In Eur. *IT* and *Or*.
[25] I have cobbled together a rough and ready text, with no great confidence in some details; Skutsch's discussion ad loc. reveals all the difficulties. 'Consilium partit' is Skutsch's emendation of the transmitted 'comiter inpertit'. 'Triuisset' is Baehrens's conjecture for the MSS 'fuisset' which Skutsch prints. (Skutsch himself throws out 'fregisset' (cf. Hor. *Odes* 2.7.7) which is attractive; he takes 'lato' as the past participle of 'fero'.)

consider Maecenas in Propertius 2.1.25 f. and Agrippa in Vergil himself (*Aen.* 8.682 ff.).[26]

We look therefore with interest at Vergil's characterization of Aeneas and Pallas together. There is virtually none. And Book 8 in particular offers ample opportunities for just such characterization. Interestingly, we can observe a signal opportunity being (so to speak) missed. When Evander offers Aeneas the martial services of his son in the affecting words I have quoted, Pallas himself is, as we know, present (see line 466 as well as 514). Is not this the moment for Aeneas to react, to respond to Evander and to Pallas with word or gesture? Does not the occasion demand some human response? Aeneas in fact responds with a brooding silence (520–3):

> uix ea fatus erat [sc. Evander], defixique ora tenebant
> Aeneas Anchisiades et fidus Achates,
> multaque dura suo tristi cum corde putabant,
> ni signum caelo Cytherea dedisset aperto.

Evander had just spoken; Aeneas son of Anchises and trusty Achates kept their expressions set, and were pondering deeply on many a hard fact in their sad hearts, and would have continued so, had not Venus given a sign in a clear sky.

And Venus' portent directs everyone's attention elsewhere. We have another 'cut-off' scene.

It is a famous scene—and has caused the commentators much trouble.[27] It bears similarities both to the Creusa and to the Dido scenes discussed above. Once more a portent effects the 'cut-off', intervening at a crucial moment. Once more Vergil shows us clearly that Aeneas did have something in mind to say, indeed he indicates *what* he had in mind to say—or at least part of what he had to say: the patronymic 'Anchisiades' indicates the direction of his thoughts (see below, p. 178). And here again it is amply clear (clearer even than in the Creusa scene) that Aeneas has time to speak, at least to start to speak,

---

[26] Cf. too (though he has an axe to grind) Velleius 2.127.1, 'raro eminentes uiri non magnis adiutoribus ad gubernandam fortunam suam usi sunt, ut duo Scipiones duobus Laeliis' etc.

[27] See very conveniently Pöschl, 71 ff. On 8.522, 'tristi cum corde', Servius comments 'propter breuitatem auxiliorum', which may serve as an amusing reminder of how wrong he can get things. But modern scholars, as Pöschl illustrates, have followed him.

The Hero and His Son

before the 'cut-off' device operates. But Vergil makes him appear completely disinclined or unable to do so. He stands thinking. And without the 'cut-off' he would have gone on thinking.[28] So once more Vergil avoids a characterizing speech, avoids characterizing Aeneas in his relationship with another. But perhaps the avoidance should be assigned to Aeneas rather than Vergil. Vergil is being provokingly inventive, in a way that awaits interpretation.

In all the rest of Book 8 no opportunity is taken to characterize Aeneas in relation to Pallas, even when their two forces leave Pallanteum together (585ff.). Nor (I would say) is any opportunity taken in Book 10. The sort of thing we are missing is interestingly shown by a little scene in Book 10 that might, *if* it had been developed, have begun to characterize the pair. Trojans and Arcadians sail towards the Trojan camp; on board ship (159–62):

> hic magnus sedet Aeneas secumque uolutat
> euentus belli uarios, Pallasque sinistro
> adfixus lateri iam quaerit sidera, opacae
> noctis iter, iam quae passus terraque marique.

Here great Aeneas sits and ponders in his heart the changing issues of war, and Pallas, cleaving to his left side asks him now about the stars, their pathway through the dark night, now about his adventures by land and sea.

Note: Pallas 'asks', Aeneas 'ponders'. Pallas makes the overture—as Ascanius did in one of his two close scenes with his father (above, p. 153), and moreover as Creusa had done. And Aeneas? He ponders. One recalls his pensiveness at Pallanteum. It seems clear that in both scenes it is because of Aeneas, and not because of disinclination or inability on Vergil's part, that characterizing conversation fails to develop. A final point. When Aeneas laments over Pallas' body in 11.42ff. and fills in details which happened during the time of Book 8 but were not mentioned in Book 8 (11.45–8; this is a frequent Vergilian technique),[29] we get more information about Aeneas' ties with Evander, but nothing more on Aeneas and Pallas.

---

[28] The conditional clause is an elliptical one: 'they were thinking [and would have gone on thinking], had not . . .': see Williams (7–12) ad loc.
[29] Heinze, 393f.

In sum, Vergil barely sketches any relationship between Aeneas and Pallas. And yet it is Pallas personally and in his own right—as well as or more than Evander—who has the powerful emotional impact on him that I have referred to (10.515 ff.):

> Pallas, Euander, in ipsis
> omnia sunt oculis, mensae quas aduena primas
> tunc adiit, dextraeque datae . . .

Pallas, Evander, all is before his very eyes, the table to which he came first as a stranger, the right hands pledged . . .

Similarly, in 12.948, 'Pallas te hoc uulnere, Pallas / immolat . . .' ['With this wound Pallas sacrifices you, Pallas . . .']. Pallas has this emotional effect on him: but Vergil is not interested—or unable—to characterize Aeneas' vital relationship with him. It seems unlikely. I detect a further voice.

I provide a small but, in the circumstances, telling reminder that Vergil can and does characterize relationships. Aeneas may not be greatly characterized in relation to Pallas, but Evander is. His warmth and love is evident enough in the lines I have quoted above (8.514 ff.), and the significance of his prayer at 8.574 ff. needs no attention drawing to it. Attention should perhaps be drawn to a passage at the opening of Evander's lament in Book 11 which, again following the frequent Vergilian practice, reveals events that took place previously—here, something that took place during the time of Book 8 not mentioned in Book 8. 11.152 f.:

> non haec, o Palla, dederas promissa parenti,
> cautius ut saeuo uelles te credere Marti.

O Pallas, these were not the promises you gave to your father, that you were willing to entrust yourself more warily to savage Mars.

That seems to me both touching and acute in its characterizing effect. Evander had asked Pallas to do what he surely knew Pallas could not possibly do (namely 'fight warily'), and Pallas had agreed knowing that he could not and would not. That is the comforting, self-deluding kind of conspiracy that happens between parents and sons on the eve of every war. Suddenly we have real insight into a human relationship—of a kind not often (I would judge) to be found in the epic.

5. Aeneas and Dido

I have glanced at Dido's feelings and behaviour towards Aeneas in Chapter I. I now look at his towards her. I concentrate on the love-affair.

We might well expect some characterization. Epic tradition did not impose reticence. Achilles professes love for Briseis in *Iliad* 9, Odysseus has affairs with Circe, Calypso, and, in a sense, Nausicaa; and in certain respects his relations with these females are richly characterized. And then we have Medea and Jason, and the other amorous Hellenistics. Rome, of course, is not Greece, and we will grant with Klingner[30] that Vergil had particular problems in the presentation of his amorous episode. On the other hand he chose to have these problems: he chose to make his hero fall in love with the Carthaginian queen.[31] We might indeed expect some characterization of the relationship, albeit delicate.

What do we find? For the 'successful' period of the love-affair we have virtually no illumination. Aeneas and Dido are not explicitly pictured in each other's company between the cave and the rupture. We have merely the loaded rumour of 'Fama', 4.193f.; and then, with Mercury, we find Aeneas 'founding citadels' in Punic dress—alone (4.260). Vergilian embarrassment at this touchy material may be operative. Before the cave scene, when Dido is patently infatuated, they are pictured together ('nunc media Aenean secum per moenia ducit . . .' ['she conducts Aeneas through the midst of the city's buildings . . .'], 74ff.). And Dido in her infatuation for Aeneas is effectively drawn: we note in particular how finely Vergil charts the way she succumbs to love at the beginning of Book 4; also the characterization by action at 4.75–85.[32] But there is no characterization of Aeneas in relation to Dido: that is to say, Vergil makes him utter no feelings, and attributes no expressive gestures or actions to him. The narrative is silent on the topic. Perhaps this is again to be imputed to Vergilian embarrassment. I doubt it. Though discreet, Vergil is not silent on a

---

[30] Klingner, 463ff.
[31] See Buchheit, 32–40; Horsfall, 'Dido in the Light of History', esp. 11f.
[32] Vergil reworks themes traceable to Hellenistic literature: cf. Heinze, 130.

more sensitive topic: the hero's intentions towards the beautiful queen (in the hind simile, discussed below). I deduce in fact that it is Aeneas, not Vergil, who is inexpressive: this is 'negative' invention again.

However this may be, Vergil does describe one major scene of interaction between the two: at the point of rupture. Does this colour in the picture of the characters in their relationship with one another? It certainly colours Dido's. Her first speech, 'dissimulare etiam sperasti . . .' (305 ff.), radiates pathos, disbelief, despair, all issuing from her passionate love for the man who stands before her; it also suggests the beginnings of the fury which will be amplified in her second speech (365 ff., 'nec tibi diua parens . . .'), the hate-filled fury into which her passionate love turns. This is fine rhetoric, fine psychology, fine characterization, and handled frequently enough by critics to make comment by me otiose;[33] though note the action which accompanies and supports the characterization by speech: how, at 296 ff., Dido races distractedly through the city before she 'arraigns Aeneas'; how, after Aeneas' reply (362 ff.) and before 'nec tibi diua . . .' (365 ff.), she is first 'turned away', then 'this way, that way, she darts her eyes'; and then, before flaring up, she stares him up and down with 'silent eyes' ['luminibus tacitis'], a most expressive phrase which is well explained by Pease.[34]

And what of Aeneas? This time we have something quite substantial. Aeneas delivers a speech (333 ff.), a reply to 'dissimulare etiam sperasti . . .'. No interchange develops: Aeneas is gestating a reply to 'nec tibi diua . . .', but it fails to materialize, in the circumstances described above (the 'cut-off'; p. 146). We have this speech; we have its introduction; we have an important description of Aeneas after Dido's second speech, and after the 'cut-off' (393 ff.); and we have another important description of him after Anna's overture (the oak tree simile at 441 ff.). This is characterizing material, and gives us something

---

[33] Klingner, 446–8 and 449, offers a fine analysis of 4.305 ff. and brief but perceptive comment on 4.365 ff.
[34] Pease on 4.364: 'Dido has kept an ominous silence during his speech, nor have her eyes given him any sympathetic response such as Ovid describes (*Am.* 2.5.17): "non oculi tacuere tui".' Cf. (and contrast) also Tibull. 2.6.43, 'oculos . . . loquaces'.

The Hero and His Son

to work on. Vergil, or Aeneas, is giving us an opportunity. The material must be scrutinized.

The first thing to notice is that, at this stage at least, Aeneas 'loves' Dido; and he feels concern and sympathy for the plight she is in. The text informs us of these emotions, while telling us that he *suppresses* them. Aeneas' speech is introduced thus, 331 f.:

> dixerat [sc. Dido]. ille Iouis monitis immota tenebat
> lumina et obnixus curam sub corde premebat.
> tandem pauca refert.

Dido finished speaking. Aeneas because of the warnings of Jupiter held his eyes steadfast and with a struggle smothered the care in his breast. At last he gave a few words in reply.

And after Dido's departure (the 'cut-off') he is described thus (393–6):

> at pius Aeneas, quamquam lenire dolentem
> solando cupit et dictis auertere curas,
> multa gemens magnoque animum labefactus amore
> iussa tamen diuum exsequitur classemque reuisit.

But pious Aeneas, although he desires to soothe the anguished queen with consolation and by his words to turn aside her care, nevertheless, with many a groan, his spirit shaken by great love, he follows the commands of the gods and returns to his fleet.

Secondly, we should not miss that Aeneas suppresses his love and resists Dido with difficulty, and at emotional cost. This is evident from the above passages and is then made more clear in the description of his response to Anna's overture. He is compared to an oak tree buffeted by Alpine north winds, and the passage concludes (447–9):

> haud secus adsiduis hinc atque hinc uocibus heros
> tunditur, et magno persentit pectore curas;
> mens immota manet, lacrimae uoluuntur inanes.

Even so the hero is buffeted from all sides with ceaseless appeals, and feels anguish in his great breast; his will stands steadfast, vain tears roll forth.

—and those tears are his.[35] But with whatever difficulty, he does suppress his love, and resist Dido. In his speech to her he tries, among other things, to explain why.

I turn to consider this speech now. It runs as follows (333 ff.):

> tandem pauca refert: 'ego te, quae plurima fando
> enumerare uales, numquam, regina, negabo
> promeritam, nec me meminisse pigebit Elissae (335)
> dum memor ipse mei, dum spiritus hos regit artus.
> pro re pauca loquar. neque ego hanc abscondere furto
> speraui (ne finge) fugam, nec coniugis umquam
> praetendi taedas aut haec in foedera ueni.
> me si fata meis paterentur ducere uitam (340)
> auspiciis et sponte mea componere curas,
> urbem Troianam primum dulcisque meorum
> reliquias colerem, Priami tecta alta manerent,
> et recidiua manu posuissem Pergama uictis.
> sed nunc Italiam magnam Gryneus Apollo, (345)
> Italiam Lyciae iussere capessere sortes;
> hic amor, haec patria est. si te Karthaginis arces
> Phoenissam Libycaeque aspectus detinet urbis,
> quae tandem Ausonia Teucros considere terra
> inuidia est? et nos fas extera quaerere regna. (350)
> me patris Anchisae, quotiens umentibus umbris
> nox operit terras, quotiens astra ignea surgunt,
> admonet in somnis et turbida terret imago;
> me puer Ascanius capitisque iniuria cari,
> quem regno Hesperiae fraudo et fatalibus aruis. (355)
> nunc etiam interpres diuum Ioue missus ab ipso
> (testor utrumque caput) celeris mandata per auras
> detulit: ipse deum manifesto in lumine uidi
> intrantem muros uocemque his auribus hausi.
> desine meque tuis incendere teque querellis; (360)
> Italiam non sponte sequor.'

At last he gave a few words in reply. 'I shall never deny, O queen, that you have deserved well of me for all the very many things you are able to list in words, nor will it displease me to remember Elissa, while I have memory of myself and while breath still rules these limbs (336).

---

[35] Cf. Pöschl, 57; this is not the general view, as Pöschl documents (see e.g. Klingner, 451)—but Augustine and Servius got it right. Austin ad loc. sees it as ambiguous. I think that context here in fact disallows ambiguity; and to compare 10.465 is instructive.

For my case I shall speak a few words. I did not hope—do not imagine it—to conceal this flight in stealth. I never held out the torch of marriage or entered into a compact of this kind (339). If the fates suffered me to lead my life on my own authority and arrange my cares according to my own will, I should be tending Troy's city before all others, and the sweet relics of my people; Priam's lofty palace would abide, and I in person would have set up a revived Pergama for the vanquished (344). But as it is Grynean Apollo and the Lycian oracles have ordered me to lay hold of great Italy, Italy. This is my love, this is my homeland now. If the citadels of Carthage and the sight of a Libyan city detain you, a Phoenician, why pray grudge the Trojans their settling on Ausonian land? For us too it is right to seek a foreign realm (350). As often as night covers the earth in dewy shadows, as often as the fiery stars rise, my father's troubled ghost warns and appals me in dreams; so does Ascanius and the wrong done to his beloved head—he whom I defraud of kingdom in Hesperia and lands his by fate (355). Now too the messenger of the gods sent by Jupiter himself (I swear it by your head and my head) has borne commands down through the swift breezes; I myself saw the god in the clear light of day as he entered the walls, and with my own ears I drank in his words. Cease to inflame both me and you with your laments (360). Not of my free will do I follow Italy.

The most important elements of this speech are: an expression of gratitude, in part coolly pitched (333–6); self-exculpation, which may seem somewhat frigid and incomplete (337–9); a relatively extensive explanation of the various factors which persuade him to leave (345–59); and a perhaps rather insensitive statement that, had he been a free agent, he would have stayed at Troy and rebuilt the city (340–4). I say 'insensitive', for surely the natural thing to say here is, even if it is a white lie: 'were I free agent, I would stay with *you*'. But perhaps I judge this subjectively. I think not—and demonstrably not; but I leave that point for the moment. What the speech certainly does not do—and we can straight away grant this—is humanly acknowledge and respond to the despair of a beloved person. It does not talk of the love he feels, in spite of which he must go. Most glaringly, it betrays no compassion.

Here, then, is evidence for Aeneas in his relationship with Dido. It is of course confined to an extraordinary situation (rupture), but for that very reason should give a concentrated view of at least certain aspects of Aeneas in his relationship with another. So what do we make of it, of Aeneas' cool speech and his consciously suppressed emotion?

Interpretations of Aeneas vary in their nuances, but what we might call a post-romantic consensus can be identified, and this consensus opinion I shall now try to paraphrase.[36] Aeneas' comportment and speech are those of a man who has responded to a moral dilemma (love versus duty), exercised moral strength, and come, albeit belatedly, to a dutiful and painful conclusion. Aeneas shows himself at this moment pretty much the Stoic; and a Stoical attitude seems to be one that the world in which he lives requires and lauds.[37] We should not be surprised, therefore, if he seems to us frigid and inexpressive. Stoicism gives rise to such misapprehensions. In fact (my paraphrase continues) Aeneas is now simply rational and self-possessed where before he was passionate and unruly. Rationally, he refuses to harp on the emotion he has subdued. What would be the use? Why stir the ashes? Rationally, he tells the plain truth (why disguise anything?): he would have preferred to stay in Troy, above all else. And of course he gives no play to compassion, for, as every Stoic will tell you, compassion is a vice.[38] To involve oneself in someone else's wrong emotion—to share in their passion, to be compassionate—is irrational, unhelpful, even dangerous: it may divert you from reason. Aeneas indeed expressly senses that danger: 'cease to inflame both me and you with your laments' (360). In sum, according to this consensus, Aeneas' actions and speech characterize him, at this crisis-point in his relationship with Dido, as a man putting Stoical virtue into practice. And this decision, this attitude, can seem to some demanded and explained by the circumstances, to others it can even seem laudable.

But is this sort of view correct? Is this *all*? Let us grant that Aeneas' response is correctly Stoical, eminently self-possessed,

---

[36] Cf. Austin on 4.331–61; Klingner, 448f., 463–6; Quinn, *Latin Explorations* (London, 1963), 47f.; La Penna, lx; Feeney, 'The Taciturnity of Aeneas', esp. 205–10 and 219. Pöschl, 44ff., faces facts in the text more honestly and sympathetically than most. Parry, 119, reacts to the consensus excessively ('Virgil deliberately presented Dido as a heroine, and Aeneas as an inglorious deserter').
[37] See Lyne, 'Vergil and the Politics of War', 190–2.
[38] Cic. *Tusc.* 4.16 and, esp., 56; Sen. *Clem.* 2.6.4.

rational, and practical. Does Vergil in fact present it as laudable, or as explained by the special circumstances? Other Vergilian invention challenges such conclusions. For instance, if we conclude that Aeneas' 'frigidity' and 'inexpressiveness' here are demanded by the circumstances and are therefore unfairly so termed, we must remember that the hero struck us—if we accepted the implications of 'negative' invention—as pretty frigid and inexpressive on other occasions, occasions which made no such demands and so provided no such explanation. Does this fact not bear on our conclusion? I think of his attitude towards Creusa, Ascanius, Pallas. Then again, earlier on in the Dido story, why are we not told that Aeneas uttered feelings, or conveyed them in gestures? I think we should infer an inexpressiveness on his part. But what cause was there for Aeneas to be inexpressive then? Aeneas' comportment as he leaves Dido clearly requires further attention: the interpretation of it put forward above is insufficient. And Aeneas' comportment in the relationship with Dido as a whole requires further attention; and so do his relationships with Creusa, Ascanius, and Pallas. Let me summarize the position. We have observed that Vergil was able and willing to characterize Priam in a human relationship with Hecuba, and Evander in a human relationship with Pallas. Then we observed that he did not so colour in a relationship between Aeneas the hero on the one hand and Creusa, Ascanius, Pallas, and Dido on the other. My conclusion is: this lack of colour is colour; and my basic argument is the simple one that if Vergil does colour in some relationships but does not colour in Aeneas', that absence must be significant: in fact, it characterizes. This is 'negative' invention; and it, and the implications it has for Aeneas, must now be carefully and positively interpreted. To date I have commented only superficially and in passing. As for Aeneas' comportment in the parting scene with Dido, Vergil provides crucial further material for us to absorb.

6. Creusa and Dido again: the 'too late' phenomenon

I return to Aeneas in his relationship with Creusa. There is a further striking fact to observe. In the description of the departure from Troy which I discussed above, Aeneas showed no human response to Creusa. I now accept the implication of this invention. Aeneas is being discreetly characterized: he was, for a reason to be identified, unresponsive to Creusa at that time. Now what is fascinating to observe is that things are very different when Creusa dies. Here are some excerpts from the description (it is Aeneas' own description) of his reaction to her loss (2.745ff.):

> quem non incusaui amens hominumque deorumque,
> aut quid in euersa uidi crudelius urbe?
> Ascanium Anchisenque patrem Teucrosque penatis
> commendo sociis et curua ualle recondo;
> ipse urbem repeto et cingor fulgentibus armis.
> stat casus renouare omnis omnemque reuerti
> per Troiam et rursus caput obiectare periclis . . .
>
> inde domum, si forte pedem, si forte tulisset, (756)
> me refero: inruerant Danai et tectum omne tenebant . . .
>
> ausus quin etiam uoces iactare per umbram (768)
> impleui clamore uias, maestusque Creusam
> nequiquam ingeminans iterumque iterumque uocaui.

Whom of men and gods did I not madly reproach? What did I see more cruel in the overthrown city? I entrust Ascanius, Anchises my father, and the gods of Troy to my companions and hide them in a winding valley. I myself seek the city again and gird on my shining arms. I am resolved to renew every risk, to return throughout the whole of Troy, and again to throw my life in the way of danger. . . .

Thence I return homewards, in the hope that perchance, perchance, she had made her way there: the Greeks had burst in and were in possession of the whole house. . . . I even dared to cast my voice through the shadows, filling the streets with my cries, and in woe I vainly called upon Creusa, again and again, groaning.

This is more than responsive. In fact the extent of emotion and love here exhibited is astonishing. Temporarily it swamps Aeneas' sense of piety and duty. By his own description he accuses men and gods 'madly'. He relinquishes his son, his father, and even the gods of Troy into the care of his companions while he returns to court danger for Creusa's sake. His rhetorical question 'what did I see more cruel in the overthrown city?' suggests the statement: 'nihil crudelius', that nothing was crueller than Creusa's loss. This, when we recall the slaying of Polites and Priam and hear—in this very same part of Aeneas' speech (766f.)—of columns of captive women and children, is, to put it mildly, a remarkable claim. What a change in priorities! This is the man who had said in reference to his wife 'longe seruet uestigia coniunx' (711)—and nothing to her. Now we find this wild, elegiac love upsetting his whole regard for piety and duty and finding anguished expression in word and action. Only the appearance of Creusa's ghost returns him to his companions, family, and commitments.

What Creusa does is invite him to see her loss from a different, a divine, perspective (2.776 ff.):

> quid tantum insano iuuat indulgere dolori,
> o dulcis coniunx? non haec sine numine diuum
> eueniunt; nec te comitem hinc portare Creusam
> fas . . .

[she then prophesies his wandering, his arrival in Italy and new wife, and so on; and concludes, 785 ff.]:

> non ego Myrmidonum sedes Dolopumue superbas
> aspiciam aut Grais seruitum matribus ibo,
> Dardanis et diuae Veneris nurus;
> sed me magna deum genetrix his detinet oris.
> iamque uale et nati serua communis amorem.

Of what avail is it to give play to frenzied anguish, my sweet husband? These things do not befall without the will of the gods; nor is it right for you to take Creusa hence as your companion . . .
I shall not look upon the proud palaces of the Myrmidons or Dolopians, or go to be the slave of Greek matrons, I a daughter of Dardanus' line and wife of the son of divine Venus: the mighty mother of the gods keeps me on these shores. Now farewell, and guard your love for the son we share.

It is, incidentally, crucial not to mistake the implications of these words. Their correct estimation is important for our assessment of Aeneas' character. I suggested above that the way Aeneas arranges the departure from Troy ('longe seruet uestigia coniunx') contributes to, if not causes, Creusa's loss. Creusa's words here do not amount to an exculpation, or not a total or objective one.[39] It is usually, perhaps always, possible to view human events from a divine perspective in the *Aeneid*, and to see a divine purpose to them. It is vital to remember, however, that the divine purpose is often accomplished in

---
[39] *Pace* e.g. Heinze, 59–62, Otis, 251.

mysterious ways. The events for which we can discern such a purpose may themselves seem and indeed be tragic or invidious or culpable in the immediate human context: the abandonment of a queen, the killing of Italian countryfolk, for instance. Creusa in her transubstantiated state can perceive the divine reason for her loss, and it is understandable that she should emphasize that perspective to Aeneas. Not only will it get him back to his fateful duty: why recriminate? But her emphasis does not mean we can or ought to forget all our previous impressions of that occasion. I am not at all sure, for example, that the reproach implied in her own words 'coniunx quondam tua dicta' (2.678; above, p. 147) was unjustified at the time, or subsequently made up for. Where *was* Aeneas' response to her, as his wife? And Creusa's words, for all their eternal and fate-enlightened perspective, do not, or should not, delete our uncomfortable knowledge that Aeneas' dynastically practical decision to order Creusa to follow behind him at least facilitated her loss. It is of course true that Creusa's death was necessary for the plan of Fate. But did she have to be lost *in that way*? Nothing says so.

But the point which I wish to select and stress here is that when Creusa is dead, Aeneas displays in abundance, in passionate superabundance, the love and emotion which, for one reason or another, he did not display when she was alive. *Too late*, we might be tempted to say. We might also be tempted, provoked by the irony, to be more particular and to ask: what if he had displayed just a little of this present warmth *earlier*? We are tempted, in short, to question those unresponsive moments, and the consequences of them. And we might conclude (for example) that Aeneas' dispassionate and logical orders for the exit from Troy might have been less dynastically logical and more affective without being fatal for the dynasty: and for Creusa that might have been more healthy. Certainly Aeneas himself would have had a more satisfyingly warm final episode with his wife to look back upon. Is all this unwarranted speculation? Are the questions unjustified? I think not. Vergil provokes questions by invention and arrangement: by revealing Aeneas in this 'too late' paroxysm—a further voice is prodding us. The point will be amplified, for the pattern *too late* is repeated: it therefore demands scrutiny and interpretation.

The Hero and His Son

There is, in fact, something very comparable in Aeneas' dealings with Dido.

Aeneas meets Dido again, in the Underworld in Book 6. And there he displays in abundance the tender emotions which he did not display at their parting in Carthage: those emotions which, so it was judged, he Stoically and necessarily, even laudably, suppressed. The scene in the Underworld is of course a famous one,[40] but its significance in conjunction with the parting scene in Book 4 is insufficiently noticed. I quote the central section (6.455–68):

>   demisit lacrimas dulcique adfatus amore est:
>   'infelix Dido, uerus mihi nuntius ergo
>   uenerat exstinctam ferroque extrema secutam?
>   funeris heu tibi causa fui? per sidera iuro,
>   per superos et si qua fides tellure sub ima est,
>   inuitus, regina, tuo de litore cessi.
>   sed me iussa deum, quae nunc has ire per umbras,
>   per loca senta situ cogunt noctemque profundam,
>   imperiis egere suis; nec credere quiui
>   hunc tantum tibi me discessu ferre dolorem.
>   siste gradum teque aspectu ne subtrahe nostro.
>   quem fugis? extremum fato quod te adloquor hoc est.'
>   talibus Aeneas ardentem et torua tuentem
>   lenibat dictis animum lacrimasque ciebat.
>   . . .
>   prosequitur lacrimis longe et miseratur euntem.   (476)

Aeneas shed tears, and spoke to her with gentle love: 'Unhappy Dido, so it was a true tale that came to me, that you were dead and had sought your end with the sword? Alas, was it death I caused you? I swear by the stars, by the gods above, by whatever good faith there is in the world below, unwillingly, O queen, I left your shore. The commands of the gods, which now compel me to pass through these shades, through lands squalid with neglect and through deep night, drove me by their ordinance; nor did I believe that I was bringing such great anguish on you by my departure. Stay your step and do not withdraw yourself from my sight. Who are you fleeing from? This is the last word which fate allows me to speak to you.' With these words Aeneas tried to soothe her fiery, fierce-eyed anger, shedding tears the while. . . . He follows her from afar with his tears, and pities her as she goes.

---

[40] Knauer, 111, makes some very interesting observations.

Here Aeneas reveals both by action and speech that he *loves* and *pities* Dido: emotions to which, at Carthage, he denied expression. He tries to *console* her, an action he then eschewed ('*although* he desired to soothe her, *nevertheless* . . .', 4.393 f.). Here, before he lists the reasons why he had to leave her, he stresses in moving and eloquent terms the fact that he wanted to stay. This would have been the naturally human thing to say at Carthage, but again, at Carthage he did not say it. Instead there was a substitute which, though it was doubtless true, I ventured to describe as insensitive ('had I been a free agent, I would actually have stayed at Troy', 4.340 ff.).

Let us grasp clearly what is happening. By meeting Dido in the Underworld Aeneas has been brought face to face with what happened to her subsequent to and, it could be argued, consequent upon his action. And he has, too, an unexpected chance to explain himself. Once again in fact, as at Carthage, Aeneas is explaining his dilemma to Dido and the reasons for his decision: it is as if he has a chance to replay the scene. And now, in the new situation, he does it very differently. He does it, in all the major points, in what we might call the opposite way. And here, as with Creusa, we might be tempted to say again: *too late*. At any rate, the question must offer itself, as it did with Creusa: what if Aeneas had acted then more like he does now? It makes us wonder about his cold comportment. In this case I think the question urges itself. Vergil's decision to dispose a complete 'replay' scene results in a clearer invitation to reconsider the earlier episode than happens with Creusa: he shows us exactly how Aeneas might have behaved rather than leaves us to conjecture. The answer to the question thus urged—what would have happened?—must ultimately of course be: we do not know for sure. But we can think our thoughts. Here are a couple of suggestions. Dido rejects Aeneas' advances in Book 6 with stony hate (469 ff.). We might infer that no amount of soft handling in Book 4 would have made any difference: Dido wanted Aeneas to love; and if she could not have him and love him, she would hate him and curse him. Dido is no compromiser—as 6.469 ff. show.

But, we could immediately respond, Dido's situation in Book 6 compared with Book 4 has changed much more than Aeneas'. She has died in the meantime. Her hatred has had

The Hero and His Son

time and cause to fester. And here is another thought. The effect of Aeneas' speech at 4.333ff. is to stir Dido to immediate fury and hatred; and this expands into a dreadful curse. I quote from the beginning of her speech (4.365ff.):

> nec tibi diua parens generis nec Dardanus auctor,
> perfide, sed duris genuit te cautibus horrens
> Caucasus . . .
> num fletu *ingemuit* nostro? num *lumina flexit?* (369)
> num *lacrimas* uictus *dedit* aut *miseratus* amantem est?

False one, no goddess was your mother, nor Dardanus author of your line. Rugged Caucasus begat you on hard crags . . . Did he *groan* when I wept? Did he *turn his gaze towards me*? Did he yield and *shed tears* or *pity* the one who loved him?

This indicates that Dido's immediate rage is directly and precisely fuelled by what *we* saw as evidence of Aeneas' Stoical, rational self-possession (unmoving eyes, no grief shown, no pity; 4.331f., 393ff., etc., above, pp. 163, 166), but which *she* sees as evidence of unfeeling hard-heartedness. And her rage expands into a hate-filled curse upon Aeneas (612ff.) and, eventually (622ff.), upon his descendants. Now, I ask, if Aeneas had not given that incorrect impression of lack of feeling, if he had acted more in the manner of Book 6, where as we have seen he does weep, does pity, and so on, might Dido's terrible historic fury have been less? Again, at the heart of the cluster of emotions that presses Dido to suicide is simply (if I may use such a word) the agony of love: 'ferroque auerte dolorem' ['be rid of your anguish ('dolorem') by the sword'], she says (4.547), in a crucial speech; and that is what is signified by the area of the Underworld which she occupies: 'here those whom harsh love has consumed with cruel wasting . . .' (6.442). If Dido had not thought that she was being left by someone callous and unfeeling, if Aeneas had managed not to give that incorrect impression, would her 'anguish' have been lessened, the love seemed less 'harsh'? Might her anguish have been lessened even to the point where life might have seemed bearable to her? These are speculations, but not, I think, idle ones, because the text—a further voice exploiting the invention of scenes and their arrangement—instigates them, and perhaps suggests that things might indeed have been otherwise, at least for Dido. If fact I would conclude as follows. It may be that for Aeneas his Stoic approach in Book 4 was the best: we can recall his conclusion 'forbear to inflame both me and you by your laments' (4.360). For Dido, however, the other approach might have been better. It certainly could not have been worse. This is a consideration we should bear in mind among all the others when we count the cost and assess the empire and its hero. I wonder, not irrelevantly, how Odysseus would have left Dido.[41]

I have reserved a detail in the text (6.463f.) to consider separately. Unless I misinterpret, 'nec credere quiui / hunc tantum tibi me discessu ferre dolorem' ['nor was I able to believe that I was bringing so great pain on you by my departure'] refers to a judgement of Aeneas' *at the time* of his departure; it is not his assessment of the credibility of the 'nuntius' of 456, *pace* Austin ad loc. Syntax and rhetoric point this way. While the sentence 'per sidera iuro . . . inuitus, regina, tuo de litore cessi' (6.458–60) recalls Aeneas' unwillingness to leave Carthage, the next sentence 'sed me iussa deum' presents a factor that pressed him at that time to do so; 'nec credere quiui' is the second limb of this sentence, syntactically bound with it, and should therefore similarly present a factor that influenced him in his conduct at that time. Aeneas therefore admits to a miscalculation at Carthage, a misjudgement of Dido's emotion, and one which apparently had some bearing on his departure. Well, what would he have done if he had not miscalculated Dido's reaction? It is hard to imagine that the 'iussa deum' would not have remained sufficient to make him move. But Aeneas surely means that something would have been different. Perhaps a consequence of properly assessing Dido's pain would have been a differently handled departure. Aeneas, admitting a miscalculation and one that influenced him at the time of his departure, opens up this possibility. Aeneas therefore may be tentatively enlisted as support for my own conclusions: his departure could have been handled otherwise and perhaps better.

It is therefore quite wrong to suppose that Aeneas had no option but to leave Dido in the way he did and wrong to

---

[41] See Griffin, *Homer*, 56–8 on Odysseus' scenes of parting from women.

think that we cannot speculate about an alternative. The Underworld meeting, in particular the provoking contrast it makes with the earlier scene, must make us query his comportment at Carthage. It shows us that he was not absolutely incapable of adopting a more human approach. It should make us ask: what factors external to Aeneas demanded that he should not? And the answer to that is: none. It also invites us to believe (I think) that treatment more in the manner of Book 6 would, for Dido at last, have been better. But Aeneas tried it *too late*—a point I shall come back to.

7. Aeneas: an interim description

The time is appropriate to summarize some provisional conclusions. Views like Heinze's may possess some truth, but they do not take account of important facts. Vergil can characterize admirably when he wants to: individuals, and people in their affective relations with one another (Evander and Pallas, Priam and Hecuba, Mezentius and Lausus). From this I deduce that if a character is shown *not* responding at times to those who merit such a response, we must interpret that character as, at those times, incapable or undesirous of so responding. The implications of silence and inaction (Vergil's 'negative' invention) must not be resisted. This conclusion seems particularly to apply to Aeneas. Aeneas cannot, will not, anyway does not, react affectively at crucial moments in the main relationships of his life (with Creusa, Ascanius, Dido, Pallas). He seems to have the essential ability so to react, as his response to the dead Creusa and to the dead Dido demonstrates; but as these episodes also demonstrate, he seems prone to doing so, if at all, *too late*. The same pattern is observable in his relationship with Pallas, as we shall see.

I am prepared to hazard a more psychological description of Aeneas in the *Aeneid*, taking up the question of 'cannot' and 'will not'. It can be tested against the text. As befits a hero, Aeneas is a man of grand passions (Ch. 3, pp. 106–7). He is also a man capable of tenderer feelings. But often he appears inhibited in the expression or communication of those feelings: often it seems that he *cannot* express them (e.g. with Pallas and Ascanius; with Creusa before the omen; and with Dido in the 'happy' part of their affair). It takes something like the trauma of death to undam him. But further, in his attempt to perform the task of fate—in his attempt to be the Stoical Roman hero—he tries not only to curb his passions but also politically to restrain his tender feelings more than they are already restrained by nature: with Dido at his departure, with Creusa (I would say) between the omen and her loss; he seems to share the Stoic view that tender emotions as much as grand passions may interfere with duty and resolve. In this latter case it is a question of *will not* rather than *cannot*, decision rather than inability. This, I maintain, is how Aeneas emerges in the poem, in the matter of his feelings and his dealings with others; this is how the insinuations of Vergil's invention and arrangement present his essential character and elected policy. And insinuations invite us to lament this type of character and this sort of policy. Further voices comment as well as contribute.

Recall Dido. At 4.390 ('multa metu cunctantem et multa parantem / dicere, above, p. 146) it may be that Aeneas, given time, would have responded sympathetically to Dido. If so, Dido's swift exit thwarts him. But he has already refused one opportunity so to respond, in his speech at 333ff., and by 393 he has explicitly decided on a Stoical resistance to compassion. This policy, or combination of policy and character, contributes (I would say) to Dido's death. Most readers lament that death. Recall Creusa. At 2.677ff. ('cui paruus Iulus . . .', above, p. 147) Aeneas fails to respond to her; his attitude to her in the exit from Troy is then firmly impersonal (711, 'longe seruet uestigia coniunx'). At 2.677ff. he is, I suggest, controlled by his inhibited character ('cannot'), at 711 by conscious policy ('will not'). When Creusa is then lost, it seems lamentable that he should have been so frigid towards her in the last scene of her life. It also seems the case that his reason-dictated, unemotional instruction at 711 contributed to if not caused her loss—and that is even more lamentable. In both these cases, therefore, Vergil's invention has organized it so that lamentable consequences follow from Aeneas' inherent character and from his chosen policy in combination: consequences that are *unnecessary*. For it should be stressed that Dido's suicide was not a *sine qua non* of Jupiter's plan, nor was Creusa's death *in that way* (cf. pp. 169–70). Nor would any of the affective responses I am talking about seriously have compromised Aeneas as a hero. A demonstration of affection towards Creusa, of warmth and even compassion towards Dido, was compatible with epic and Augustan if not with strictly Stoic dignity. Now if Vergil's invention shows unnecessary as well as lamentable consequences ensuing on Aeneas' typical character and elected policy, must we not be meant, at these times, to lament that type of character and policy? Is there not a voice here which we should hearken to?

8. The 'too late' phenomenon analysed: Pallas again

Now let us assess the 'too late' phenomenon. In both Creusa's and Dido's story there are sequels. Whereas Aeneas could not and would not respond affectively to these women at crisis-points in their lives, he is quite different after their deaths: *too late*. Towards Dido he reveals sympathy, love, compassion; towards Creusa a wild, mad love according more with his passionate nature. Such gentle handling might, I argued, have produced a different end to Book 4, and just a little of that passionate expression of love could have served Creusa well. So, Aeneas has it in him to react more helpfully, and does in fact do so, but not until it is *too late*. This clearly is a desperately ironic situation. But to what do we impute it?

The 'too late' phenomenon may be seen in two ways, both legitimate. The first of these I have not yet mentioned, and it is simple but important. The 'too late' phenomenon may be seen as a natural enough event in the plot. It can be imputed to Aeneas' own character and policy in combination with the sort of world in which he, being such a man, finds himself: a harsh and unrelenting world. We can call it the product, within this harsh world, of Aeneas' luckless dose of inhibition and his ill-timed, ill-starred adherence to dogma (on this, see further below: the 'cut-off', s. 9). But we can also see it, as I was suggesting above, as a device of invention and arrangement by which a further voice discreetly but persistently expresses itself. For the irony produced by the 'too late' phenomenon calls attention to Aeneas' lamentable missed chances, and to the contribution he arguably makes (through character and policy) to those missed chances. It prompts us to searching thoughts, such as: 'What if Aeneas had displayed such feelings before, when they might have proved vitally efficacious . . .', 'If only

...'. The irony of the 'too late' phenomenon may therefore be said to be, as well as Aeneas' burden, Vergil's inventive means to provoke us to questions and to views.

We may feel without prompting that Aeneas' failure to establish much of a relationship with Ascanius and Pallas is lamentable. Ascanius I shall consider later. The story of Pallas again produces the motif of ironic 'too lateness'—Aeneas' burden, and Vergil's means to prompt us to questions and to views. One scene may be recalled which strikingly demonstrates how inhibited in this relationship Aeneas is. At 8.514ff. (cf. above, p. 158) Evander affectingly offers him the martial services of his son. As we know, Pallas is present. And Vergil indicates that Aeneas is indeed struck by this gesture on the part of father and son. In a characteristic manner Vergil conveys his character's feelings through the style (see Ch. 6 pp. 227ff.) and, with the patronymic 'Anchisiades', suggests the line of Aeneas' thoughts: fathers and sons. Aeneas *is* moved by the gesture from the father and son before him—as moved as he is at 10.822 by the action of a son for a father, when he is similarly equipped with the patronymic 'Anchisiades'.[42] Surely it is the moment for an expressive response on his part, to Evander and in particular to Pallas, to the father and son who are in his thoughts, and standing before him. However: 'multaque dura suo tristi cum corde putabant' ['then [he and Achates] reflected on many harsh things in their gloomy breasts'] (8.522). Inhibited, and/or turning his mind to other politic things, Aeneas does not respond or cannot respond (for Achates, of course, response was neither necessary nor appropriate). And this sets the pace for the rest of the story. Except at the end. When Pallas is *dead*, there is Aeneas again undammed: uninhibited in the expression of his affection and gratitude—keenly sensitive, too, to the father's sacrifice (11.42ff.):

> 'tene,' inquit 'miserande puer, cum laeta ueniret,
> inuidit Fortuna mihi, ne regna uideres
> nostra neque ad sedes uictor ueherere paternas? (44)
> ...

---

[42] See Warde Fowler, *Site of Rome*, 88, and Ch. 1 n. 16. On what passes through Aeneas' thoughts see too Pöschl, 72f.

The Hero and His Son

> et nunc ille quidem spe multum captus inani (49)
> fors et uota facit cumulatque altaria donis,
> nos iuuenem exanimum et nil iam caelestibus ullis
> debentem uano maesti comitamur honore.
> infelix, nati funus crudele uidebis! (53)
> . . .
>   ei mihi quantum (57)
> praesidium, Ausonia, et quantum tu perdis, Iule!'

'Was it you, unhappy boy, that Fortune begrudged me in her happy hour, begrudged that you should look upon my kingdom and ride back in victory to your father's palace? (44) . . . He now perchance, much beguiled by empty hope, is offering vows and heaping altars with gifts; while with empty honour we in sadness attend the youth, lifeless and now owing a debt to none of the gods above. Ill-starred man! You will look upon the unkind funeral of your son (53) . . . Alas, how great a protection is lost to you, Ausonia, and to you Iulus!'

The situation is different from that with Creusa or Dido, in that no tangible consequences ensued from Aeneas' lack of response to Pallas. But we feel Aeneas' burden again: inhibition and/or ill-timed, ill-starred adherence to dogma once more producing a pathetically ironic end. And we note the effect of Vergil's invention. We should be prompted to ask: why did not Aeneas say such things, or a version of such things, during Pallas' life, during Book 8, indeed at 8.522? What if he had? It might have served Pallas and Evander well. The utterance in Book 11 does, I think, strike us as too late, ironically too late—as with Creusa and Dido; and so prompts us to questions and to views about the fact that no such utterance was made during Pallas' lifetime. A further voice suggests there is cause for regret.

9. The 'cut-off' phenomenon analysed. The hero described again

I should now like to recall the 'cut-off' technique: how in certain scenes conversation seems deliberately cut short by the poet. Heinze saw this as Vergil's device to avoid retardation in the action. I shall grant some truth to this view. But there is something more. The scenes which contain such 'cut-offs' are dramatically plausible, and they are symptomatic of the world as Vergil understands it.

I gather the instances. Though Aeneas had other chances to

react humanely to Dido, her rapid exit at 4.390 dramatically 'cuts off' one. At 2.680 the omen, and the shift of attention it causes, leaves Aeneas mere moments to respond to Creusa. More time seems allowed to Aeneas at 8.520ff. with Pallas and Evander, but that scene too is fairly swiftly 'cut off'. Helenus' arrival and a shift of focus prevent a familial interchange between Aeneas and Andromache at 3.345. At 6.538ff. the Sibyl prevents any exchange developing between Aeneas and Deiphobus. These scenes are certainly swift-moving. They also indicate that Aeneas' world is of a certain type.

Aeneas finds himself in a harsh world, one in which there is little time for mere individuals and for their affective relationships and interactions, or little time anyway for individuals who are also men of history. 'More important' things—or, simply, other things—overshadow and displace the individual and his affective relationships. This means that if an occasion offers, or requires, an affective response, the chance must be seized, for it may pass in an instant and be lost for ever, as more important matters supervene. This, I maintain, is the point which the 'cut-off' technique is designed to make. To put it another way, in the Vergilian world 'cut-off' moments are naturally and remorselessly produced. This is the fact (see above, p. 177) which makes Aeneas' character and policy so particularly lamentable in effect. Being that sort of a man in this sort of a world, he finds himself again and again reacting *too late*.

Consider the individual examples and the lessons they teach. Aeneas and Deiphobus have some time for their human interchange, but it is ruthlessly limited. A question, an emotional reply containing questions—and then the authoritative voice of the Sibyl interrupts the tears. The work of Fate must proceed and mere human relations must be put back into perspective. At Troy Aeneas has no more than a moment for a vital human response: Creusa appeals, the seconds tick by, and then comes the omen which emphasizes a larger, historic perspective; and the moment is gone. Creusa's death then ensues, and there can be no further chance for Aeneas to respond to her. And yet: in the subsequent scene, when Creusa's generous ghost appears, just such a possibility may seem in prospect. But it is not to be. After her speech, Creusa immediately disappears, leaving Aeneas weeping and, characteristically, groping for expression.

A *second* and cruelly abrupt 'cut-off' (2.790) rubs in the point. This is indeed a harsh world, where chances of affective response must not be missed: one was crucially required of Aeneas, and a moment was granted to him, but the moment passed and when it passed it went for ever. With Pallas, too, there is a moment which obviously requires an affective response from him; but Aeneas misses it, and it passes (8.520), as the focus is shifted to higher, historic things. Aeneas misses other chances, and soon finds he has lost the possibility for affective interaction, with Pallas as with Creusa. Compare Dido. Aeneas spoils rather than misses one big chance, in his speech at 4.333 ff. Then, when he is 'preparing' to speak at 4.390, he is 'cut off'. That earlier speech was destined to be his only chance at Carthage. Then, rather as with Creusa, it may seem that he receives another opportunity: in the Underworld, in Book 6. And he does get to speak to her. But it does not work. His belated sympathy falls on deaf ears. His only opportunity does prove to have been the one at Carthage, and he spoilt it. Again Aeneas confronts the lesson, rubbed in: if an occasion offers or requires affective response, the moment must be seized. Fate hurries people and history on, and does not squander time on second chances.

Such is the picture these 'cut-off' episodes help to create. Nor (and this is an important point) is the world that is thus suggested an implausible one. In particular, the necessity for generous and warm reactions to be swift and decisive will strike many as only too true, and not just those who are men of history. How often does the moment pass! People die, they go away, or in some other way the crucial moment is lost for ever.

Now it seems to me that the fact that this is the sort of world in which Aeneas operates has an effect on our judgement of Aeneas. It affects it in two ways. We have noted that dire consequences ensue upon Aeneas' inhibited emotions. But if Fate allows so cruelly little time for vital human responses, there is reason to sympathize with Aeneas. If only (we may feel) he had had more time at those crucial moments . . . On the other hand, since the world as Vergil sees it and represents it is thus—urgent and unrelenting—it increases the *importance* of an ability to respond humanly and naturally, and with it the *lamentability* of a character as inhibited as Aeneas'. And it presses us to ask more fiercely whether it was right to try to reinforce that inhibition by policy.

Vergil invents another suggestive fact which may incline us to a troubled view of Aeneas and his policy: another irony. We should remind ourselves again that Aeneas battles with grand passions as well as with tenderer 'passions' (like compassion) in his bid to obey the will of destiny. He must, for example, suppress his heroic and passionate impulse to die at Troy; he must suppress his own passionate love (if that is what it was) for Dido. And we should remind ourselves that at times, for a time, he fails in such suppression—which is one of the reasons why he is interesting as a character. Not just at Carthage: he succumbs to the passion of revenge in Book 10, and prosecutes a cruel slaughter; similarly at the end of the poem he succumbs to a vengeful killing, neglecting the instructions of Anchises.

If we now consider the struggle of Aeneas versus passion as a *single* struggle, in the manner of the Stoics and in the manner that the *Aeneid* itself encourages,[43] we shall perceive the irony. For is it not ironic that an aspiring Stoical Augustan, who *does* admit the passion of revenge and in consequence slaughter helpless victims, does *not* admit the 'passion' of compassion[44] and perhaps save a beloved queen's life? Is it not ironic that frightful passions causing destruction are admitted while humaner 'passions' that might have averted destruction are excluded? Does not Aeneas seem to have an ironic propensity to drop his Stoical, reasoned self-possession at what might be called particularly the wrong moments (Books 10 and 12) and not to drop it at what might be termed right moments (Books 2 and 4)? Is not this in fact lamentably, tragically, ironic? The irony points us to lament and perhaps to criticize. In the invented irony we hear a further voice.

Let me phrase the irony in other, more general terms. It has always been acknowledged, and Vergil makes it abundantly clear, that Aeneas' grand Stoic and imperial mission entails a large and unavoidable cost, to Aeneas and to others. It has also been acknowledged that Aeneas' failure to uphold Stoic princi-

---

[43] See Lyne, 'Vergil and the Politics of War', 190, giving references.
[44] On the passion of compassion, see above, n. 38.

ples (duty before passion) in the prosecution of the mission causes avoidable human damage. It is less often acknowledged that Aeneas' success in upholding Stoic principles (the suppression of 'passion') sometimes causes avoidable human damage too—as well as accentuating the barrenness of a life that is already barren enough by nature. But that too is a point which is made to us by further voices. If we listen to all the voices in Vergil's poem, we should find that his hero and his hero's story encourage us to approach the Stoical attitude to life and the imperial attitude to life (which the *Aeneid* may appear to espouse) warily and critically. It is fallible and inadequate.

10. The exit from Troy (and the end of the poem)

In my previous glances at this scene I have been particularly concerned with Aeneas and Creusa; I now consider Aeneas' actions and attitudes towards Anchises and Ascanius as well. Here it might be felt that evidence exists to qualify the above conclusions about Aeneas in his relationships with others: here he is more responsive. In my opinion the qualification necessary is small, if any. The scene—in its entirety—in fact well characterizes Aeneas in his relationship with his family, but not in the way some imagine. We must examine the invention and not resist implications.

It is necessary to identify the factors which first prevent Aeneas from leaving the city, and then persuade him. This is a momentous and difficult decision for him. The factors that operate in it are therefore vital for an assessment of his character. I shall summarize the sequence of events baldly but, I hope, fairly.

During the bulk of Book 2 Aeneas ignores the clear instruction of Hector's ghost (289 ff., 'heu fuge nate dea . . .') to fly the city taking with him the gods of Troy. Instead, he rushes madly into battle, committing himself to a last and hopeless fight (314 ff., 'arma amens capio . . .'). Thus, in the bulk of the book, the heroic passions of despair, revenge, hatred, *vel sim.*, outweigh for Aeneas the call of duty and fate, and, for that matter, the call of his family.

The sight of the dead Priam, however, prompts Aeneas to think of his family (559 ff.). Then something—perhaps it is the sight of Helen, but here we are in the quagmire of the 'Helen episode' problem[45]—revives heroic fury in him; and Venus has to intervene to recall him from his passionate course (whatever it is), and to urge him to think of his family again (594ff., 'nate, quis indomitas tantus dolor excitat iras?' ['my son, what great anguish arouses this indomitable wrath?']). She repeats Hector's instruction to him to flee (619), but her emphasis unlike Hector's (and it is characteristic of the goddess) is on his family and not on a new future, new city, and so on (596–8).

Instructed by Venus to attend to his family—specifically, to Anchises, Creusa, and Ascanius—Aeneas is minded to attend primarily to Anchises: about this he is emphatic (635f.). However, Anchises refuses to leave (637ff.), and resists the tearful entreaties of everyone assembled. This refusal on Anchises' part revives Aeneas' passionate impulse, inciting him to return to the doomed battle, in search once more of a desperate, heroic death (655ff., 'rursus in arma feror' ['again I am borne off into battle']).

At this point Creusa, confronted by Aeneas' despairing, heroically egoistic, and for her potentially disastrous decision, supplicates him most affectingly, putting him in emotional terms right on the line (673–8; cf. s. 1 and 2): she begs him pitifully to consider 'paruus Iulus', Anchises, herself. Aeneas does not respond. The portent intercedes (fire plays around Ascanius' head, 682ff.). This persuades Anchises that it is right to leave; and with Anchises convinced, Aeneas is persuaded too.

The portent is therefore the most vital factor in engineering the departure from Troy. Its significance, which would be clear to every Roman reader and is obviously clear to Anchises (he reacts to it 'happily' ['laetus'], 687), is that it designates Ascanius as a future ruler.[46] This is the information which, once it has been confirmed by Jupiter (692ff.), persuades Anchises to quit the city. And *his* decision moves Aeneas. Aeneas responds to Anchises' change of heart, forgets his heroic intention to

---

[45] Conte, *Il genere*, Ch. 5 offers an agile argument in favour of the Helen episode's authenticity.

[46] See Austin (and Servius) on 2.683. We are reminded most immediately of the portent that attended Servius Tullius (Liv. 1.39). It is worth remembering that tradition endowed Anchises with a knowledge of divination: Naev. *Bell. Poen.* fr. 9 Strz.; Enn. *Ann.* 15f. Sk.; Austin on 2.687; Horsfall, review of Fordyce, 222.

return to battle, and immediately organizes the departure from Troy (707 ff.). And he attends to his father first, to his son second, and to his wife emphatically third (cf. s. 2): 'longe seruet uestigia coniunx' ['let my wife follow in my footsteps at a distance'] (711). He attends to his father in that famous, pious gesture: 'ergo age care pater ceruici imponere nostrae' ['come then, dear father, be supported on my shoulders'] (707).

Thus the bald summary, and some minimal explanation. Let us now be precise about what does and does not move Aeneas: to see what his priorities are. First and very importantly, the bulk of the book shows that Aeneas can forget *everything*—duty to fate, the call of his family—when in the grip of great heroic passion. Second, a divine instruction (Venus') can confirm his own inclination and make him think of his family again. But the priorities he then displays in regard to his family suggest Roman dutifulness rather than love and compassion. For he attends first and foremost to his father, the authoritative head of his house, not to those whose appeal would be more clearly affective: his pathetic wife and son. Not only first and foremost: his attention to his father is for a time his exclusive familial concern. When his father refuses to leave, no concern for his wife and son then supervenes to prevent him from forming the heroic, suicidal plan (returning to die in battle) which is his response to Anchises' refusal. And what dissuades him from putting this disastrous plan into action? Again it is dutifulness, 'pietas', almost we might say patriotism, rather than tender concern. For it is *not* Creusa's pathetic and eloquent appeal on behalf of his son, his father, and herself in their human, affective capacities that moves him. It is his father's response to a dynastic Iulus, Iulus designated by an omen as a king. Anchises sees Iulus' omen, expresses his confidence in a Trojan future under divine protection; this confidence infects Aeneas: and Aeneas then duly, dutifully, *piously* attends to Anchises (below, p. 188), and then to Iulus, and last and indeed very least to Creusa. We may conclude as follows. In this scene mighty passions on the one hand and duty (patriotism, 'pietas') on the other contend for control of the hero's actions; but tenderer considerations and affective relationships have little practical influence, for one reason and another (inhibition, conscious policy, see s. 7). This is the picture the hero presents in the scene; and, interpreting it properly, we find material to confirm and amplify the sort of conclusion we have reached before.

I shall strengthen this conclusion shortly. Meanwhile there are a couple of points to draw out. There is much in Aeneas' narrative that might have given Dido, who is listening to the story, food for thought: an interesting point, of which Ovid had an inkling.[47] Aeneas, as I have said, shows in the story of Troy that he can forget *everything*—duty to fate and family—in the grip of great passion. That is precisely what he is going to do in Carthage, though there the great passion is love. But equally the narrative of Book 2 shows that authority—first Venus, then Anchises and divine signs—can recall him to sense, responsibility, and duty. That will be Mercury's function at Carthage. Then, as I have said, while grand passion and 'pietas' contend for Aeneas' allegiance at Troy, Book 2 shows us that more tender, affective claims do seem to stir him little. It is not Creusa's pitiful appeal, it is not *compassion* that sways him, but Anchises and history. Similarly at Carthage. When Dido has witnessed Aeneas deny the grand passion of love and acknowledge the claims of duty and history, she will be astounded to find him apparently impervious to pity, and will observe with incredulity how in his scheme of things she and her human plight seem irrelevant. Of course Dido is far from completely right in her analysis (cf. pp. 162ff.)—but far from completely wrong. In any case she should not have been surprised. The evidence was there to forewarn her that such might be the behaviour of the hero.

While duty and great passion contend for the allegiance of Aeneas, tenderer passions and tenderer claims weigh little: this is evident at the end of the poem.[48] The wounded Turnus appeals thus (12.931ff.):

[47] See the intriguing lines which Ovid assigns to his Dido at *Her.* 7.81–6.
[48] I have published my views on the end of the poem in 'Vergil and the Politics of War': see esp. 199ff.; the present paragraph takes up a point not considered there. See too Barchiesi, 91ff., and G. Thome, *Gestalt und Funktion des Mezentius bei Vergil—mit einem Ausblick auf die Schlussszene der Aeneis* (Frankfurt, 1979), 328ff., both estimable discussions. Suerbaum, 46ff., 105ff., provides a convenient and interesting summary of other scholarly opinion on the subject.

'equidem merui nec deprecor' inquit;
'utere sorte tua. miseri te si qua parentis
tangere cura potest, oro (fuit et tibi talis
Anchises genitor) Dauni miserere senectae
et me, seu corpus spoliatum lumine mauis,
redde meis. uicisti et uictum tendere palmas
Ausonii uidere; tua est Lauinia coniunx,
ulterius ne tende odiis.' stetit acer in armis . . .

'I have earned it, and I make no entreaty,' said Turnus. 'Use your fortune. If any consideration for a wretched parent can touch you, I beg you—for you too had such a father in Anchises—pity Daunus' old age, and give me or my lifeless body, if you prefer it, to my kin. You have conquered and the Ausonians have seen me stretch forth my hands in defeat. Lavinia is yours as wife. Press no further in hatred.' Aeneas stood, fierce in his armour . . .

This appeal for clemency which, it should be stressed, Turnus makes not on his own selfish behalf, is based on both emotion and reason. The emotional part is directed to pity ('consideration for a wretched parent . . . I beg you . . . pity . . .'). Turnus' reasoning (implicit) is this: since, as he points out, he is patently defeated, since moreover his own side has seen him defeated, his death is now unnecessary. For he no longer poses any threat; and his time as a proud leader of men is surely over. His reasoning, in fact, is like that which helped Anchises to command clemency (6.853), a command which was as much political as humanitarian: peace, and the reconciliation necessary for it, will not be hazarded and may best be served by judicious granting of clemency.[49] And, of course, the way Turnus is described ('humilis', 'supplex', 12.930) and the way he himself speaks should remind us, and Aeneas, of Anchises' actual order. We could say, therefore, that Turnus' appeal, wittingly or unwittingly, brings into play Aeneas' duty as well as pity: Aeneas has a duty to uphold his father's solemn and considered imposition. We wait to see what happens. 'Aeneas stood, fierce in his armour . . . and stayed his sword' ['. . . dextramque repressit']. He is inclined to clemency. Why? Through pity (the appeal by Daunus) or through duty, in remembrance of Anchises' solemn instruction? Through duty, I infer: a man described as 'fierce in his armour' may have duty

[49] Cf. Lyne, 'Vergil and the Politics of War', 195 and Ch. 1 n. 62.

but has little thoughts of pity in his head. And why does he not spare him in the end? Because of grand passion, as Turnus had feared ('Press no further in hatred'), in particular because of the passion that consists, according to Stoic doctrine, in the desire to avenge.[50] Aeneas sees the baldrick, the symbol of Pallas' dishonour, and that seals Turnus' fate. Duty and grand passion contend for control of Aeneas, and here grand passion wins; meanwhile, tenderer 'passion', compassion,[51] weighs little. The ingredients are familiar. Our hero undergoes no metamorphosis in this poem.[52]

But to return to the exit from Troy in Book 2, and to its climax. For some, the picture of Aeneas shouldering his father and leading his little son out of Troy (707ff.) reveals a warm and tenderly motivated hero. This is not, I think, quite on the mark. Aeneas' priorities, if we do not resist implications, tell against such an interpretation. We remember Creusa. And we remember Iulus: in what capacities he did and did not move Aeneas. 'Paruus Iulus', Iulus exhibited by Creusa in his capacity as Aeneas' weak and defenceless little boy, did not have a noticeable effect on Aeneas; Iulus designated as a king, dynastic Iulus, in an effect mediated through Anchises, did. Similarly with Anchises himself. Anchises radiating dynastic confidence and authority moved Aeneas, not the pitiable figure that Creusa drew his attention to. Aeneas then responded affectionately to Anchises, it is true: 'ergo age, care pater'. But affection is not what the Augustan reader retains as his lasting memory of Aeneas' action. Rather, it is something historic and national. Aeneas' reactions to his father here are governed by 'pietas'—

---

[50] Cf. Cic. *Tusc.* 4.21, 'quae autem libidini subiecta sunt, ea sic definiunt, ut 'ira' sit libido poeniendi . . .' (cf. 4.44, 'est enim ira, ut modo definiui, ulciscendi libido'). The Stoics would of course accept Turnus' description of Aeneas' passion as 'odium'. 'Odium' is 'ira inueterata' (Cic. *Tusc.* 4.21) and 'ira' is the desire to avenge, 'ulciscendi libido' (4.44)—and all such emotions are anyway 'libidines' (*Tusc.* 4.16) (or, ultimately, 'perturbationes', 'animi commotiones' (4.11)). For full discussion of the motives behind Aeneas' killing of Turnus see 'Vergil and the Politics of War', esp. 200f.

[51] See above, n. 38.

[52] But this is a common view: Heinze, 271ff., esp. 275ff.; Bowra, 'Aeneas and the Stoic Ideal'; Otis, index *sub* 'Aeneas—development of'. Correctly, La Penna, lxv.

'pietas' to his father and, through and beyond him, to the future of the Trojan and Roman peoples. What this scene offers, therefore, is a hesitant demonstration of that quality which makes the Augustan hero, the quality which Aeneas pursues. Shouldering his father in this scene, Aeneas gives us a foretaste of the Aeneas who, at the end of Book 8, shoulders the burden of Roman history, 'attollens umero famamque et fata nepotum' ['lifting on his shoulder the fame and destiny of his descendants']. In neither of these scenes does he fully understand the 'burden' he is taking on,[53] but he understands that there is a burden, a historic burden, and piously—on these occasions—he accepts his historic role. The scene in Book 2 is richly symbolic, a moment pregnant with fatefulness—and so on. But it is not a scene that is affectingly familial. It is not, for example, to be compared with scenes in *Iliad* 6.

Such, then, is the picture of Aeneas in Book 2. Even when Aeneas himself narrates, invention is manipulated and further voices intrude stimulating thoughts on the hero's priorities, motivations, and behaviour. Perhaps we should remind ourselves that most Roman sensibility would applaud Aeneas' positive attainments in this episode, his acknowledgement of the sovereignty of patriotism and the overriding claim of history and nation. Vergil shows us these achievements. But he also shows us Aeneas ignoring individuals with personal claims upon him: ignoring them, forgetting them, dismissing them; and he shows us this when such attitudes are unnecessary to his positive attainments and lamentable in their consequences (so the situation is different from, say, showing the necessary personal grimness of Brutus the Liberator).[54] This is disturbing. When the tenderer 'passions' are displaced for whatever reason, it causes suffering. So the further voices insinuate.

11. Aeneas and Ascanius again

I now take up a scene which fleetingly involves Aeneas and Ascanius. At 12.110f. Aeneas is reported as consoling his son before the aborted duel with Turnus:

---

[53] For discussion of Aeneas and the shield, see Ch. 5 pp. 207–9.
[54] See *Aeneid* 6.819ff.

> tum socios maestique metum solatur Iuli
> fata docens . . .

Then he comforts his comrades and sad Iulus' fear, teaching of fate . . .

How do we interpret a detail like this?

As often there is an untroubling interpretation invited by the epic voice. There is, we could say, nobility in this picture. It is austere but grand. Aeneas consoles his son, eschewing sentiment—Ascanius is as it were just another 'socius'—teaching him the designs of destiny. Self-denying—and denying Ascanius—Aeneas keeps his attention firmly on the purpose that transcends mere individuality and subsumes them both: 'fata docens'. And his teaching seems to be inspirational. At 12.168f. Ascanius is described alongside his father at the initiation of the truce, duly and confidently present in his dynastic role, 'the second hope of great Rome'. Both these scenes are stirring. The first may be considered touching: a splendid evocation of the Stoical 'pater patriae' in his hour of crisis, and beside him the heir who will inherit his fate, learning from his lips.

But something troubles me through the splendour, and perhaps mars the splendour; it certainly reduces the ability of either scene to touch. It is a question of *context*—or rather, lack of it. Attention to Vergil's invention elsewhere in the poem—the invention that gives these scenes their context—puts them in a different light. Context properly considered changes their impact. Invention, in fact 'negative' invention, supplies a further voice.

My point is this. What Aeneas here exhibits is heroic single-mindedness, heroic commitment, and in this respect he is a relation of other heroes to whom he is otherwise most alien. Now, a key factor in the capacity of such heroes to appear noble and to inspire admiration is surely the *sacrifice* that their path involves. Sophocles' supremely egoistic Ajax is heroically single-minded in his commitment to his pride, honour, and hate; and for this he sacrifices his life. Antigone is committed (as it turns out) to an instinctive religious feeling and to love of her brother; and for this she too sacrifices her life. Hector feels the compulsions of honour and the responsibilities of a man who protects his city, and for these he austerely sets aside the emotional pull of the wife and child he loves. In each of these cases the ability of the hero to excite our admiration, respect, and so on, depends upon our appreciation of the sacrifice he makes. We certainly need to be assured that a sacrifice is indeed involved. Otherwise the heroism might seem facile or inhuman.

To some it might seem that at 12.110f. Aeneas exhibits a heroism something like Hector's. Thus, sacrificing what may after all be his last opportunity for warm familiarity with his son, he keeps his attention on the grand duty that involves them both. But I would contend that Vergil's invention gives us no reason to believe that any such sacrifice is being made. For we need evidence of that desired and normal familiarity between father and son. What we have been given is a context of silence (s. 3). Aeneas, as we saw, ignored or passed up chances when familiarity with his son was both possible and appropriate. Whether we judge that he was moved at those times by inhibition, policy, or whatever, the fact remains: at this point in Book 12 we have no evidence that any abnormal sacrifice is being made. Who is to say that Aeneas' noble self-denial cost anything? When we attend to all of Vergil's invention, the scene in Book 12 does indeed seem different. The epic voice presents a heroic, self-denying Aeneas. Further voices colour him less attractively, indeed less heroically.

Consider too the grim lines 12.432ff., referred to in s. 3. I quote them now in full:

> postquam habilis lateri clipeus loricaque tergo est,
> Ascanium fusis circum complectitur armis
> summaque per galeam delibans oscula fatur:
> 'disce, puer, uirtutem ex me uerumque laborem,
> fortunam ex aliis. nunc te mea dextera bello
> defensum dabit et magna inter praemia ducet.
> tu facito, mox cum matura adoleuerit aetas,
> sis memor et te animo repetentem exempla tuorum
> et pater Aeneas et auunculus excitet Hector.'

After the shield was fitted to his side and the cuirass to his back, Aeneas clasps Ascanius in an iron embrace, and lightly kisses him through his helmet, saying: 'Learn valour[55] from me, my son, and true endurance of toil. From others learn good luck. Now my right hand will defend you in war and lead you where there are great rewards. But do you, when soon your age has grown to ripeness, be mindful; and, as you recall the examples of your kin, let your father Aeneas and your uncle Hector spur you on.'

This is the only time Aeneas embraces Ascanius in the poem, and the embrace is obscured by armour. These are the only words that Aeneas is quoted as addressing to Ascanius, and they consist of this austere, martial, rather gloomily heroic exhortation.[56] And Aeneas is about to embark on what may be fatal combat. It is, we could say, tragic that Aeneas' great and destined duty should mean that his rare contact with his son should be of such a sort, and that what may be his last embrace and his last words should happen in such a bleak manner. But that would, I think, be to hearken too much to the simple epic voice; it would be to forget those silences that Vergil provokingly invents. For we could only say with certainty that the situation was tragic if we knew that Aeneas longed for and was familiar with another sort of embrace and another sort of communication: if we knew that this stark scene cost him. But such evidence is lacking. We remember rather that sterility in relationships, even the relationship with his son, is Aeneas' natural and elected way, produced by his own character and policy. It should in fact be hard to find Aeneas in 12.432ff. particularly tragic. This stark scene is simply, if strikingly, part

---

[55] On 'uirtus' and its translation, see Ch. 1 p. 8.

[56] They are not what we should expect of an Augustan and Stoic hero, whom some see Aeneas as at this point (cf. Ch. 1 p. 9). 'Disce, puer. . . . fortunam ex aliis' suggests a man not adjusted to his lot; 'disce puer uirtutem ex me' suggests either a lack of insight into the 'uirtus' required of an Augustan ruler or a lack of self-knowledge: see below, pp. 205–6. (For lack of self-knowledge in Aeneas, see Ch. 5 p. 214). And of course there is that ominous recall of the tragic Ajax (p. 9). Pöschl, 66f., correctly perceives that the speech is not all Stoicism and adjustment. It has been strikingly misinterpreted by many, e.g. Heinze, 277 ('aus denen die abgeklärte Seelenruhe spricht, wie dem Weisen ziemt'); Otis, 381 ('he reveals, as it were, the secret of his heroism. He is the divine man'); Quinn, 261; Johnson, 140f. Highet, 31f., misses the tone, but is otherwise useful. E. Belfiore, *Phoenix*, 38 (1984), 27–30, suggestively compares Hector's embrace of Astyanax in *Iliad* 6 with Aeneas' of Ascanius in *Aen.* 12, spotting an important allusion. I would put her suggestions to different use, but they are perceptive.

The Hero and His Son

of his generally stark life—the starkness of which is his own product. Perhaps we should pity the general starkness; but, as for the particular episode in Book 12, Aeneas himself could hardly find it wracking. Unlike Hector and his dutifulness, there is no evidence to suggest that it cost him.

12. Ascanius and Aeneas

My intention now is to focus more particularly on the poet's treatment of Aeneas' son. Ascanius has aroused admiration in critics, not without reason.[57] But Vergil wants us to do other things besides admire. Further voices invite disquiet.

Ascanius grows up in this poem: a little boy in Book 2, he is by Book 9 an incipient warrior, and by Book 12 on equal terms with Aeneas' 'socii' (above, p. 190). Twice he features in hunts (4.156ff. and 7.477ff.), and it has been remarked[58] that his growing up is illustrated thereby: ancillary in the first, he leads the second. It has also been remarked[59] that hunting was regarded in Rome as a healthy and toughening exercise; Vergil, we could therefore say, shows Ascanius manfully employed, wholesomely maturing, the mythical counterpart of, say, the young Scipio Aemilianus.[60] That may be true enough. But something else is going on.

Rome viewed hunting as healthy and manly. The *Aeneid* establishes a rather different tone for it. Vergil imparts his own resonances to it, and constructs sequences of *linked* imagery/motifs out of it. In this practice of linking imagery/motifs Vergil's model was most probably the Greek tragic dramatists.[61] I have already pointed to instances in Chapters 1 and 3;

[57] Heinze, 157–9, 266 ('freilich den Heroenknaben'); R. D. Williams on 5.545f.; N. Moseley, *Characters and Epithets, A Study in Vergil's Aeneid* (New Haven, 1926), 47ff.; Maurach, *passim*; L. H. Feldman, *CJ* 48 (1952–3), 303 ('Virgil had, indeed, fallen in love with the young son of his hero'); Warde Fowler, *The Death of Turnus*, 87–92 ('Ascanius is meant to represent [the ideal Roman] in boyhood . . . Virgil loved dearly this boy of his creation').

[58] Moseley, op. cit., 51f.

[59] See e.g. Hor. *Serm.* 2.2.9f., *Epist.* 1.18.49ff., *Odes* 3.24.55f., and cf. Horsfall 'Numanus Remulus', 1111.

[60] Cf. above, p. 152, and see Polybius, 31.29 (Büttner-Wobst, Paton), Diodorus, 31.27.7–8.

[61] Cf. e.g. Oliver Taplin, *The Stagecraft of Aeschylus* (Oxford, 1977), 311–15, and index *sub* 'imagery, sustained'; R. P. Winnington-Ingram, *Euripides and Dionysus* (Cambridge, 1948), *passim* (see below, n. 69); and see n. 62. On linked imagery in Vergil see Pöschl, index *sub* 'Aeneis—Symbolverknüpfung, Verwandte Symbole'.

his most striking are, I think, the 'fire' and 'wound' sequences in the story of Dido, with which we might compare the linked 'blindness' motifs in Sophocles' *Oedipus Tyrannus*.[62] 'Hunting' also makes a linked sequence in the story of Dido. This I shall illustrate, in order to show the sort of associations hunting accumulates in the *Aeneid*—and because it partners a sequence ('siege'/'sack') that I discussed in Chapter 1. Via it a further voice comments on Aeneas and Venus.

The salient moments are as follows.[63] When Venus in 1.314f. appears disguised, it is in what is for her the very paradoxical garb of a huntress, reminding Aeneas of Diana (329). Dido at her arrival in 1.498ff. is compared to Diana, and there is an intimation in the simile of Diana the huntress (she carries a quiver on her shoulder). The great and disastrous love-scene in Book 4 arises out of a hunt (129ff.) in which Aeneas and Dido participate. And before that, Dido smitten with love had been pictured as the pitiable hind struck by a hunting shepherd (4.69ff.):

> qualis coniecta cerua sagitta,
> quam procul incautam nemora inter Cresia fixit
> pastor agens telis liquitque uolatile ferrum
> nescius: illa fuga siluas saltusque peragrat
> Dictaeos; haeret lateri letalis harundo.

Like a hind shot by an arrow, an unwary hind which a shepherd hunting with darts has pierced from afar amid the Cretan woods,

---

[62] Dido's love-wound, her 'tacitum uulnus', is converted remorselessly and seemingly inevitably into the frightful 'uulnus stridens' of her suicide; the fire of her passion is similarly actualized: see Ch. 3 pp. 120–1. Cf. Oedipus' 'blindness' in the *OT*. The idea of blindness is tossed to and fro in the Oedipus–Teiresias scene (371, 389, 412f., 454), establishing itself as a motif and raising the question: who is blind, and in what way? (cf. the question raised by the hunting motif in the *Aeneid*, below). The play demonstrates that Oedipus is the blind one, mentally blind (venially so, nevertheless blind), and his blindness and the motif culminate in the terrible scenes of his physical blinding (1313ff.). (I have not found this point expressed with quite the necessary clarity, but cf. Kamerbeek on *OT* 370–1, 1183, 1385; H. Musurillo, *The Light and the Darkness, Studies in the Dramatic Poetry of Sophocles* (Leiden, 1967), 86–8; G. Méautis, *Sophocle* (Paris, 1957), 127.)

[63] On hunting imagery in the *Aeneid* in general see Otis, 75f. Pöschl, 92, comments on its function in the story of Dido: he overstresses the contribution of Dido's Diana simile, but is otherwise quite suggestive ('die Bilder erscheinen als Chiffern eines tragischen Schicksalszusammenhangs').

The Hero and His Son

leaving in her the winged iron, not knowing that he has: she in flight ranges through the Dictaean woods and passes; the deadly arrow clings to her flank.

I must pause briefly here. For this simile needs to be carefully assessed for what it does and does not imply. In the discreet medium of imagery a further voice is telling us important things.

How, first of all, do we interpret the image as a whole, the 'hunt', in this simile? The wound which the hind, figuring Dido, sustains clearly stands for the 'wound' of love. The hunt therefore is the 'hunt' of love (the tracking down of beloved by lover, *vel sim.*), a simple point which must not be resisted: what is happening is that Vergil is adapting to his epic context an image which is common enough in other, lighter (erotic) contexts[64]—a habit of his with which we are by now familiar.[65]

Next, the shepherd-hunter in this hunt of love must stand for Aeneas. Again this point must not be resisted. The specification 'pastor' helps the identification, since Aeneas is prominently figured in this role elsewhere in the poem.[66] And the other possible candidate, Cupid, has been excluded—almost ostentatiously excluded, I should say. When Vergil composed the Cupid scene in 1.657ff., ominously switching from Homeric to Apollonian, Jason–Medea material (Ch. 3, p. 123), he chose not to make Cupid an archer as he had been in Apollonius. Comparison with sources (in a sense, allusion) thus shows that Vergil's Cupid is emphatically not an archer. That role is reserved for his half-brother: for Aeneas, here in 4.69ff.

---

[64] Cf. Xenophon, *Mem.* 1.2.24, 'On account of his beauty Alcibiades [was] hunted (θηρώμενος) by many grand ladies'; Callimachus, *Epigram* 1 GP = 31 Pf., summarized by Hor. *Serm.* 1.2.105f., advancing the notion that the 'hunt', not possession, supplies the interest; Plaut. *Epid.* 215f.; Ov. *Am.* 2.9.9, *Ars* 1.89, 'sed tu praecipue curuis uenare theatris' ['do your hunting particularly in the theatres'], 1.253; Phaedrus, 4.5.4; E. Fantham, *Comparative Studies in Republican Latin Imagery* (Toronto, 1972), 39f.; cf. too Eur. *IA* 960. (At *Arg.* 4.12f. Apollonius compares Medea to a fawn, but this is primarily a 'fear' simile, something essentially different; but such similes could acquire erotic nuances: cf. e.g. Hor. *Odes* 1.23, and (probably) Anacreon, 408, also 417 (a filly).)

[65] Cf. Ch. 1 pp. 14, 22f.

[66] See 2.304–8, 12.587–92; Anderson, '*Pastor Aeneas*', esp. 1–10. Anderson well remarks the unexpectedness of the word 'pastor' in 4.71 in the place of, say, 'uenator': this unexpectedness facilitates the recall of 2.304ff. and thus the identification with Aeneas.

Thirdly, what is the significance of 'nescius'? This is vital to understand, since the commentators in general misunderstand it.[67] Our hunting shepherd is not, as is often implied, totally 'ignorant', 'nescius', of his actions (how could he be?). He *has*, Vergil tells us, been vigorously and purposefully hunting the hind: 'quam . . . agens telis' ['which, hunting with darts']. What he is ignorant of is that one of his shafts has struck: that he has hit the 'cerua', that the 'cerua' in fact carries a lethal wound inflicted by him. The implications of this last point, together with the identification of the 'pastor' as Aeneas, are crucial: discreetly but definitely we are told something about the hero's role at Carthage. He has courted the queen, made up to the queen, 'hunted' her in the hunt of love. What he does not know—yet—is that his courtship has been devastatingly and lethally successful: Dido is already mad with love for him, beyond recall; his charm, enhanced by Venus (1.589–93), has been fatal.

I return to the sequence of hunting motifs and to its meaning; I draw select conclusions, not intending to be exhaustive. 'Hunting' seems to mark the downward course of the tragic story of Dido like an ominous leitmotiv. To mention another example, even Aeneas' slaughter of stags, 'cerui', on arrival in Libya (1.184 ff.) may seem different when one rereads the poem: it is the first in a sequence of gradually ominous motifs, a premonition (note the repeated phrase 'agens telis', 1.191, 4.71). But we have to do with more than a leitmotiv. Hunting gives us one way of viewing and interpreting the Dido story. Dido is fleetingly imaged and for a time acts the huntress. But this proves to be an irony. She is more memorably and truthfully characterized as the hunted. It is Aeneas and his mother who are properly imaged, in their separate ways, as hunters.

The 'cerua' simile of 4.69 ff. reveals, as I have said, a determined pursuit, some sort of vigorous courtship of Dido by Aeneas in the 'hunt' of love: this is not to be ducked. And it is shown, too, that Dido herself feels hunted by Aeneas: a nightmare version of Aeneas the hunter appears in Dido's dream at 4.465, 'agit ipse furentem / in somnis ferus Aeneas' ['in her

---

[67] 'nescius' is misinterpreted at Pöschl, 105 (in other respects however Pöschl's discussion is good); Putnam, 155, 188; Johnson, 79–81. Anderson, '*Pastor Aeneas*', 9, is closer to the truth.

The Hero and His Son

dreams wild Aeneas himself drives her raving']; note the repetition of 'ago' from 4.71 and 1.191. And Aeneas' mother is a 'huntress'. Her role as such, and her leading role in the pathetic story of Dido, are stressed. She stands out at the beginning of the story, conspicuous in her paradoxical huntress garb as she introduces Dido to us and to Aeneas. Why, we should ask, is she dressed like that?[68] What is she hunting? As the plot proceeds, the answer becomes clear. Venus puts Cupid to work, exploits his fire and poison, plots with Juno, all in her single-minded pursuit of one event: that Dido should fall in love with Aeneas. It becomes an irresistible conclusion: like her son, Venus too is set upon ensnaring the queen. But 'hunting' in her case has a different implication.

Aeneas the 'hunter' is based on a conventional amatory image: the lover hunts his beloved. His implied role and actions may be culpable, but they are familiar and human enough, and therefore venial. Venus 'hunts' with a larger perspective, not just to entice a lover: she is after a victim, to fulfil plans. And, on the track of her victim, a goddess hunting for her own ends, she allusively recalls another divine 'hunter', as Vergil himself signals: Dionysus in the *Bacchae*, a sinister and ruthless relation.[69] And again, Vergil tells us that Dido herself senses something of this. In the nightmare passage referred to above, she is compared to Pentheus (4.469f.); and 'sibi . . . uidetur' in 467 suggests that this is her own perception. Anyway, once more the imagery offers bad press for Venus; worse press than for Aeneas.

There is another insinuation in the imagery concerning

---

[68] Interpretations of this striking and significant disguise are notably reductive: Klingner, 397; Knauer, 159 n. 1; Wlosok, *Die Göttin Venus*, 101f.

[69] I owe much in this part of the chapter to the perceptiveness of Andrew Crompton.
On Dionysus the 'hunter' in the *Bacchae*, see R. P. Winnington-Ingram, *Euripides and Dionysus* (Cambridge, 1948), *passim* (see index *sub* '*Bacchae*', words and themes—hunt'), esp. 100, 107f. For Vergilian 'signals' to Dionysus and the *Bacchae*, note, as well as Dido's comparison of herself to Pentheus (4.469f., see text; 4.470 is effectively a translation of Eur. *Bacch.* 918f.), Dido's metaphor 'bacchatur' (4.301) and the Bacchic simile that then ensues (301–3). It is possible that Vergil wishes to put us in mind of a version of the *Bacchae* by Pacuvius (see Servius on 4.469); this could explain the presence of 'Eumenidum' in the simile at 4.469f. (see further Austin ad loc.); on the other hand 'Eumenidum' may have arisen from contamination with the next simile (on which see Ch. 1 n. 51).

Aeneas, emphasizing his junior role but deleterious to his dignity. The imagery of bows and arrows, displaced from Cupid and applied in adapted form to him (see above, p. 195), might suggest a role *vis-à-vis* Venus as junior as, and comparable to, the one normally played by his half-brother: not very glorious.

Imagery again makes suggestions that the action itself does not. The explicit action, the epic voice, offers very little information on Aeneas' role in the love-affair at Carthage. Further voices fill in the picture. Compare the situation with Venus. The epic voice tells us merely that she inflamed Dido with love. Motif and imagery, a further voice, align her with Euripides' Dionysus. Motif and imagery (hunting) also associate her directly with the tragic consequences of Dido's love: she the huntress is associated via her son's hunt with Dido's consequent wound and death. But this has been done before. Compare Vergil's use of military imagery in the story of Dido, in particular the images of siege and sack (above, pp. 19–20).

As not infrequently happens when I talk about Dido, I get carried away. The points I wish to have established for my immediate purpose (Ascanius) are as follows. First, whatever reputation hunting may have in Roman culture at large, in the *Aeneid* it turns out to be an ominous motif. After Book 4 we learn to greet it with apprehension. Secondly, and more particularly, we have observed that Aeneas imaged in the role of a hunter is, however intentionally or unintentionally, disastrous for other people. That is the impression we take away with us from the 'cerua' simile in 4.69ff.

Aeneas in the role of a hunter is, however intentionally or unintentionally, disastrous for other people. So is his son. Consider what happens at 7.476ff.:[70]

> Allecto in Teucros Stygiis se concitat alis,
> arte noua, speculata locum, quo litore pulcher
> insidiis cursuque feras agitabat Iulus.
> hic subitam canibus rabiem Cocytia uirgo
> obicit et noto naris contingit odore,
> ut ceruum ardentes agerent; quae prima laborum
> causa fuit belloque animos accendit agrestis.
> ceruus erat forma praestanti et cornibus ingens,

[70] On this scene see the excellent comments of J. Griffin, 'The Fourth *Georgic*', 66f.

The Hero and His Son

> Tyrrhidae pueri quem matris ab ubere raptum
> nutribant . . . (485)
> adsuetum imperiis soror omni Siluia cura (487)
> mollibus intexens ornabat cornua sertis
> . . .
> hunc procul errantem rabidae uenantis Iuli (493)
> commouere canes . . .
> ipse etiam eximiae laudis succensus amore (496)
> Ascanius curuo derexit spicula cornu;
> nec dextrae erranti deus afuit, actaque multo
> perque uterum sonitu perque ilia uenit harundo.
> saucius at quadripes nota intra tecta refugit
> successitque gemens stabulis, questuque cruentus
> atque imploranti similis tectum omne replebat.

On Stygian wings Allecto sped herself towards the Trojans, a new wile in mind, spying out the point on the shore where splendid Iulus was hunting wild beasts with snare and coursing. Here the hellish maid cast a sudden frenzy on his hounds, touching their nostrils with a familiar scent, so that they should give fiery chase to a stag. This was the first cause of sufferings, and fired rustic minds for war. There was a stag of excelling beauty and mighty in its antlers: this, snatched from its mother's breast, the sons of Tyrrhus, who were young, nurtured . . . Their sister Silvia had trained him to obey commands, and with devoted care would deck his antlers by winding soft garlands round them . . . While this stag was straying far afield, the frenzied hounds of huntsman Iulus started him . . . Ascanius himself too, fired by love of outstanding renown, aimed a shaft from his bent bow; nor did a god fail his uncertain hand; the arrow was driven with a loud rush and pierced both belly and flank. The wounded animal fled back within his familiar roof and moaning moved into the shelter of his stall; bleeding and like someone asking for help he filled the whole house with his plaints.

The parallel is striking. Ascanius wounds a deer that compels our sympathy: very clearly Vergil paints this episode as pathetic rather than athletic. So, like his father in image (4.69ff.), Ascanius in actuality wounds a pitiable deer, 'ceruus/cerua'. And this triggers off the Italian war. Of course it is not in any obvious way Ascanius' fault that his action should have this effect. Although his pursuit, like his father's, was determined, he had no idea, and he could have had no idea, of the terrible consequences that were to ensue. Nevertheless this fact remains: terrible consequences ensued. Like his father, Ascanius as a hunter turns out to be disastrous for other people.

The parallel between father and son is clear, established by the repeated hunting motif; and it needs to be interpreted. A further voice, exploiting invention and arrangement, as well as in a sense imagery, is commenting. Through it Vergil is saying, I think, nothing personally critical of Ascanius. Rather, he is insinuating something about patterns of behaviour, or patterns of fate. He is saying something about *cost*: the cost of the Trojan/Roman progress, and how it may be repeated. Aeneas in Book 4 did not intend to bring, or to help to bring, destruction upon Dido, but he did. Ascanius in Book 7 did not intend to bring, or to help to bring, destruction upon Italy, but he did. The son is falling into the same lamentable pattern as his father, as the repetition of the hunting motif helps us to perceive. And perhaps the pattern will go on being repeated, the regrettable cost go on being paid. The sinister and exact recall of father by son within the space of the *Aeneid* makes us wonder whether it is not, in Vergil's view, part of the fate of the 'Aeneidae' to cause or to contribute to the cause of suffering among those who were getting on tolerably well, until the Trojans and the Romans came along.[71] All sorts of prices had to be paid for 'imperium sine fine'. Thoughts along these lines are invited.

The character of Ascanius in Book 9, in the context of and in comparison with Nisus and Euryalus, has not been accorded the critical attention it merits. An article by Maurach is an important exception.[72] With much of what Maurach says I can agree. But in my reactions to Ascanius' first feat of arms, his shooting of Remulus Numanus (9.621ff.), I differ. I can appreciate that it is an important event for the Trojan cause. But I cannot accept that we can flatly interpret it as 'echte virtus' or see in it, without qualification or perturbation, the 'symbol of Ascanius' ability to fulfil what the fates have given him as his task'.[73] It is not surprising that critics fight a little shy of the scene. It has its puzzling aspects.

[71] With this remark cf. Parry's comments on the lamentation for Umbro (7.759f.), 107–10.
[72] G. Maurach, 'Der Pfeilschuss des Ascanius'.
[73] Maurach, 362, 368.

The Hero and His Son

Here is a summary of what happens. Remulus Numanus, Turnus' brother-in-law, taunts the Trojans, who in the absence of Aeneas are cooped up in their camp, with effeminacy, cowardice, and so on (9.598ff.). He boasts of the toughness of the Italians in a speech which develops into a manifesto of hardy Italian virtues. Ascanius cannot endure his boasts. He prays to Jupiter; Jupiter gives a favourable sign. Ascanius shoots an arrow, transfixes Numanus' head, and delivers a pungent vaunt. The Trojans are rapturous. Apollo in heaven enthusiastically praises the 'victorious Iulus'—and then he comes down from heaven, adopts a disguise, and advises Iulus to desist from further battle. That in outline is the episode. I shall quote the intervention of Apollo (638ff.):

> aetheria tum forte plaga crinitus Apollo
> desuper Ausonias acies urbemque uidebat
> nube sedens, atque his *uictorem* adfatur *Iulum*:
> 'macte noua uirtute, puer, sic itur ad astra,
> dis genite et geniture deos. iure omnia bella
> gente sub Assaraci fato uentura resident,
> nec te Troia capit.' simul haec effatus ab alto
> aethere se mittit, spirantis dimouet auras
> Ascaniumque petit; forma tum uertitur oris
> antiquum in Buten . . .
>   ibat Apollo   (649)
> omnia longaeuo similis uocemque coloremque
> et crinis albos et saeua sonoribus arma,
> atque his *ardentem* dictis adfatur *Iulum*:
> 'sit satis, *Aenide*, telis impune Numanum
> oppetiisse tuis. primam hanc tibi magnus Apollo
> concedit laudem et paribus non inuidet armis;
> cetera parce, puer, bello.' sic orsus Apollo
> mortalis medio aspectus sermone reliquit . . .
> ergo *auidum pugnae* dictis ac numine Phoebi   (661)
> Ascanium prohibent . . .

Then by chance from the region of heaven long-haired Apollo was looking down on the city and the Ausonian ranks, enthroned on a cloud, and with these words addresses *victorious Iulus*: 'A blessing, child, on your young valour! Thus does one climb to the stars, O born of gods and sire of gods to be! Rightly will all wars destined by fate to occur settle to rest beneath the race of Assaracus; and Troy cannot contain you.' As soon as he had said this he darts from high heaven, parts the sighing breezes, and seeks Ascanius. Then he changes his aspect to that of ancient Butes . . . On went Apollo, in all respects like the aged man, in voice, complexion, white hair, and savage-sounding arms, and with these words addresses *fiery Iulus*: 'Let it be enough, *son of Aeneas*, that Numanus has fallen by your weapons, unavenged: great Apollo grants you this first glory and does not grudge you weapons that match his own; for the rest, my child, refrain from war.' . . . And so, at the will and instruction of Apollo they [the Trojan chieftains] prevent Ascanius, *eager for war* . . .

There are various disturbing or complicatory factors. First, much of what the insulting Numanus says about the Italians would appear true and attractive to Italian ears, in other words, to Vergil's Roman readers; at times indeed his speech echoes Vergil's own enthusiasm for Italy and the Italians in the *Georgics*.[74]

Next, it may strike us that Ascanius' first feat of arms, a long-range shot with a bow, is a little *easy*, even invidious. That is not simply a subjective or anachronistic feeling. In Vergil's time the ethics of archery were a centuries-old and much debated problem.[75] Why, we may ask, did not Vergil give his young hero a clearly heroic first action? It does not ease one's concern to find that Vergil leads into Ascanius' feat with the bow via his love of hunting (590–2), that now ominous motif:

> tum primum bello celerem intendisse sagittam
> dicitur ante feras solitus terrere fugacis
> Ascanius . . .

Then first is Ascanius said to have aimed a swift arrow in war, accustomed before that to affright fleet wild beasts . . .

Thirdly, Apollo the archer-god, the Augustan god, praises him from heaven: but in his disguise, dressed as Ascanius' aged companion, he tells him as we have seen to desist. 'Let that be enough,' he says. Apollo seems, perhaps, in two minds.

A fourth point. Apollo's words to Ascanius recall the Homeric Apollo's words to Patroclus in *Iliad* 16.707–9. In that

---

[74] See Klingner, 515f; Horsfall, 'Numanus Remulus'; R. F. Thomas, *Lands and Peoples in Roman Poetry*, 98–100. Pöschl, 69, pertinently compares Evander. Some of Numanus' insults against the Trojans probably hit home too.

[75] Cf. Hom. *Iliad* 11.385–9; Eur. *Heracles* 157ff.; G. S. Kirk. *The Songs of Homer* (Cambridge, 1962), 290; Bond on Eur. *Her.* 161. There were, of course, social as well as ethical objections to archery.

passage there is a very clear implication that in one way or another Patroclus is, in Apollo's view, 'going too far'. Now if we sense Vergil's Homeric source and respond to the allusion, it must reinforce our impression that all is not totally well in Apollo's view. Apollo disguised as Butes seems definitely less enthusiastic than Apollo the archer-god in heaven.

A final point. Apollo restrains 'ardentem Iulum' ['the fiery Iulus']; and when the Trojan chieftains recognize and respond to Apollo's instruction, it is an 'auidum pugnae Ascanium' ['an Ascanius greedy for war'] that they hold back. Fieriness and greed for battle are, of course, familiar attributes of the epic hero. But the world of the *Aeneid* is not, so we have learnt, simply epic and heroic. Fieriness causes the Trojan mission problems (see below). Greed for battle causes us anxiety at another stage in the poem: when it is displayed by Ascanius' father (see below).

Complicatory factors: this is teasing invention. We should be prepared for further voices. I shall now attempt to synthesize and interpret the observations I have made. Numanus is by no means wholly admirable; and he stands in the way of the Trojan march to empire. But again we find the Trojans, in the person of Ascanius, involving people in regrettable *cost*. For, other things being equal, we would very much rather he did not kill Numanus, a hardy, estimable Italian. And Ascanius' own motive and behaviour here are open to question. We may find his honourable impulse to silence Numanus admirable, and deem the passion, 'ardor', that he displays as essential in an epic hero. But in an Augustan hero such passions are potentially problematic. They may conflict with the Augustan hero's Stoical duty—as the example of Ascanius' father demonstrates. Consider what happens in Book 4. Or consider Book 10. In Book 10 Aeneas is led into a sequence of enraged and pitiless killings that conflict with the Augustan ideal (enunciated by Anchises, 6.853) of clemency for the defeated.[76] Why? Because of passion, anger, a sense of honour outraged (the young Pallas' honour). This, in fact, affords us a parallel: here in Book 9, Ascanius his son is passionate, angry, his sense of

---

[76] Cf. 10.513f., 'proxima quaeque metit gladio latumque per agmen / ardens limitem agit ferro . . .', and the pitiless killings immediately ensue. Cf. further pp.155ff.

honour outraged. What does he do? He kills someone with an arrow at long range. This is not so disturbing a response as his father's will be in Book 10. But it is morally questionable, it is worrying, it perhaps does not bode well. Ascanius, it seems, is in danger of developing those aspects of his father's character which are the least desirable. His similarity to his father, in respect of undesirable traits of character, is seen even more clearly from the perspective of Book 12. The phrase 'auidus pugnae' recurs but once in the poem, of Aeneas at 12.430. That is the memorable moment discussed above when Aeneas embraces his son, and then returns darkly, Ajax-like, to a grim slaughter (on this scene, see Ch. 1 s. 1).

The problems presented by Ascanius' character and behaviour are perceived and understood by Apollo. We can see that Apollo is in two minds about Ascanius; and we can, I think, attempt to explain why: we can attempt to explain what is governing Apollo's thoughts and actions. Ascanius in this scene is victorious; and Apollo praises him for being victorious, 'his *uictorem* adfatur Iulum: "macte *noua uirtute, puer* . . ."' ['with these words he addresses *victorious* Iulus: "A blessing, child, on your valour . . ."']. Apollo knows that a will and capacity to conquer enemies, 'debellare superbos' (also Anchises' instruction, ibid.), a will and capacity to be victorious, is indispensable to the Roman hero, to the divine line of imperial rulers—and so he praises him. He praises him in connection with precisely this quality: 'his uictorem'. But Ascanius is also 'ardentem', 'fiery', and the 'ardentem Iulum' Apollo restrains, 'atque his *ardentem* dictis adfatur Iulum: "sit satis . . ."'. Why? Because Apollo *also* knows that such fiery passions can conflict with the Augustan hero's Stoic and Augustan duty. He knows this, of course, if from nowhere else from the example of Aeneas.[77] The affinity of father and son, which we have seen, is in fact something that is preoccupying Apollo in his 'sit satis' speech. He calls Ascanius 'Aenides'.

We should note Apollo's use of this patronymic. It is the only occurrence in the poem. It is therefore very emphatic. It focuses, I think, what is in Apollo's mind, the exact direction of

---

[77] Note too 'ardentem' at 9.198, 'ardentem adfatur amicum', Euryalus to Nisus; 'ardeo' also of, e.g., Pyrrhus (2.529), Dido (4.101, 6.467), Amata (7.345), the enraged Aeneas (10.514, 552), Turnus (12.55), etc.; but also of 'uirtus' (6.130).

The Hero and His Son

his thoughts. For, emphatically addressing Ascanius as '*son* of Aeneas', he is calling attention to his successor role, to his dynastic and imperial responsibilities—as son of Aeneas. But equally, addressing him as 'son of *Aeneas*', he is also calling attention to the fact that he is the son of a man who has qualities that conflict with as well as serve such grave imperial responsibility; and he, the son, is exhibiting the same dubious mixture at the moment. And so Apollo thinks it wise, dressed in the wise garb of old age, to restrain him as well as praise him. In fact he thinks it appropriate to withdraw him from the war altogether. Ascanius, it is to be hoped, will be a more successful hero than Aeneas, greater than Aeneas in Aeneas' role. And though he needs to mature and change, to develop unequivocally Augustan and Stoic virtue, he does have the time. There is hope. It is wise to keep him out of this war. This is, I think, Apollo's perception; it is the reason why he acts as he does. The interpretation fits the facts.

Finally, I should like to turn once more to that scene in 12.432 ff. where Aeneas addresses his son for the first and last time in the poem (see s. 11). In the light of what I have just argued, there is a point to be noted. Here is what he says (435–40):

> 'disce, puer, uirtutem ex me uerumque laborem,
> fortunam ex aliis. nunc te mea dextera bello
> defensum dabit et magna inter praemia ducet.
> tu facito, mox cum matura adoleuerit aetas,
> sis memor et te animo repetentem exempla tuorum
> et pater Aeneas et auunculus excitet Hector.'

From me, my child, learn valour and true endurance of toil. From others learn good luck. Now my right hand will defend you in war and lead you where are great rewards. But do you, when soon your age has grown to ripeness, be mindful; and, as you recall the examples of your kin, let your father Aeneas and your uncle Hector spur you on.'

Aeneas, like Apollo, perceives that Ascanius has time to mature ('when soon your age has grown to ripeness'). He does not, however, share Apollo's sense of Ascanius' need; Ascanius' need to develop other qualities different from or stronger than his own. For he says 'disce, puer, uirtutem ex me uerumque laborem' ['learn valour and true endurance of toil *from me*']; and he tells Ascanius to follow *his* and Hector's 'exempla'. He does so, even as he himself displays that troubling quality of greed for war, 'auidus pugnae' (430)—and when his own inclemency towards Turnus is imminent.[78] The two scenes of advice to Ascanius, Apollo's in Book 9 and Aeneas' in Book 12, seem to me suggestively linked, and divine and human perceptiveness compared and contrasted. So the character of Ascanius is adumbrated: he is like his father. But how he will develop is anybody's guess. We sense a plan on Apollo's part; but we hear Aeneas' last grim words to him. The rest is silence.[79]

---

[78] On 'auidus pugnae' see above. Anchises' authoritative instruction to Aeneas concerning clemency (above, pp. 4, 187) should be constantly in our thoughts in the last scenes of the poem, and, when Aeneas talks of 'uirtus', we should remember the ethical connotations of the word (Ch. 1 n. 12); we might in particular recall Publilius Syrus, 690 Duff (= 682 Meyer = S48): 'supplicem hominem opprimere uirtus non est sed crudelitas' ['to crush a suppliant *is not valour* but savagery'].

Andromache at 3.343 asks as a question what Aeneas at 12.440 issues as an instruction: 'et pater Aeneas et auunculus excitat [sc. Ascanium] Hector?' The simple viewpoint that this implies is of course excusable in her, less so in Aeneas.

[79] Barchiesi, 15: 'l'uomo della pace sarà piuttosto [than Aeneas], come chiaramente si intravede, il figlio'. I wonder.

5

Dramatic Irony

*Aeneas and the Shield; Aeneas and Aeneas;
Anchises and poetry*

At 8.523 ff. thunder and lightning occur in a clear sky, and clashing arms are seen. Aeneas remembers Venus' words and interprets the omen: war is imminent, and his mother will now bring him arms forged by Vulcan. With his Arcadian allies he leaves Pallanteum and camps in a numinous grove within sight of Tarcho and the Etruscans, from whom he will receive further assistance (597 ff.). Then, apparently, he retires to a 'secluded vale', for here Venus appears to him bearing the divine arms. It is obviously a special and climactic moment, and is marked as such by, among other things, Venus herself. She behaves quite differently from the tantalizing goddess who met Aeneas in Book 1 (314 ff.)—an episode which from more than one point of view is interesting to compare with this one. She appears here undisguised: it is a real epiphany (611). And instead of eluding her son, she actually seeks his embrace (615), a gesture unparalleled in the *Aeneid*. Above all, the moment is marked out by the provenance and splendour of the arms. Aeneas is astounded, unable to sate his eyes with looking upon them (617 ff.). The *pièce de résistance* is the shield with its 'indescribable texture' ['non enarrabile textum'] (625).

On this Vulcan has depicted salient moments of Roman history (626–9):

> illic res Italas Romanorumque triumphos
> haud uatum ignarus uenturique inscius aeui
> fecerat Ignipotens, illic genus omne futurae
> stirpis ab Ascanio pugnataque in ordine bella.

There the Lord of Fire, in full awareness of [the predictions of] prophets and in knowledge of the ages to come, had fashioned the story of Italy and the Romans' triumphs, there every generation of the stock to spring from Ascanius and the wars fought one by one.

And Vergil proceeds to describe these depictions for nearly one hundred lines. The centre-piece is a vivid display of the battle of Actium (675ff.).

For the reader this is indeed a climactic moment. As the battle narrative is about to begin, he finds this revelation—the third major revelation (cf. 1.257ff., 6.756ff.)—of the destiny for which Aeneas is struggling. For Aeneas too it is a climactic moment. With war imminent, he receives these splendid arms—and finds the shield inscribed with a majestic revelation of the destiny for which he is struggling. It is, it appears, his second such revelation, and one which we should suppose to be welcome. For the parade of heroes in the Underworld, his first clear sight of the future (he was not privy to 1.257ff.), had been splendid but not exactly seductive in the way it presented Roman history—and Aeneas was not seduced. It did not obscure the continuing need for a fearful *price* to be paid, and it had in fact been the spectacle of cost rather than splendour which had finally moved Aeneas, after long and significant silence, to utterance (6.863ff.).[1] So with war imminent this second revelation seems timely. And, as the pageant on the shield unfolds and the tale of triumph is disclosed, we may imagine Aeneas taking heart and being inspired in his purpose: here is the future for which he struggles and must fight, definite, tangible, his own. When finally he shoulders the shield, the action might seem to symbolize his state of mind: as he 'lifts on his shoulders the fame and fate of his descendants' (8.731)

---

[1] The major portion of Anchises' revelation provokes no expressed reaction from Aeneas (6.756-853). Anchises in a kind of coda (855-9) then draws his attention to the illustrious M. Claudius Marcellus (cos. 222 BC). This hero too elicits no response from Aeneas, but, tellingly, a pathetic descendant of his who walks by his side (Marcellus son of Octavia who dies in his twentieth year in 23 BC) does. Anchises' revelations are thus very far from inspiring Aeneas to confidence or jubilation; and for more than one reason, e.g. the heavy emphasis throughout on pain, cost, and suffering, this is not surprising. See further the important forthcoming article (*CQ*) of D. C. Feeney, 'Two Visions of History from Hell: Verg. *Aen.* 6.679–886, and Luc. 6.777–820'; also Clausen, 86. Other scholars badly mistake the effect of Anchises' revelations on Aeneas: e.g. Otis, 306f. ('his spiritual regeneration is finally accomplished'), Klingner, 489. La Penna, lxii–iii, ducks this important question: 'In ogni modo ciò che conta nell'incontro è la rivelazione in sé, rispetto alla quale gli attori finiscono col restare secondari.'

we might infer an Aeneas shouldering the burden of his people's future, convinced and determined in his knowledge of fate.

The above account is true except in one vital respect. Vergil's description of the shield discloses a tale of triumph and reveals Aeneas' destiny *to us*. What Aeneas gazes on are marvellous, meaningless images (8.729–31):

> talia per clipeum Volcani, dona parentis,
> miratur rerumque ignarus imagine gaudet
> attollens umero famamque et fata nepotum.

Such things he marvels at on the shield of Vulcan, the gift of his mother, and *knowing nothing of the events rejoices in the image of them*, lifting on his shoulder the fame and fate of his descendants.

Aeneas therefore shoulders the burden of his people; but he cannot meantime take heart from a revelation of the future, because for him there is no such revelation. Vulcan's 'full awareness of prophets and knowledge of ages to come' is not extended to him (for Aeneas there is more than one sense in which the 'texture' is 'indescribable'); and Venus is cheating him almost as much with this 'image' as she did with the 'false images' he complained of in their meeting in Book 1 (1.407f.): even when a god tries to be kind to Aeneas, the kindness is incomplete. The pictures on the shield in fact mean one thing to us, another to Aeneas: what we have here—when we recall or reread lines 626ff.—is something akin to *dramatic irony*.[2] And our knowledge relative to Aeneas' ignorance should focus that ignorance. Vergil's invention is here underlining a feature of the poem that is important throughout it. Aeneas toils in the service of gods and nation without the sort of knowledge of the function of that toil which would make it more easily supportable. The path of gods and nation is hard and comfortless. So it is for Aeneas, even at this late stage in Book 8: the point is focused by dramatic irony, by a further voice.

'The pictures on the shield mean one thing to us, another to Aeneas.' Compare the depictions on the temple of Juno in 1.456ff. *Aeneas* sees episodes that warrant the deduction (461f.): 'here too [in Carthage] honour has its due; here tears

---

[2] Useful comments on dramatic irony in W. B. Stanford, *Ambiguity in Greek Literature: Studies in Theory and Practice* (Oxford, 1939), 66f.

fall for men's lot, and mortality touches the heart.' *We* see brutal, unpitied moments in the downfall of Troy. Aeneas must think that the pictures radiate sympathy and esteem for the gallant and pathetic defeated. We realize that they were erected in triumph over the defeated, and in celebration of the victors. For this is the temple of Juno, one of the arch-enemies of Troy.[3] Thus, when we read Aeneas' words (461 f.) 'sunt hic etiam sua praemia laudi, / sunt lacrimae rerum', then survey what is actually on the temple, and remember whose temple it is, we should again have a sense of dramatic irony: the pictures on the temple mean one thing to Aeneas, another to us. I should interpret this irony to be exposing a need to believe in our disheartened hero, an act of wish-fulfilment, credulity.[4] A further voice operating by dramatic irony is commenting on him, and I am not sure that it is sympathetic.

A further voice operating by dramatic irony comments on Aeneas on other occasions (cf. how it was used to show up Evander, and Evander's views about heroes and monsters, pp. 32–8). In Book 2, for example, Aeneas unwittingly comments on Aeneas and the Trojans, and in the process creates a thought-provoking dramatic irony.

Consider 2.379–82:

> improuisum aspris ueluti qui sentibus anguem
> pressit humi nitens trepidusque repente refugit
> attollentem iras et caerula colla tumentem,
>   haud secus Androgeos uisu tremefactus abibat.

As one who firmly planting his foot on the ground has trodden on a snake unforeseen amid rough briars and in terror shrinks suddenly back as it rears up in anger with dark swelling neck: likewise did Androgeos draw away, terrified by the sight.

The Greek Androgeos comes across Aeneas' band of Trojans and, after a few moments, realizes he has fallen in with ene-

---

[3] Thus, more or less, Horsfall, 'Dido in the Light of History', 8; Coleman, 150; Johnson, 103 ff. *Contra* e.g. Servius on 1.461, 'omnis Aeneae sollicitudo de moribus Afrorum est, quam nunc picturae contemplatione deponit. qui enim bella depingunt, et uirtutem diligunt et miseratione tanguntur'; Austin on 1.461 f. with bibliography.

[4] Slightly differently, Johnson, 104: 'There is nothing in the pictures to cheer Aeneas, and in fact he is not cheered. He deludes himself into feeling heartened because the realities he confronts are, literally, intolerable.'

mies. He starts back, and Aeneas the narrator gives him this simile. Clearly the snake figures the Trojans, and the unwary treader Androgeos. Aeneas, we may infer, wishes to bring the Greek's sudden timidity and startled movement vividly before his audience's eyes. That was the sort of expressive power the comparison would have for him—as it had done for Homer.[5] For us it means something more. It fits into a linked sequence of imagery and motifs (cf. Ch. 4 s. 12), extending through Book 2; and in this way Vergil makes it insinuate ideas that Aeneas could not possibly intend. Snakes were a familiar symbol of, among other things, death and deceit.[6] Their ominous and ugly associations are strikingly activated early on in Book 2 when monstrous serpents devour Laocoon and his sons (201ff.); the dreaded Pyrrhus, a 'reborn Achilles', is shortly to be compared to a snake that has sloughed off its skin (471ff.); meanwhile and subsequently, further more or less obvious details fill out the sequence.[7] So Aeneas, in his heroic account of the Trojans' desperate deeds, gives Androgeos' movement vivid pictorial illustration; but unwittingly, in *Vergil*'s context, he is associating the Trojans with unTrojan and invidious symbols. While Aeneas makes his point, Vergil's point is to comment on imminent Trojan actions. In the next moments they will disguise themselves in Greek armour and, protected thereby, will embark on a sequence of slaughter. They will, in fact, match the hated deceit of the Greeks with their own brand.[8] The simile at 379ff. is a presage of this, designed to disturb. Deceit in warfare was something that the Trojans' descendants, the Romans—leastwise, the moral and traditional among them— deplored and eschewed.[9]

[5] Cf. *Iliad* 3.33ff. (The simile there describes Paris' reaction on seeing Menelaus, thus Trojan fear in the face of a Greek. Vergil transfers it to Greek fear of Trojans.)
[6] See Knox, esp. 379f., 392; Eden on 8.697. Knox has a summary of the role of snakes in the *Aeneid* at 384 n. 9.
[7] See Knox.
[8] Note 2.62, 'dolos' (of Sinon); 65, 'accipe nunc Danaum insidias et crimine ab uno / disce omnis'; 252, 'Myrmidonumque dolos' (the wooden horse, etc.). Then note Coroebus' 'dolus an uirtus, quis in hoste requirat?' (2.390).
[9] Cf. Livy, 1.53.4, 'postremo minime arte Romana, fraude ac dolo, adgressus est' and 42.47.1ff., 'legationem . . . ita renuntiarunt, ut nulla re magis gloriarentur quam decepto per indutias et spem pacis rege. . . . pars senatus adprobabat; ueteres et moris antiqui memores negabant se in ea legatione Romanas agnoscere artes' (the whole chapter bears interestingly on our passage).

The simile means more to us than it means to Aeneas who utters it: we could call this dramatic irony. Linked imagery insinuates into the simile a comment on Aeneas[10] and the Trojans: that is one further voice. Dramatic irony shows this comment to issue from an opinion of the hero different from the hero's own. It focuses the fact that Aeneas' own simple and heroic way of viewing himself is by no means the only one, and thereby suggests perhaps a certain lack of self-knowledge in the hero (similarly below). Dramatic irony supplies another further voice.

An earlier simile in Book 2 is comparable in its effect. Aeneas describes the Trojan band as they begin their desperate foray in the following manner (2.355–9):

> inde, lupi ceu
> raptores atra in nebula, quos improba uentris
> exegit caecos rabies catulique relicti
> faucibus exspectant siccis, per tela, per hostis
> uadimus haud dubiam in mortem . . .

Then, like robber wolves in a dark mist who are driven blindly on by irresistible, savage hunger, and whose cubs at home wait for them with thirsty jaws, we pass through swords, through enemies to certain death . . .

Aeneas, we may infer, wishes to illustrate the Trojans' desperation, their valour, viciousness, and so on.[11] That is the sort of expressive power that wolves have in the heroic, Homeric tradition: they are fearsome, heroic creatures.[12] Wolves have positive expressive power in the Roman 'heroic' tradition, too,[13] and Aeneas might be thought—though it is of course strictly anachronistic—to have that sort of resonance in mind as well. What he cannot have in mind is another implication in the

---

[10] Some think that Aeneas' mode of expression in 2.391ff. is meant to suggest that he personally did not participate in the deceit; see Heinze, 37; Stahl, 167. It does seem that Aeneas or Vergil words himself carefully here; but at 396, 'uadimus immixti Danais haud numine nostro' (on which see Conington-Nettleship), Aeneas certainly identifies himself with the stratagem, without comment; and that is quite sufficient for the point I am making.

[11] Cf. R. D. Williams (1–6) ad loc.: 'The effect here is to reinforce the concept of 'furor', and to suggest the wild and violent anger of the Trojans'. Neither he nor any other commentator I have consulted sees any more in the simile.

[12] Cf. *Iliad* 11.72, 12.299–306, 16.156; H. Fränkel, *Die homerischen Gleichnisse* (Göttingen, 1921), 73–5.

[13] See Ogilvie on Livy, 3.66.4.

simile, something that *Vergil* contrives. Once more the simile means more to us than it does to Aeneas.

As often, it repays us to examine Vergil's sources for points of difference as well as similarity. Important details may be highlighted thereby. We remember Vergil's change from 'goat-herds' to 'farmers' at 12.451ff. (p. 7)—and we can note that the crucial idea of skin-sloughing in Pyrrhus' simile at 2.471ff. is an addition to Vergil's main Homeric source.[14] In the present simile we find that there is no authority for the salient detail of the cubs whose hunger is part of the wolves' reason for prowling. Vergil, it seems, wishes to present a slightly different type of 'fearsome, heroic creature' from his epic model, one differing in point of *motive*. We must therefore ask: why this difference: why this added detail?

The addition does not in fact correspond with Aeneas' situation. It does not correspond rather glaringly. Aeneas and the Trojans do *not* have the motive of needful young driving them into battle. On the contrary: Aeneas' explicit and vividly expressed motive was a glorious but senseless and strictly selfish death (314–7; 353, 'let us rush into battle and die'; 359, above; and Aeneas still boasts of his efforts to die at 2.431–4, from the perspective of Carthage). The only way Aeneas might have served his dependants, his 'cubs', was to do what Hector's ghost had expressly told him to do: flee the city. Of this very duty Venus had subsequently to remind him—and it also took much time and prodding before Aeneas with no great grace complied (Ch. 4 s. 10). Vergil's added detail therefore highlights *contrast*. Aeneas may see himself and his band as similar to heroic wolves, but Vergil's context and Vergil's presentation of those wolves points up a difference: while Aeneas thinks of the Trojan actions as despairingly heroic, Vergil insinuates the point that this heroism was at the expense of Aeneas' dependants (a further voice comments). So, once again, the simile means more to us than it does to Aeneas; and again the difference has an effect like that of dramatic irony—and another further voice. Dramatic irony emphasizes the fact that

---

[14] The main source is *Iliad* 22.93–6. Vergil draws on Nicander and his own *Georgics* for the skin-sloughing and other details: see the discussion by E. J. Kenney, in *Creative Imitation and Latin Literature*, eds. D. West and T. Woodman (Cambridge, 1979), 105 ff.

while the hero has one interpretation of his actions, there is another which is less flattering: one again senses a suggestion of a lack of self-knowledge in the hero.[15]

Dramatic irony focuses a viewpoint different from that of another authoritative character in the poem, the hero's father. This occurs at one of the most significant moments of the poem. The famous, commanding epilogue to Anchises' revelation of the Roman future runs as follows (6.847–53):

> excudent alii spirantia mollius aera
> (credo equidem), uiuos ducent de marmore uultus,
> orabunt causas melius, caelique meatus
> describent radio et surgentia sidera dicent:
> tu regere imperio populos, Romane, memento
> (hae tibi erunt artes), pacique imponere morem,
> parcere subiectis et debellare superbos.

Others will shape bronze so that it breathes in softer lines (yes, I am sure), and will mould from marble living features; they will plead causes better, and with the rod trace the journeyings of heaven and tell the risings of stars: do you, Roman, remember to rule the nations with your power—these will be the arts for you—and to impose civilization upon peace, to spare the subject, and to war down the proud.

Aeneas, now addressed as 'Roman', hears his imperial mission, stirringly summarized. We may, incidentally, see Anchises as speaking outside and beyond the dramatic situation to the 'Roman' of the future; but it is also right in context for him to address Aeneas in this way. At this critical moment the hero's gaze is being turned from the past to the future, from Troy to Rome: so that the appellation is appropriate and pregnant.

And it is a stirring summary, with what seems a clear message. The structure 'excudent alii . . . tu memento . . .' is of a familiar rhetorical type in which one course of action or belief is more or less politely dismissed in favour of another: cf. Hor. *Odes* 1.7.1 ff., 'laudabunt alii claram Rhodon . . . me . . .' ['others will praise illustrious Rhodes . . . as for me'], 1.1.3 ff., Tibull. 1.1.1 ff., and so on. Anchises is dismissing the arts as an appropriate occupation for Aeneas and the Romans, imposing

---

[15] Cf. above, p. 212, and see Ch. 4 n. 56 for a not dissimilar suggestion concerning Aeneas.

Dramatic Irony

upon them instead the more worthy and manly task of empire, government, and civilization. This is a patriotic and imperial view of the Romans' function that is easily and respectably paralleled: Cicero for example, though he is amusingly different on the topic of oratory, says something very similar.[16] Anchises' message is in fact patriotic, orthodox, inspiring, and, we might say, unambiguous—as befits his position and character.

We might say it is unambiguous. But there is a striking paradox to notice, introducing ambiguity.[17] Anchises' dismissal of art occurs, of course, within Rome's greatest work of art, the *Aeneid*. This is not a paradox of which Vergil will have been unaware, or thought that we should ignore. Anchises himself unwittingly calls attention to it by his ironical play on the word 'artes': claiming for the Romans the manly arts ('hae tibi erunt artes') he alludes also to the fine arts he disclaims: and in so doing surely reminds *us* that his disclaimer occurs within a work of consummate fine art. Another fact adds to the paradox: immediately preceding these art-eschewing lines, Anchises is made to include a resounding quotation from the poet Ennius.[18] There is in fact a great irony to the passage, again a type of dramatic irony. Considered *in character*, as Anchises' speech, the lines require the clear, patriotic interpretation given to them above. Considered in *Vergil's* context, they have a different colour: to us, in this context, they should mean something different.[19] At the very least we could say that

---

[16] Cic. *Tusc.* 1.1 ff. (oratory at 1.5). Further interesting parallels for the sentiments in Norden on 6.847–53: he quotes from the imperial encomiast Aristeides.

[17] This point is missed by the commentators, who see nothing but the patriotic imperialism: e.g. Klingner, 493f.; Otis, 314 with n. 1; R. D. Williams, *GR* 11 (1964), 61; G. Williams, 208f. Even critics generally receptive to Vergilian doubt and equivocation see none here: Clausen (whose instincts were seen to be sound above, n. 1), 86, Parry, 121. Comments by Johnson, 108, promise well, but dissolve into dissolving pathos.

[18] 6.846, 'unus qui nobis cunctando restituis rem' is from Enn. *Ann.* 363 Sk., 'unus homo nobis cunctando restituit rem'. And there are most probably further Ennian echoes in lines 841 ff.: Vergil ends his catalogue 'not with the chronologically latest figures, but with the heroes of Ennius's narrative described in Ennian language': see Wigodsky, *Vergil and Early Latin Poetry*, 72. In a variety of ways, therefore, Vergil manages to give his great poetic predecessor prominence at a crucial and paradoxical moment.

[19] Cf. very interestingly what they mean to J. Griffin at 'The Fourth *Georgic*', 65 f.

Vergil's context and the irony it produces suggest that Vergil cannot be at one with his character in his view of art, government, and the Roman mission. How much at odds with it we cannot, from this evidence, say. But the dramatic irony must make us wonder. It intrudes a striking further voice at this crucial part of the epic.

6
Further Voices

I hope that I have now given practical demonstration of Vergil's modes of communication in the *Aeneid*, of the ways in which he insinuates unexpected material and opinions. In particular I have shown that unexpected political material is insinuated: the *Aeneid* probes, questions, and occasionally subverts the simple Augustanism that it may appear to project;[1] and it does this by means of its further voices. It is now time to pick up and expound more fully this idea of voices, the epic voice and further voices,[2] and show how they relate to each other, and to other more familiar topics in epic narrative technique. And I shall provide more examples.

Vergil can be shown to adhere, or to appear to adhere, to many classic, 'Homeric' principles of epic narrative. To a surprising

---

[1] It should follow from this that I sympathize with what Johnson, 11, calls the 'pessimistic Harvard school' of Vergilian criticism, best represented by the works of Parry, Putnam, and Clausen. I find this company congenial, always stimulating, but just occasionally embarrassing. (American 'pessimists' tend to laud a paper by R. A. Brooks: '*Discolor Aura*', *AJP* 74 (1953), 260–80; I got little or nothing out of this.) We pessimists are by the by still vigorously attacked: see, e.g., A. Wlosok 'Der Held', 19–21, and, by the same author, 'Vergil in der neueren Forschung'. For an unequivocally patriotic and imperial Vergil see the works of Otis, Klingner, Perret, and Brisson—these scholars have hearkened too much to the epic voice.

For an excellent and balanced survey of the ways in which the *Aeneid* has been read, see R. D. Williams, 'Changing Attitudes to Virgil'; also Suerbaum. (Wlosok, 'Der Held', provides a similar survey for the figure of Aeneas.)

[2] With my notion of a variety of voices, we may compare other scholars' description of the *Aeneid* as 'polysematic'. Cf. Conte, *Il genere*, 106, 'è pur vero che alla critica moderna la poesia virgiliana va rivelando una complessità strutturale (ai più vari livelli) che invita a non mortificare la polisemia del testo ma a percorrerne attentamente le stratificazioni nascoste'; Johnson, Ch. i, esp. 17–20. Polysematic the *Aeneid* of course is, but I find this a rather lifeless and unnecessarily impersonal way of articulating Vergil's devious, searching communications. By contrast, the notion of 'two voices', a public and a private voice (cf. Parry; R. D. Williams, 'The Purpose of the *Aeneid*', 32, 41; R. O. A. M. Lyne, 'La "Voce privata" di Virgilio nell'Eneide', *Museum Patavinum*, 2 (1984), 5–21; also G. Williams, *Technique*, 164ff.), seems to me naïvely intentionalist and vastly over-simple: see my comments, Introduction, pp. 2–3.

degree he, like Homer, pursues techniques contributing to the self-effacement of the author, and to the consequent 'objectivity'[3] of the epic story; like Homer, he seems to have wished to create an action able, within certain bounds, to stand free from its author and to develop independence, conviction, credibility: to approximate, in short, to the condition and impact of a stage drama. When he does this, to the extent that he does this, he is using what I call his epic voice (cf. Introduction). I shall now illustrate and amplify this point. And I shall seek by degrees to identify with greater exactness—if it is possible—the point at which further voices make themselves felt. The question to which I attend first is therefore this: how does the anonymous epic narrator remove himself from the stage to allow his action to develop credibility? Or to put that question another way: what is the characteristic behaviour of the epic voice? I comment sparingly on Homer side by side with Vergil.

Both poets are careful in the matter of *plot*. Homer, especially in the *Iliad*, makes event follow upon event with *plausibility*, if not the rigid 'probability' that Aristotle imputes to him.[4] Vergil likewise.[5] Event motivates event: even an episode like the catabasis is prudently and plausibly prepared for in the action, more plausibly in fact than the *Odyssey*'s *Nekyia*.[6] There may be many reasons for such scrupulousness; but one result of it is credibility. It is a way of assisting authorial self-effacement. Consider the alternative. An improbable sequence of events must remain personal, the product of a creator: the obvious, or only, explanation of why one event leads to another is that the author's whim so ordains. Credibility can hardly establish itself in such circumstances: we register an author's tall story rather than experience something resembling a lifelike drama. Vergil and Homer seem to have aimed at the latter. Contrast, interestingly, the splendidly inconsequential 'plots' of the Callimachean

---

[3] I shall shortly dispense with this familiar but misleading term: below, p. 225.
[4] Cf. A. Lesky, *A History of Greek Literature* (London, 1966), 23 ff.; Aristotle, *Poetics*, 1451^a (and 1450^b), 1459^{a-b}.
[5] See Heinze, 436 ff. (and *passim* in Part I); Quinn, 64–71.
[6] Aeneas' despair after the ship-burning (5.604 ff.) makes Anchises' intervention (5.723 ff.) natural and necessary. And what Anchises promises to show him (737) is or should be just what Aeneas needs: knowledge of what his suffering is for. Cf. Otis. 278–80. But see Ch. 5 p. 208.

poets, Callimachus in the *Hecale*, Catullus in 64. The sequence is not plausible, we *are* constantly aware of the ingenious creators present and controlling the sequence; and the whole is incredible, gloriously so. But Callimachean poets do not aim at self-effacement and an epic voice, 'objectivity' and credibility. They exploit narrative genres for, precisely, self-advertisement and artificial display.

We may now note something in the practical business of narration, something we can call *symmetry of treatment*.[7] It is a temptation for a story-teller to dilate upon his more colourful episodes, to hurry over duller stretches: to produce, therefore, an elliptical and unbalanced narrative serving interest or novelty. But to do that is also, inevitably, to obtrude the presence of the narrator and hence to impede the story's independence: the reader must remain conscious of the contriving creator who produced such an idiosyncratic, unnatural account. Now this sort of technique is again exactly what the unrepentant Callimacheans exhibit—Catullus in 64, Callimachus in *Hecale*. They flout symmetry of treatment just as they cheerfully ignore plausibility of plot, producing spectacularly unbalanced narratives. They do not care for self-effacement and its consequence, credibility. On the contrary they are bent on self-advertisement and a parade of their own 'ars', τέχνη.

Homer and Vergil on the other hand, constructing an epic voice, caring for self-effacement and credibility, avoid all obvious imbalance, and respect symmetry of treatment. Mostly: on occasion both of them admit precisely what I have been describing.[8] For example, in the wanderings of Aeneas in *Aeneid* 3, in the episode of Hercules and Cacus in Book 8, in the wanderings of Odysseus in *Odyssey* 9, in Phoenix's account of Meleager in *Iliad* 9. The reason for this is clear, and most illuminating. I have said that such abandonment of natural symmetry suggests the contriving decision of an author, an authorial *presence*—and Vergil and Homer are unwilling for their presence to be felt in this way, since they want their voices to be epic and their narratives to achieve independence from

---

[7] Cf. Heinze, 359.
[8] References in Heinze, 357 ff.; cf. too 21 ff.

them, and thus credibility. But on the occasions in question Vergil and Homer are not themselves narrating; a *character* is: Aeneas, Evander, Odysseus, Phoenix. And clearly a character who is part of the story can credibly let himself and his inventiveness be evident in a way that the author, who is not a character in the story, cannot.

I interrupt this list of self-effacing features in Homer's and Vergil's technique to look more closely at an example, and to make an important point. At *Aeneid* 12.872 ff. Juturna laments. It seems surely plausible, credible, 'symmetrical'; only Juturna's revelation of her relationship with Jupiter (878) is, on reflection, provoking (above, p. 87):

> 'quid nunc te tua, Turne, potest germana iuuare?
> aut quid iam durae superat mihi? . . .
> . . .
>   cur mortis adempta est   (879)
> condicio? possem tantos finire dolores
> nunc certe, et misero fratri comes ire per umbras.
> immortalis ego? aut quicquam mihi dulce meorum
> te sine, frater, erit? . . .

'How, Turnus, can your sister avail you now? What awaits me now hard at heart with grief? . . . Why has the condition of death been taken away? Now surely would I be able to end such anguish, and pass through the shadows a companion to my poor brother. I immortal? Will anything of mine be sweet to me without you, my brother? . . .

Now this speech, even without taking account of the reference to Jupiter, should affect our response to surrounding events.[9] For instance, to the death of Turnus. Aeneas kills Turnus at the end of the poem, fulfilling an admirable human impulse, to avenge dishonour. Juturna's lament reveals an equally admirable human impulse: love for a brother. And Aeneas is going to kill that brother, causing Juturna to lament for ever. Admirable human impulses are shown to be in conflict. Again: to Aeneas in the last two lines of the poem Turnus is the slayer and dishonourer of Pallas. Perhaps that is how we should see him

---

[9] Quinn, 374, disagrees and, I think, spectacularly misinterprets the speech ('It is . . . of no great consequence what Iuturna says'). A. Barchiesi, *MD* 1 (1978), 99–121, has some fine comment. (The point I make above is unaffected by whether we understand the speech to be a monologue or not: see Ch. 2 n. 49).

too, without Juturna. To Juturna he is a beloved brother—as she vividly communicates in the lament. In consequence we may not be able to see Turnus in Aeneas' black and white terms either. In short, Juturna's lament (leaving aside the reference to Jupiter) gives important and suggestive context to the concluding scene. In its wake we should find it difficult to pretend that Aeneas acts in splendid isolation.

Of course it is not Juturna's own intention to generate this sort of implication. She is simply, and plausibly, bound up with her own grief. Vergil's invention of her speech, and his arrangement of it, generates the implications. And this is what I wish to assess. What is the relation of this use of invention and arrangement to those I discussed above as examples of communications by further voices? If one considers Juturna's lament as I have just now considered it (that is, excluding the reference to her loss of virginity), it is not perceptible that Vergil is provokingly including unexpected material or tendentiously juxtaposing it—or wilfully dilating upon it; it is not perceptible that the epic voice is being relinquished. The situation with this material is different from, say, the timely and provoking reference to Iarbas' parentage at 4.198 and indeed from the pointed disclosure of Juturna's own past affair with Jupiter (12.878). And yet: is it? We find that her lament, in its basic form, prompts us to troubling questions—the effect, we might think, of a further voice; and perhaps, on reflection, such an *extensive*, *proleptic* lament is somewhat artificially contrived at this hectic point in the action. The point I wish to make is that there is not an absolute dividing line between 'objective', 'epic' invention and arrangement and the workings of a further voice. All epic and indeed dramatic poetry may exploit invention and arrangement for tendentious purposes, 'encouraging' us, we might say, to certain views; and Vergil's tactics with, for example, Iarbas are simply an extension, though a large extension (his tactics with Juturna's basic lament are a small extension) of what Homer does with the proleptic quasi-laments of Hecuba and Priam at the beginning of *Iliad* 22[10] or Sophocles with the

---

[10] Lamentation concludes and quasi-lamentation introduces the climactic duel. We are encouraged to see the *tragic* significance of what might have been a simply heroic scene.

second stasimon and the action of the *Oedipus Tyrannus*.[11] In conclusion, what I wish to stress is on the one hand that a further voice which exploits invention and arrangement in this way is simply an extension of epic technique and the epic voice, and not rigidly separable; on the other hand, I would stress that the effects which Vergil achieves by it can be (as we have seen) very distinctive and, I would say, even personal.

I revert to features in Homer's and Vergil's technique which show them interested in epic self-effacement and dramatic credibility. Consideration of *general action* will take us to a relevant point. Drama cannot easily present general action. Nor does it want to. Built around vivid individuals it more easily focuses our imagination and commands our belief. And indeed it is true to life. In the common experience of mankind, life is a matter of individuals and particularities, not masses and generalities. Vergil and Homer have the means for general description. But like dramatists, and to be dramatic, they prefer in their epic voices to focus on individuals.[12] They want us to respond to free, created people, rather than read their own descriptions and comment. Warfare is typically a question of personal combats in both Homer and Vergil, often a long sequence constructed around a single hero: an *aristeia*. War is presented to us through individuals. So are the trials of civilians under siege, so is the contempt of a vigorous native army for soft Asiatics: Andromache, Helen, Hecuba in *Iliad* 6 and 22, Remulus Numanus in *Aeneid* 9; and so on. Homer's and Vergil's narratives are again made to approximate to drama; and to life.

Our epic poets do not just build their actions around individual characters. They exploit characters' *direct speech*.[13] A

---

[11] Cf. R. P. Winnington-Ingram, *Sophocles: An Interpretation* (Cambridge, 1980), 179–204. Note this remark (202): 'they [the chorus] have been made to give, proleptically, an explanation of the fall of Oedipus. And it is the wrong explanation. It is shown to be the wrong explanation by an elaborate chain of ironies . . .'. The action of the *Oedipus* thus encourages us to certain views about the beliefs underlying the chorus's song.

[12] References in Heinze, 355–7.

[13] See Bassett, 57 ff., Heinze, 403 f. Plato and Aristotle were sufficiently struck by Homer's use of direct speech to form an exaggerated view of its role: *Rep.* 393 A, *Poetics* 1460ᵃ.

large part of stage drama's own ability to achieve independence and conviction is of course due to the fact that it is entirely made up of characters speaking their own words: in one sense the author of stage drama effaces himself entirely. An obvious way for an epic poet to increase his poem's approximation to drama is for him to construct his action so far as possible likewise: in direct speech. Homer and Vergil do. According to a calculation of Bassett's,[14] three-fifths of the Homeric poems are taken up by the 'ipsissima uerba' of characters. In the *Aeneid*, if we include Aeneas' narration of Books 2 and 3, nearly half the epic is direct speech.[15]

Both poets, to maintain their epic voice, make direct speech do unexpected jobs, ingeniously. The value they attach to its dramatic quality becomes clear. Andromache and the other women of course utter their trials, Numanus utters his scorn. There are more striking examples. Consider how often epic poets must be tempted to give us a whole range of information themselves, for example what the repercussions of an action will be, what is going on in characters' minds, and, simply, mere factual information (who's who, and so on). But if they were constantly to tell us such things themselves, we should become too aware of them and the impersonality of the epic voice would be compromised. So characters often do the job for them. Andromache tells us what will be the repercussions of Hector's death in her lament at the end of *Iliad* 22; Venus tells Aeneas, and us, who Dido is; Tiberinus tells us about Evander;[16] in both poets (though in Vergil much less than Homer) characters utter their own moods and motivations—in the dramatic manner.[17]

The whole of an epic poem cannot, of course, be conducted in characters' 'ipsissima uerba'. There must be reported action. What is the policy of the epic voice here? Our attention must now shift more narrowly to style.

Homer composes the direct speeches of his epic in such a way as to be vividly mimetic, colourfully reflective of the speakers'

[14] Bassett, 85.
[15] To be precise, 46.75 per cent: see Highet, 302.
[16] Cf. Heinze, 375, 390f.
[17] Cf. Heinze, 333, 427–31.

feelings. Not so his own narrative.[18] At the beginning of the *Iliad* he asks (1.8): 'Who then of the gods brought the twain to strife and contention?' The answer comes:

Even the son of Leto and Zeus. For he in anger with the king sent an evil plague on the army, and the people perished, because the son of Atreus had dishonoured Chryses his priest . . .

and the epic proceeds to unfold 'objectively', reflecting in its style none of the author's personal feelings or idiosyncrasies, and little or none of his subjective reactions. In this way authorial self-effacement is continued. As little as possible is put between us and the (reported) actions. Credibility is again the result. Consider the alternative. If we were constantly aware that *Homer* was telling the story—larding the narrative with his feelings, constantly introducing his reactions, playing with the style—we should be constantly reminded that the story was someone's fiction, and credibility would be hazarded. Hence the epic voice chooses an epic, 'objective', reporting style. Homer is (again) quite unlike Callimachus who, presenting himself as personally inspired to an individual role, speaks in a personal, idiosyncratic, subjectively affected style. Homer reports in the epic style, dutifully relaying dramatic truth from the Muse. So (approximately) he presents himself,[19] and so he acts.

The epic voice in reported action has accepted and traditional habits: this statement has important and misunderstood implications. In the course of reporting the actions themselves Homer's epic voice will, with the same stylistic neutrality, with the same authorization from the Muse, supply 'obituary' information on fallen heroes, switch to the present tense to describe localities (ecphrasis), give reasons with the conjunction 'for', foreshadow the future, inform us 'what would have happened' in another set of circumstances, make comparisons, and

---

[18] On Homer's 'objective' narrative style (and the mimetic style of his speeches), see Fränkel, 37–44; Bassett, Chs. 2 and 3; Griffin, *Homer*, Ch. iv; Effe. La Penna, xlix, has brief but admirable remarks on both Homeric and Vergilian 'objectivity'.

[19] On Homer's view of the Muses and their significance for his epic, see Bassett, 28–31. At salient points in the poem Homer then reminds us—by fresh invocations—that it is his role to relay truth from the Muse; he reminds us, to use my terminology, that he speaks in an epic voice. So does Vergil. See Norden on *Aen.* 6.264 ff.

employ other such 'interpositions'. But such interpositions are not narrator's 'interpositions' which 'break the Epic Illusion' (to use someone else's terminology).[20] They are part of the resources of the epic voice, part of its stock in trade, and do not disturb it (to use my terminology). Nothing disjoins narrative of reason or comparison from narrative of event, nothing that imposes itself upon an audience.[21] What imposes itself upon an audience is that Homer presents all such narration—events, reasons, similes, circumstantial information, and so on—similarly: as all deriving from the Muse. Of course from one point of view reasons do not have the *objectivity* of events. But 'objective', although customary, is not really a satisfactory epithet to describe Homer's reporting mode. Better to say that he neutrally reports what may plausibly 'derive from the Muse', but *only* (usually) what may 'derive from the Muse'. And in Homer reasons and events have the same status—*qua* deriving from the Muse. To conclude: the epic voice makes comparisons and so on: but it does not cease thereby to be the epic voice. When Homer tells us not just that Achilles rushed upon Aeneas but that he rushed upon him like a lion (*Iliad* 20.164ff.), we do not have the impression of a 'further voice', of something intruding and interrupting the tenor of the epic voice.

I acknowledged above that invention and arrangement in the epic voice can in fact encourage us to views. So can these smaller items in the reported narrative. For instance, the 'obituary' information supplied about Hippothous (*Iliad* 17.300f.) might encourage us to the view that Hippothous' death was not heroic but pathetic.[22]

---

[20] Bassett, Ch. 4. Effe, 172ff., is better than most on this topic.
[21] Differences in the language of the similes, perceptible to the philologist (cf. G. P. Shipp, *Studies in the Language of Homer* (2nd ed., Cambridge, 1972); some summarizing remarks, 208ff.), do not, I think, force themselves upon a natural and rapt audience. In general scholars overemphasize the distinction between narrative of event and narrative of comparison: e.g. Fränkel, 40, Shipp, op. cit., 212, Quinn, 432. It may be that similes evoke scenes more familiar to the audience than the general heroic context (as ancient critics were fond of observing or prescribing: Aristotle, *Topica*, 8.1, 157ᵃ 14ff., Σ A on *Il.* 16.364 (and cf. Σ T on *Il.* 15.362–4), Quint. 8.3.73, with an interesting hedge in ref. to Vergil). But that does not mean that the audience will sense a change in the voice of its obliging and authoritative narrator. On the contrary; it becomes used to the narrator providing these comparative narrations as part of his received stock in trade.
[22] Cf. Griffin, *Homer*, 108f.

At the beginning of the *Aeneid* (1.8) Vergil asks: 'Musa, mihi causas memora' ['O Muse relate to me the reasons']. And at line 12 the answer starts to roll forth:

> urbs antiqua fuit (Tyrii tenuere coloni)
> Karthago, Italiam contra Tiberinaque longe
> ostia, diues opum studiisque asperrima belli,
> quam Iuno fertur terris magis omnibus unam
> posthabita coluisse Samo.

There was an ancient city, the home of Tyrian settlers, Carthage, confronting Italy and the faraway mouth of Tiber, rich in wealth and most harsh in the pursuits of war. This city Juno is said to have cherished above all other lands, holding even Samos less dear.

The answer starts to unfold on the face of it in much the same sort of dispassionate way as Homer's. In his reported action, as well as in matters of plot and so on, Vergil makes a considerable attempt to maintain an epic voice, like Homer. Of course, vast qualifications of that statement necessarily follow. But Vergil does base himself in a traditional language. Not much overt or immediate stylistic idiosyncrasy is put between us and the reported actions (contrast, say, Catullus in 64). Vergil does use an epic voice—and employs the traditional habits of the epic voice: deriving similes, circumstantial information, reasons, as well as events, from the Muse, like Homer. It is true that he gives himself more prominence in the first line of the poem than Homer gives himself ('arma uirumque cano' ['*I* sing of the arms and man'])—in the manner of the cyclic poets in fact.[23] But 'Musa mihi . . . memora' still firmly disjoins the poem from the dark-complexioned Mantuan's personal imagination;[24] this is no Hesiodic-Callimachean *Dichterweihe*. And the voice is consonant: substantially epic. Before we dissociate Homer and Vergil in the way they conduct reported action, we must as in everything else acknowledge the extent of their association. To identify Vergil's new modes of 'further voices' we must identify what are not such. Vergil uses 'obituary' information with 'encouraging' effect: compare, for example, Galaesus at 7.536–9, who, in an attempt to make peace, dies 'iustissimus unus' ['of all men the most just']. We are encour-

[23] See Austin on 1.1; Effe, 182; Buchheit, 13.
[24] Buchheit, 18.

Further Voices

aged to sensations of irony, pathos, and so on.[25] But Homer uses obituary information likewise. When Vergil suggests to us that Aeneas was like a bull it is not immediately clear that this interrupts the tenor of the epic voice any more than when Homer tells us that Achilles was like a lion. But I should stress the word 'immediately'.[26]

I shall now concentrate more particularly on the task, already essayed above (p. 221), of trying to identify the precise point at which further voices actually impinge. In the process I shall include for consideration passages in which some scholars believe that not just a further voice but a *personal Vergilian voice* is evident.

A striking feature of Vergil's style in reported action is that it can reflect and convey the feelings of participating characters, 'die Empfindung der handelnden Personen', in Richard Heinze's words. This is the phenomenon which Brooks Otis discusses in his chapter *The Subjective Style*.[27] When Vergil writes thus, it might seem a point at which he is departing from the epic voice. Certainly it is not an objective style—but I have already indicated the unsatisfactoriness of that term in this connection (p. 225).

To illustrate how Vergil's style can convey characters' feelings, I cite a couple of unobtrusive examples taken from Heinze.

At 6.5ff. the Trojans arrive in Cumae:

iuuenum manus *emicat ardens*
litus in Hesperium; quaerit pars semina flammae
abstrusa in uenis silicis, pars densa ferarum
tecta *rapit* siluas inuentaque flumina monstrat.

---

[25] Schlunk, 20, has interesting comment on this obituary.
[26] See below, p. 237.
[27] See Heinze, 169ff., 362–6 (the quoted phrase, 362); Otis, 41ff., esp. 46–8; Pöschl, 175ff., develops the idea. For something similar in Homer see below, pp. 231–2, and note too this comment of N. J. Richardson (*CQ* n.s. 30 (1980), 276) on the *Iliad* scholia: 'their comment on the passage describing the return journey of the Greeks from Chrysa after the appeasement of Apollo is surely very acute (BT.1.481): "the poet shares in their joy and now paints a fair picture . . . of their return-journey, in contrast to the journey out . . .". This must in fact be one reason why Homer expands in a lyrical way the "typical scene" of a voyage at this point, whereas the outward journey to Chrysa is very matter-of-fact.' See further Richardson ad loc.

> at pius Aeneas arces, quibus altus Apollo
> praesidet, *horrendaeque* procul secreta Sibyllae,
> antrum *immane*, petit . . .

In *hot haste* the youthful band *dashes* forth onto the Hesperian shore. Some seek the seeds of flame hidden in veins of flint, some *raid* the woods, the thick home of wild animals, and point to streams they have found. But pious Aeneas seeks the citadels which lofty Apollo watches over, and the *tremendous* cavern hard by, hidden haunt of the *awesome* Sibyl . . .

The language reflects the aggressive vigour in the young men's minds as they land and explore. It also reflects the awed reaction of Aeneas to surroundings he finds fearsome (though as often in these cases there is an ambiguity, a not unproductive one: here, between Aeneas' and the epic voice's reaction; cf. below, p. 231). Next, 8.86ff.

> Thybris ea fluuium, quam longa est, nocte tumentem
> leniit, et tacita refluens ita substitit unda,
> mitis ut in morem stagni placidaeque paludis
> sterneret aequor aquis, remo ut luctamen abesset.

All that night long Tiber calmed his swelling river and flowing back with silent wave stood fast, in order to smooth the surface of his water like a gentle pool or peaceful fen, that the oars might have no struggle.

The description of Tiber's actions here contains clear suggestions of Tiber's benevolent motives (notice especially 'mitis', 'placidae', 'luctamen').

Now this is not something that Homer typically does (though see above, p. 227 n. 27 and below, pp. 231–2). But I would maintain that there is no distinctive further voice here. There is nothing that we could not say 'derived from the Muse', nothing that is inconsonant with a dutiful epic voice, nothing intruding an unexpected opinion. An epic voice is no more compromised by suggesting information on characters' feelings or indeed by stating it (note how, for example, Nisus is said to be 'iam uictor ouans' ['already rejoicing in victory'], at 5.331) than it is by stating that Galaesus was 'most just' or suggesting that Aeneas was 'like a bull'. Vergil may be extending the scope of the epic voice, but not, as yet, anything more.

I select a more interesting example, this time a simile. Eurya-

Further Voices

lus' head drooping in death is given the following comparison (9.435–7):

> purpureus ueluti cum flos succisus aratro
> languescit moriens, lassoue papauera collo
> demisere caput pluuia cum forte grauantur.

As when a purple flower, cut by a plough, wilts in death; or as poppies with wearied neck bow their heads when weighted by some chance shower.

The poppy simile derives from Homer and so fits happily into the epic voice.[28] It is suggestive enough, conveying to us the idea of youth cut down, fragile and evanescent youth, pathos, and so on; but it is suggestive in the manner of the epic voice. The simile of the flower cut down by a plough derives from Catullus (62.39ff., 11.22ff.) and through Catullus from Sappho (105c LP); and it adds an additional and unexpected nuance. It is an erotic image, as the literary history confirms.[29] More particularly, it suggests the death of love, the destruction of innocent beauty, and so on. Now the source which would most naturally give rise to this sort of thought is Nisus. The simile therefore conveys his, a character's, feelings,[30] and what we have here is again a character's feelings conveyed in the style: in the moment of Euryalus' death the text communicates to us Nisus' reactions at the death of his lover.[31] Now, in conveying a character's feelings the simile is of course doing nothing unexpected. But conveying these feelings in this way at this time it is. For death naturally prompts thoughts of love in elegy, not the epic;[32] the image is generically unepic; and in a 'Homeric' poem homosexual love is in itself odd.[33]

Are we therefore tempted to talk here of something other

---

[28] *Iliad* 8.306f.
[29] Sappho's context was probably epithalamial: see D. Page, *Sappho and Alcaeus* (Oxford, 1955), 121.
[30] This type of 'character-subjectivity' (in similes) happens not infrequently: see e.g. Otis, 59–61. An interesting case is made by Pöschl, 89f., that Dido's Diana simile at 1.498–502 reflects among other things *Aeneas'* reactions to Dido. See too Pöschl, 172; and on this simile see further p. 123 n. 41.
[31] Cf. Klingner, 564f., Otis, 388f. (but Otis glosses an important point: see below, n. 33).
[32] See below, p. 235.
[33] See Griffin, *Homer*, 104 n. 4. The passionate homosexual nature of the love of Nisus and Euryalus should not be glossed over (as happens at Otis, 49, Pöschl, 139); cf. Cydon and Clytius at 10.325, and see further below, p. 235.

than an epic voice? On the face of it the answer to this might seem: no. The situation here is the same as at 6.5ff. and 8.86ff. (above). On the other hand, the insinuation of this information at this time in this way is individual. Invention, arrangement, and style are idiosyncratic and teasing: Vergil's presentation of Nisus puts a climactic moment of the epic action in an unexpected and thought-provoking light. Perhaps, counting all the factors, we should grant that our impression is of something else besides an epic voice obediently relaying information from a Muse. At the very least we might say that Vergil is radically extending the epic voice's scope.

Consider now the use of the epithet 'infelix' of Nisus at 5.329 and of Dido at 1.712, 749, 4.68, 450, 529; consider too the description of Dido as 'misera' at 1.719 and 4.697. On what authority, in what voice, are Dido and Nisus said to be 'unfortunate' and 'pitiable'?

The most eminent Vergilian scholars detect here a striking intrusion into the epic voice: they detect Vergil's personal voice.[34] They regard these epithets as examples of subjective authorial empathy, Vergil's own personal reaction to the character. I think that this interesting judgement is faulty. We must recall (above, pp. 224ff.) that in his epic voice Vergil delivers a great deal of information about his characters: their circumstances, their motives (in the manner of Homer), their feelings. Are these new instances radically different? I do not in fact see that Vergil's revelation that Dido is 'infelix' is markedly different from his revelation in Galaesus' obituary that Galaesus was 'iustissimus'. With both I would compare Homer's epic voice reporting that a character is 'foolish'[35] and indeed that a character is 'pitiable', οἰκτρός.[36] I do not see that any one of these reports clearly differs from another, or from the other information that the poets 'derive from the Muse' and report in their epic voices. If we want clearly to except one (Dido's infelicity— or Iphidamas' pitiableness) some good reason for doing so should be given. And certainly—to look at it a different way—

---

[34] Otiš, 50, 70ff.; Heinze, 371; Klingner, 385, 386 n. 1; La Penna, li–lii; Effe, 184.
[35] On this cf. Fränkel's terse but useful comment, 37 n. 31.
[36] Contrast Griffin, *Homer*, 110.

Further Voices

it is possible to discover communications from voices besides the epic one, which are more striking and intrusive than the intimation that unfortunate Dido was unfortunate.

But I am the last person artificially to reduce possibilities in Vergil's text, or to deny ambiguities. I do not, of course, rule out Vergil's personal participation in the belief that Dido was unfortunate. What I deny is that we can exclusively assign the above epithets to a personal voice of his as opposed to the epic voice of the narrative poet. The same situation obtains, it seems to me, when it is said that Dido 'merita nec morte peribat' ['did not die by a death she deserved'] (4.696).[37]

And ambiguity in voice, in the authority for an opinion,[38] exists on innumerable other occasions, with most productive consequences. For example, when at 1.21f. we are told that Juno had heard 'hinc populum late regem belloque superbum / uenturum excidio Libyae; sic uoluere Parcas' ['that from this source [the Trojans] would come a people wide in power and proud in war for the downfall of Libya; for such was on the scroll of the Fates'], whose opinion does 'superbum' reflect? The epic voice's? Juno's? The Fates'? (These last two would be examples of characters' feelings conveyed in the style.) Or another voice's, even Vergil's personal voice? I suppose the most obvious answer is Juno's, but the text does not let us exclude the others—even, ultimately, the last. And that thought is provoking: in general, and especially in retrospect from 6.853, the epithet seems not one that its recipient would welcome. Again: in whose view are the Carthaginian lands at 4.281 'dulcis'? It would be wrong, I think, to *confine* this opinion to Aeneas[39] (though it certainly does reflect Aeneas' opinion: character's feelings in the style again). And lest we be tempted to think that we are dealing with an entirely un-Homeric phenomenon, consider the dogstar simile at *Iliad* 22.25–33:

---

[37] Contrast, e.g., Austin ad loc.: 'Virgil's judgement here is explicit . . .'.
[38] The topic I am touching upon here could be called ambiguity in *point of view*, on which see conveniently W. C. Booth, *The Rhetoric of Fiction* (Chicago, 1961); cf. too Conte, *Il genere*, 65ff., 153ff. For a recent treatment of the topic in relation to the *Aeneid*, see M. Bonfanti, *Punto di vista e modi della narrazione nell' Eneide* (Pisa, 1985).
[39] La Penna, lxxxviii, Otis, 83, do so confine it.

Further Voices

> Τὸν δ' ὁ γέρων Πρίαμος πρῶτος ἴδεν ὀφθαλμοῖσι,
> παμφαίνονθ' ὥς τ' ἀστέρ' ἐπεσσύμενον πεδίοιο,
> ὅς ῥά τ' ὀπώρης εἶσιν, ἀρίζηλοι δέ οἱ αὐγαὶ
> φαίνονται πολλοῖσι μετ' ἀστράσι νυκτὸς ἀμολγῷ·
> ὅν τε κύν' Ὠρίωνος ἐπίκλησιν καλέουσι.
> λαμπρότατος μὲν ὅ γ' ἐστί, κακὸν δέ τε σῆμα τέτυκται,
> καί τε φέρει πολλὸν πυρετὸν δειλοῖσι βροτοῖσιν·
> ὣς τοῦ χαλκὸς ἔλαμπε περὶ στήθεσσι θέοντος.
> ᾤμωξεν δ' ὁ γέρων . . .

Him [Achilles] the aged Priam was the first to behold as he raced all-gleaming over the plain: like the star which comes at harvest time, whose rays shine most brightly among the many stars in the darkness of night; men call it the dog of Orion; it is the brightest, but it is an evil sign, and brings much fever on wretched mortals; in this way did the bronze shine on Achilles' breast as he ran; and the old man groaned . . .

The development ('but it is an evil sign . . .') clearly foreshadows the destruction that Achilles is bringing. This sense of foreboding could be Priam's (character's feelings in the style), or it could belong to the epic voice. Or, much better, we could assign it to both.[40]

My final example in this category is the most provoking. At 5.3f. the Trojans in their ships see Carthage ablaze. The text then makes this observation (4–7):

> quae tantum accenderit ignem
> causa latet; duri magno sed amore dolores
> polluto, notumque furens quid femina possit,
> triste per augurium Teucrorum pectora ducunt.

What reason kindled such a fire is obscure. But the thought of the harsh anguish caused when a great love is desecrated, and the knowledge of what a frenzied woman can do, led the hearts of the Trojans along paths of gloomy foreboding.

Whose opinion does 'polluto' ['desecrated'] reflect? In what voice is that uttered? R. D. Williams (1–6) ad loc. comments: 'I take the word to reflect not the attitude of the Trojans, but their thoughts about Dido's attitude . . . We cannot say how far Virgil identifies himself with Dido's feeling . . .'. In short, he takes this extraordinary description to be an 'indirect' example

---

[40] For another example of character's feelings conveyed by Homer's style, see above, n. 27.

Further Voices 233

of characters' feelings in the style (the Trojans' opinion about Dido's opinion)—and tentatively canvasses more disturbing ideas. That is right, or on the right lines. It is impossible to prove that 'polluto' reflects more than, ultimately, Dido's own attitude.[41] But it is also impossible to prove that the epic voice which utters it does not endorse its utterance; and impossible not to wonder whether this abruptly discordant participle does not issue from a further voice, from a personal voice.

Comment should finally be made on actual 'interventions' in the text by Homer and Vergil: apostrophe, exclamation, and the like.[42] Homer uses such devices sparingly, Vergil also sparingly but more strikingly. These, particularly when uttered 'to the audience', may seem patently the product of a further voice, perhaps a voice personally Homer's or Vergil's. But they should be judiciously weighed.

When Homer switches to an apostrophe in 'But when for the fourth time he rushed on like a god, then for you, Patroclus, did the end of life appear; for Phoebus met you, a dread god, in the fierce conflict' (*Iliad* 16.786–8), and to a question to the audience in 'And how would Hector have escaped the fates of death, had not Apollo for the last and latest time come near to him . . . ?' (22.202–4), do we get a sense of a different, indeed a personal voice (some ancient scholiasts seem to get such an impression)?[43] Or do we respond to what are certainly vivid devices, unusual devices, but devices of the epic voice nonetheless? I think in fact that when we abandon the misleading term 'objectivity' (above, p. 225) and ponder instead what may or may not be a habit of the epic voice, we find ourselves less tempted to facile distinction—and more inclined to be truthful to the text. I should myself prefer to call these interventions vivid devices of the epic voice.[44] Certainly they do not uncover Homer in the way in which some further voices seem to me to uncover the personal Vergil in some of the passages discussed in this book.

What of Vergil's own interventions? A prominent example is

---

[41] Vergil is far more evasive than, say, Parry, 120, believes.
[42] Vergilian references in Heinze, 370–2, Pease on 4.65; I disagree with their interpretation.
[43] See Σ T on 16.692f., 787, and M.-L. von Franz, *Die aesthetischen Anschauungen der Iliasscholien* (Zurich, 1943), 35.
[44] Not dissimilarly, Effe, 177.

the exclamation and comment in response to the despoiling of Pallas at 10.501 ff. This greatly exceeds the scope of interventions in Homer and, if it does not suggest a different voice, is certainly a surprising extension of the epic voice. However, what is actually said here must be carefully appraised, and is in fact neither as decisive nor as striking as many scholars infer: no unexpected or vital opinion is dramatically revealed.[45] The intervention at 12.452, though formally far less conspicuous, reveals a further voice much more perceptibly and interestingly (Ch. 1 p. 5).

Among Vergil's other examples, two will strike us particularly. Vergil promises to Lausus, and to Nisus and Euryalus, immortality in his verse. He responds to the death of Nisus and Euryalus thus (9.446-9):

> fortunati ambo! si quid mea carmina possunt,
> nulla dies umquam memori uos eximet aeuo,
> dum domus Aeneae Capitoli immobile saxum
> accolet imperiumque pater Romanus habebit.

Happy pair! If my song avails anything, no day will ever remove you from the memory of time, so long as the house of Aeneas shall dwell on the Capitol's immovable rock, and the Roman Father hold sway.

He apostrophizes the dead Lausus thus, in an abrupt parenthesis (10.791-3):

> hic mortis durae casum tuaque optima facta,
> si qua fidem tanto est operi latura uetustas,
> non equidem nec te, iuuenis memorande, silebo

Harsh death's misfortune and your noble deeds—if it shall be that antiquity makes so great an exploit believable[46]—I shall indeed not leave unsung, nor you, O unforgettable youth.

Now Heinze (whose interpretation is very different from, say, Klingner's)[47] emphasizes that in these examples Vergil intervenes *as a poet*; and he argues that they are generically allied to turns of phrase in the catalogues, 10.185, and 7.733, 'nec tu carminibus nostris indictus abibis / Oebale' ['nor will

---

[45] See Lyne, 'Vergil and the Politics of War', 195f.; also Barchiesi, 43-52, esp. 46.

[46] Conington-Nettleship ad loc.: 'i.e. if a deed, which if reported of modern times would be justly disbelieved, should be thought credible because it is sufficiently ancient. Virg. means to say that the deed was only possible in antiquity'.

[47] Heinze, 372; Klingner, 561, 563.

you, Oebalus, pass unhonoured in our song']—which, in turn, are based on formulae deriving from Homeric invocations of the Muse. He does not think that these interventions are therefore very striking.

There is some truth in Heinze's position, but it misses a couple of vital points. Heinze is particularly wrong concerning 9.446ff. I first of all leave aside the exclamation 'fortunati ambo'. What Heinze's opinion boils down to is, in my terminology, that Vergil makes his interventions in the epic voice: the epic poet, deriving authority from the Muse, exclaims about his duties and their effects. This is not quite the case. We have seen (p. 226) that Vergil is not unambiguous in his deference to a Muse, even at 1.1ff.; the same situation obtains at 7.37ff.— though not at 7.641ff. And at 9.446ff., at least, his inclination *not* to be deferential to the Muses is amplified into self-assertion: '*mea* carmina'. Vergil therefore enters his text at this point certainly as a poet, and not in a more personal and private capacity: to this extent Heinze is right. But he does not enter as a conventional epic poet using a conventional epic voice. He promises perpetuation in *his* poetry. That is provoking invention, suggesting a further, indeed personal, voice.

When we bring into play 'fortunati ambo', we find Heinze more strikingly wrong. It is vital to understand this particular part of the intervention correctly. It has been misunderstood, in more than one way.[48] It is not (for example) uttered with reference to Nisus' and Euryalus' prospective felicity in being hymned by Vergil. It is a romantic response to the preceding text, and is occasioned most immediately by 'placidaque ibi demum morte quieuit': it is a reference to Nisus' and Euryalus' felicity *in love*, in particular to their elegiac union as *lovers in death*.[49] In content therefore, and timing, this particular phrase

[48] A mixed bag of misinterpretations is provided by La Penna, lxxviii; Quinn, 206; G. Williams, 205f.
[49] Vergil may well have in mind Bion's comment on a romanticized and eroticized Achilles (xii Gow; I owe this reference to Jasper Griffin): 'Happy are those who love, when passion is equally reciprocated . . . Blessed was Achilles when his companion was alive; happy was he in dying since he did not keep dread fate from him.' For elegiac love and death, see Prop. 2.20.18, 'ambos una fides auferet, una dies' ['one selfsame day shall bear us both away in one selfsame love'], also Tibull. 1.1.59f. A felicitous death like this is what Nisus and Euryalus achieved, and Vergil is moved to apostrophize them in consequence. (A death such as this is also, we might remember, what Amata vowed: Ch. 3 p. 116, 12.61–3.)

is most striking, and in its content and timing—rather than in its form—we must detect a further voice: it is invention and arrangement of a most provoking kind to offer this elegiac and romantic opinion at this point in an epic story. Compare the implications of Euryalus' 'cut flower' simile (above, p. 229); but a further voice is yet more distinct here. I would be inclinded to say: a personal voice.

Study of Vergil's interventions therefore reveals what I think we should by now expect: no hard and fast rule, but a sliding scale. Some of them cohere quite closely with the practice of an epic voice. On other occasions the invention and arrangement are provoking enough to suggest a further voice. And other instances are indeterminate.

It will be noted that in the above discussions I keep returning us to the basic headings: invention, arrangement, and style. It is at this level that we can best describe the workings of further voices in Vergil's *Aeneid*. A seemingly promising category like 'interventions' is revealed to be too crude or too large. Further voices in Vergil's *Aeneid* operate by the provoking inclusion of unexpected material and by placing material at tendentious moments; or they effect their communication by leaning on devices of style like imagery, ambiguity, and so on. And they do so discreetly. Although further voices are irremovably there, a reader inclined to hearken to the epic voice need not be irritatingly diverted. And, being thus discreet, further voices do not fatally hazard, although they do impair,[50] the credibility of the action, the achievement of the epic voice.

The *discretion* of further voices (Introduction) may now be more exactly described. It may be imputed to a fact alluded to above. All voices in the *Aeneid* exist on a *sliding scale*. The modes of communication operated by further voices are an extension, not a replacement, of those operated by the epic voice. The epic voice deploys invention, arrangement, and style; further voices deploy invention, arrangement, and style of a not radically dissimilar sort, but more provokingly, suggestively: provokingly and suggestively enough to introduce communications that seem idiosyncratic and disturbing. The result of this is: a sliding scale. As we have seen, invention and

[50] See e.g. my comment on characterization, Ch. 1 p. 44.

arrangement in the epic voice may at least *encourage* us to views, and Juturna (p. 221) is just one point on a sliding scale on which Iarbas (p. 85) is another. Style and invention in the epic voice convey the feelings of the young Trojans at 6.5 ff.; style and invention convey the feelings of Nisus at 9.435–7, but there both style and invention are provoking enough to suggest, perhaps, a further voice. Vergil apostrophizes Lausus at 10.791–3, Nisus and Euryalus at 9.446–9. At 9.446–9 we detect a further voice. But can the invention and arrangement of 10.791–3 be exclusively assigned to the epic voice? And between 9.446–9 and (say) 10.185 f. would there be any point at which we would be able to draw a clear line? Another example: is the simile at (say) 1.148 ff. qualitatively or quantitatively different from 12.451 ff. (pp. 5 ff.)? In all cases we must realize: we have to do with a sliding scale. Further voices are simply more provoking with the modes of, and in the same area as, the epic voice. Hence their unobtrusiveness, their discretion.

Their unobtrusiveness in operation may be particularly appreciated in the light of the following consideration. An individual passage may shift its point on the sliding scale, depending on how we look at it, depending on whether we approach it in the expectation of an epic or further voice. Thus a reader inclined to hearken to the epic voice need by no means be irritatingly diverted. I give a final example (most of those discussed in this book would serve).[51] At 12.715 ff. the clash of Aeneas and Turnus is compared to the clash of two bulls. We may hear an epic voice. Aeneas and Turnus are like bulls: fierce, formidable, massive, and so on. Such is the sort of inference we may make—hearkening to the epic voice, paying attention to the sort of connotations the simile would bring with it from the epic tradition[52]—and then the drama may proceed. Or we may pause, in the expectation of a further voice—and find one (if not more). We may note that the simile at 12.715 ff. is linked to one at 12.103–6 in which Turnus alone, frenziedly preparing for battle, is compared to a bull in similar prep-

---

[51] Cf. e.g. what I say above, p. 12 on 12.451 ff.
[52] The simile is based on one used by Apollonius of the boxers Amycus and Polydeuces, *Arg.* 2.88 f. But much of the material comes from *Georg.* 3.219 ff. This is a significant fact in view of what I proceed to say. It could be argued that *Aen.* 12.715 ff. independently allude to the context of *Georg.* 3.

aration; and then note that that simile strikingly alludes to—it quotes—a passage in the *Georgics* (3.232–4) in which a bull in such preparation provides an *exemplum* of frustrated, fruitless passion. Turnus' destructive and wasteful motivations are adumbrated; and a further voice associates Aeneas, on the threshold of Augustan victory, in the same sterile passion.[53] The passage has shifted its point on the sliding scale. A further voice with a disturbing communication has intruded—but with the devious unobtrusiveness that we should expect of Vergil.

[53] This passion is, among other things, sexual. First we should note that the fruitless passion of the bull in *Georg.* 3.232–4 is sexual, so the simile at 12.103–6 imports that motive into the *Aeneid*; this is obviously pertinent for Turnus whose motives are at least in part demonstrably sexual (12.70, 'illum turbat amor', etc.). Next we note that Apollonius' bulls, Vergil's primary source at 12.715ff., are simply and plainly sexual in their motivation ('for a grazing heifer', *Arg.* 2.89), and so of course are the bulls of *Georg.* 3.219ff. (see n. 52); and we note that Vergil, although he has discreetly blurred such a motive at 12.715ff. and suggested others to accompany it, has not eliminated it: note 'mussantque iuuencae' (718). If we sense allusion to Apollonius, this sexual motive is of course focused; it is similarly focused when we pick up the link between 12.715ff. and 103ff.—and there is the possibility that 12.715ff. directly allude to *Georg.* 3.219ff. (n. 52). Further voices emphatically reinforce the point: the heroes struggle for their Helen. A gloomy thought at this stage in the poem. Gloomier ones follow.

Select Bibliography

The works listed below are referred to by author's name, or author's name and abbreviated title.

Standard commentaries on Vergilian and other classical texts are cited similarly, but I think it unnecessary to list them all here. There is, however, a possibility of confusion in the case of R. D. Williams's commentaries on the *Aeneid*. I therefore specify that by 'R. D. Williams on *Aeneid* 3' and 'R. D. Williams on 5' I mean his separate commentaries on those books (Oxford, 1962 and 1960); and by 'R. D. Williams (1–6)' and 'R. D. Williams (7–12)' I mean his general commentaries on *Aeneid* 1–6 (London, 1972) and *Aeneid* 7–12 (London, 1973) respectively.

Much other bibliographical material is cited in full at relevant points in the book.

Abbreviations of periodical titles generally follow the conventions of *L'Année philologique*.

ANDERSON, W. S., 'Vergil's Second *Iliad*', *TAPA* 88 (1957), 17–30.
——'*Pastor Aeneas*: On Pastoral Themes in the *Aeneid*', *TAPA* 99 (1968), 1–17.
BAILEY, C., *Religion in Virgil* (Oxford, 1935).
BARCHIESI, A., *La traccia del modello: effetti omerici nella narrazione virgiliana* (Pisa, 1984).
BASSETT, S. E., *The Poetry of Homer* (Berkeley, Calif., 1938).
BOWRA, C. M., 'Aeneas and the Stoic Ideal', *GR* 3 (1933–4), 8–21.
BOYANCÉ, P., *La Religion de Virgile* (Paris, 1963).
BRIGGS, W. W., 'Virgil and the Hellenistic Epic', *Aufstieg und Niedergang der römischen Welt*, II.31.2 (1981), 948–84.
BRISSON, J.-P., *Virgile: son temps et le nôtre* (Paris, 1966).
BUCHHEIT, V., *Vergil über die Sendung Roms* (Heidelberg, 1963).
CAMPS, W. A., *An Introduction to Virgil's Aeneid* (Oxford, 1969).
CLAUSEN, W., 'An Interpretation of the *Aeneid*', *HSCP* 68 (1964), 139–47, reprinted in a revised version in Commager, 75–88; I refer to the latter pagination.
COLEMAN, R., 'The Gods in the *Aeneid*', *GR* 29 (1982), 143–68.
COMMAGER, S. (ed.), *Virgil: A Collection of Critical Essays* (Englewood Cliffs, NJ, 1966).

CONTE, G. B., *Memoria dei poeti e sistema letterario* (Turin, 1974).
——*Virgilio: Il genere e i suoi confini* (Milan, 1984).
Those parts of these two books which most pertain to Vergil are to be published in an English translation by Cornell University Press.
EFFE, B., 'Epische Objektivität und authoriales Erzählen', *Gymnasium*, 90 (1983), 171–86.
FEENEY, D. C., 'The Taciturnity of Aeneas', *CQ* n.s. 33 (1983), 204–19.
——'The Reconciliations of Juno', *CQ* n.s. 34 (1984), 179–94.
FRÄNKEL, H., *Early Greek Poetry and Philosophy*, translated by M. Hadas and J. Willis (Oxford, 1975).
GALINSKY, G. K., 'The Hercules–Cacus Episode in *Aeneid* viii', *AJP* 87 (1966), 18–51.
——*The Herakles Theme* (Oxford, 1972).
GIGANTE, M. (ed.), *Lecturae Vergilianae. Volume terzo: L'Eneide* (Naples, 1983).
GRIFFIN, J., 'The Fourth *Georgic*, Virgil, and Rome', *GR* 26 (1979), 61–80.
——*Homer on Life and Death* (Oxford, 1980).
——*Latin Poets and Roman Life* (London, 1986).
HEINZE, R., *Virgils epische Technik*, 3rd. ed. (Leipzig/Berlin, 1915).
HIGHET, G., *The Speeches in Vergil's Aeneid* (Princeton, NJ, 1972).
HORSFALL, N., 'Numanus Remulus: Ethnography and Propaganda in *Aen.* ix.598f.', *Latomus*, 30 (1971), 1108–16.
——'Dido in the light of history', *PVS* 13 (1973–4), 1–13.
——Review of: C. J. Fordyce, *P. Vergili Maronis, Aeneidos Libri vii–viii* (Oxford, 1977): *CR* n.s. 29 (1979), 219–23.
JOHNSON, W. R., *Darkness Visible: A Study of Vergil's Aeneid* (Berkeley/Los Angeles, Calif., 1976).
KLINGNER, F., *Virgil* (Zürich/Stuttgart, 1967).
KNAUER, G., *Die Aeneis und Homer* (Göttingen, 1964).
KNOX, B. M. W., 'The Serpent and the Flame: The Imagery of the Second Book of the *Aeneid*', *AJP* 71 (1950), 379–400. This is reprinted, with some footnotes omitted, in Commager. I refer to the original article.
LA PENNA, A., 'Virgilio e la crisi del mondo antico', in: *Publio Virgilio Marone: Tutte le opere*, ed. E. Cetrangolo, 2nd. ed. (Florence, 1967).
LYNE, R. O. A. M., 'Vergil and the Politics of War', *CQ* 33 (1983), 188–203.
——'Diction and Poetry in Vergil's *Aeneid*', *Atti del Convegno mondiale scientifico di Studi su Virgilio* (Milan, 1984), 2.64–88.

MAURACH, G., 'Der Pfeilschuss des Ascanius', *Gymnasium*, 75 (1968), 355–70.
OTIS, B., *Virgil: A Study in Civilized Poetry* (Oxford, 1963).
PARRY, A., 'The Two Voices of Virgil's *Aeneid*', *Arion*, 2 (1963), 66–80; reprinted in Commager, 107–23. I refer to the latter pagination.
PERRET, J., *Virgile: l'homme et l'œuvre* (Paris, 1952).
PÖSCHL, V., *Die Dichtkunst Virgils: Bild und Symbol in der Äneis*, 3rd. ed. (Berlin/New York, 1977).
PUTNAM, M. C. J., *The Poetry of the Aeneid* (Cambridge, Mass., 1965).
QUINN, K., *Virgil's Aeneid: A Critical Description*, 2nd ed. (London, 1969).
RIEKS, R., 'Die Gleichnisse Vergils', *Aufstieg und Niedergang der römischen Welt*, II.31.2 (1981), 1011–110.
SCHLUNK, R. B., *The Homeric Scholia and the Aeneid* (Ann Arbor, Mich., 1974).
STAHL, H.-P., 'Aeneas—An "Unheroic" Hero?', *Arethusa*, 14 (1981), 157–75.
STEINER, H. R., *Der Traum in der Aeneis* (Bern/Stuttgart, 1952).
SUERBAUM, W., *Vergils Aeneis: Beiträge zu ihrer Rezeption in Gegenwart und Geschichte* (Bamberg, 1981).
THOMAS, R. F., *Lands and Peoples in Roman Poetry: The Ethnographical Tradition* (Cambridge, 1982).
WARDE FOWLER, W., *Aeneas at the Site of Rome: Observations on the Eighth Book of the Aeneid* (Oxford, 1918).
——*The Death of Turnus: Observations on the Twelfth Book of the Aeneid* (Oxford, 1919).
WEINSTOCK, S., *Divus Julius* (Oxford, 1971).
WIGODSKY, M., 'The Arming of Aeneas', *C & M* 26 (1965), 192–221.
——*Vergil and Early Latin Poetry* (Wiesbaden, 1972).
WILLIAMS, G., *Technique and Ideas in the Aeneid* (Yale, 1983).
WILLIAMS, R. D., 'The Purpose of the *Aeneid*', *Antichthon*, 1 (1967), 29–41.
——'Changing Attitudes to Virgil', in *Virgil*, ed. D. R. Dudley (London, 1969), 119–38.
WLOSOK, A., *Die Göttin Venus in Vergils Aeneis* (Heidelberg, 1967).
——'Vergil in der neueren Forschung', *Gymnasium*, 80 (1973), 129–51.
——'Der Held als Ärgernis: Vergils Aeneas', *WJA* 8 (1982), 9–21.

General Index

'Absumptae uires', 57
Achilles
    and Aeneas, 108ff.
    and Turnus, 108f.
'Acri fixa dolore', 51, 56
Actions, and consequences, 70, 84–7
Aemilius Paulus, 152
Aeneas
    allusively compared to Achilles, 109–13
    allusively compared to Ajax, 9–12, 113f.
    allusively compared to Odysseus, 104–7
    an Augustan hero?, 4, 9, 12, 30–1, 110–13, 113f., 176f., 182f., 188f., 192 with n.56, 203f., 238
    attitude to war, 4–5, 30–1, 111–13
    character and characterization of, Ch. 4 *passim, esp.* 175–7, 179–83
    character develops?, 188
    and compassion, 6, 165f., 172f., 182, 185f., 187f.
    comportment when leaving Dido, 164–7, 171–5
    contributes to Creusa's death, 151, 169f., 176
    contributes to Dido's death, 173–5, 176
    courted Dido, 195–6
    and Cupid, 195, 197f.
    dilemma at Carthage, 84f.
    dilemma at end of poem, 86f., 187f.
    and Diomedes, 132–5, 137–9
    echoes Cacus, 28–32
    explains himself to Dido, 164–7
    a Homeric hero, 106f.
    horses of, 137–9
    as hunter, 195–7, 198
    individuality of his role, 106f.
    as Jason, 123f., 132
    lack of self-knowledge, 192 n.56, 212, 214
    and Laomedon, 131f.
    and Medea, 126ff.
    meets Dido in Underworld, 171–5
    motives in killing Turnus, 35, 111–13, 155f., 187f.
    as Paris, 109
    and passion, 4f., 31, 106f., 168f., 172f., 175–83, 183–9, 203, 238
    'pastor', 195
    a plague-bringer, 123–5
    reactions to parade of heroes in Underworld, 208 with n.1
    relationship with Anchises, 183–6, 188–9
    relationship with Ascanius, 151–5, 185, 188, 189–93
    relationship with Creusa, 147f., 149–51, 167–71, 176, 177, 180–1, 184f.
    relationship with Dido, 20–3, 161–7, 171–5, 176, 177, 180f.
    relationship with Pallas, 155–60, 178f., 180f.
    repressed/suppressed emotions, Ch. 4 *passim, e.g.* 164–7, *and esp.* 175–7, 179–83
    responsible for his actions, 70, 84–7
    role at Carthage, his bad press, 23, 125, 195–7
    and sacrifice, 189–93
    and sexual passion, 238 n.53
    suffers in answer to Dido's prayers, 130f.
    tactless, 22
Aeneid
    apparent lack of characterization in, 55–6, 148f., *and see* Ch. 4 *passim*
    characterization, *see* Characterization
    characters' feelings in the style, 227ff.
    crucial tension in, 106f.
    debt to Tragedy, 17f., 193f.
    direct speech in, 222f.
    emphasizes cost, 137, 174, 182f., 200, 203, 208

Index

end of, 35, 86f., 112f., 135–7, 143f., 155–7, 160, 186–8, 206, 220–2, 238
exit from Troy scene, 183–9
general action in, 222
Great Irony of, 182f.
interventions in, 5, 233–6
Muse in, 226, 235
narrative technique of (epic voice), 218ff.
obituaries in, 226f.
plausibility of plot in, 218f.
reported action in, 226f.
and Stoicism, 30, 36–9, 73, 75, 176f., 182f., 192 n.56
'subjective style', 227ff.
'symmetry of treatment' in, 219f.
world of, 179–81
'Aenides', 205f.
Agrippa, 158
Ajax, and Aeneas, 9–12, 113f.
Allecto, 13ff., 24–6, 68, 90, 93
exploits sexual passion, 15
ingenuity of, 68, 69
'works with'
Amata, 13ff., 26 n.50, 68
Turnus, 68f.
Allusion (*see esp.* Ch. 3 *also*), 7 with n.9, 9, 10, 16, 17, 40f., 43, 126ff., 197, 202f., 237f.
characters have views on, 108f., 133f.
connects two passages in *Aeneid*, 129
in English literature, 101 n.1
and Ennius, 113 n.23
extends to smallest detail, 103
function of, 102f.
reverses Aeneas' defeat in *Iliad* 5, 132ff.
Vergil's views conflict with characters', 109f.
Amata, 13ff.
mode of suicide, 17
name Vergil's invention, 14f.
a Phaedra figure, 15–17
recalls Dido, 17, 116f.
sexual passion of, 15, 116f.
Anchises (*see also* Aeneas)
differs from Vergil in view of Roman mission, 214–16
divination of, 184
imperial instructions of, 4, 30 n.62, 31, 80, 111, 187, 203, 214–16
'Anchisiades', 10, 158, 178
Antonius, Marcus, 12, 28

Apollo
in two minds about Ascanius, 201–6
understands problem presented by Ascanius, 204f.
Apollonius of Rhodes, alluded to, 43, 123, 126ff., 238 n.53
Archery, 202
'Ardeo', 'ardor', 203f.
Aristotle, on plot, 218
Arrangement ('Dispositio'), 2, 37 *and passim*
Arts, and the Romans, 214–16
Ascanius (*see also* Aeneas), 193–206
an Augustan hero? 203–6
grows up in *Aeneid*, 193
as hunter, 198–200
like his father, 198–200, 203–6
and passion, 203f.
shoots Remulus Numanus, 200–6
acts invidiously?, 202–6
Athena, reason for hostility to Troy, 76
Augustanism (*see also under* Aeneas *and* Augustus), 217
Augustus
in the *Aen.*, 27–32
as a father, 152
'Auidus pugnae', 5, 203f., 206
Author's overheated imagination, 17

Blushes, 118

Cacus
echoed by Aeneas/Augustus, 28–32
monstrous opponent of Hercules, 28–32
'Caelique marisque', 58
Callimachus, narrative style and technique of, 218f., 224
Camilla, 136–7
entails Dido, 136 with n.57
a Penthesilea figure, 136 n.57
tragic figure recalled at end of poem, 136f.
Cato the Elder, 151f.
Catullus
echoed by Vergil, 16
narrative style and technique of, 218f., 226
61. 185ff., 122
65. 19–24, 118
'Ceu', 54f.
Characterization, *see esp.* Ch. 4, *also* 44–56

Index

by action, inaction and interaction, 45, 149, 162
by diction, 50–3
Vergil's compared with Homer's, 44
'Cisseis', 58
Clemency ('clementia'), 4, 111, 187
Compassion, 6, 165f., 166, 172f., 182, 185f., 187f.
Conversation, limited in *Aeneid*, 145ff.
Cost, *see under Aeneid*
Credibility, in epic narrative, 218ff.
Creusa, *see* Aeneas
Cupid, 123, 195, 197f.
'Cut-off' technique, 146–9, 150, 158f., 179–82

Dawn, descriptions of, 38
Deceit
  adopted by Trojans, 211
  eschewed by Romans, 211
  practised by gods, 84ff.
'Deum genitor', 58
Diction
  poetic, function of, 51, 54
  prosaic/colloquial, function of, 52, 54
Dido
  'Amazonian', 136 n.57
  ambivalences of, 47f.
  as an Evadne, 49
  and Camilla, 136
  characterization of, 45–9
  curse of, 130f., 173
  dies of love, 173
  grim verbal ambiguities of, 48
  as Hector, 20
  her ghostly presence, 131
  hunted, 196
  lesson for her in story of Creusa, 186
  as Medea, 128ff.
  as Nausicaa, 123
  as Orestes, 27 n.51
  and Penthesilea, 136 n.57
  as Pentheus, 197
  prepared to stoop, 45
  significance of wound and fire imagery, 121, 194 with n.62
  'spoils' of, 21–3
  tragic impact of, 46
  victim of Aeneas, 23, 176
  victim of Venus, 20, 23
'Dignus deo', 36f.
Diomedes, 132ff.
Direct speech, 222f.

'Dispositio', *see* Arrangement
'Doto', 58
'Ductor Rhoeteius', 10f.

'Effundit pectore dicta', 51, 57
Empire, etc., and the Romans, 214–16
'Encouragement to views', 221f., 225
Ennius 268ff. Sk., 157
  echoed by Vergil, 19 n.41, 215
  Juno in, 94f.
Euryalus, 228–30, 234–6
Evander
  gullibility of, 32–4, 36f., 38
  and Pallas, 160
'Exclusus amator', 14
'Excutio', 52, 58–9
'Exuuiae', 22f.

'Fari' and 'fatum', 74
Fate, 71–5, 89
Fathers and sons, in epic and Roman tradition, 151–2
'Fatum', *see* Fate
'Flammas/ignem uomere', 27ff.
Foreshadowing, 155
'Fortunati ambo', 235f.

Galaesus, 226f.
General action, in epic, 222
Georgics
  alluded to, 7f., 237 n.52, 238
  1.511ff., 139f.
Gifts, 22, 138
'[G]natus' ('[g]nata'), 54f.
Gods
  bend facts, 79–84
  'concilium' in Book 10, 88–90
  difference of Vergil's to Homer's, 65, 71ff.
  inclemency of, 78
  irresponsibility and *Unernst* etc. of, 36ff., 40, 44, 84ff., 95, 98f.
  participate in war in Italy, 90
  perspective of, 86ff., 98, 169f.
  plausibility of Vergil's system, 65
  polytheistic system in *Aeneid*, 64f., 74f., 84
  similarity of Vergil's to Homer's, 62–5
  as symbols, 61, 65ff.
  and war in Italy, 78ff., 87ff.
  'work with', plausibility of system, 67
  'work with' in *Aen.*, 15, 18, 26 n.50, 66–71

'work with' in Aesch. *Agam.*, 67
'work with' in Eur. *Bacch.*, 67

Hanging, a degrading death, 17
'Haurire', 47f.
Hector
  and Astyanax, 151
  characterized by Homer, 147 with n.5
  and Turnus, 110
Hercules
  the Benefactor, 29 with n.56
  as paradigm of Aeneas/Augustus, 27–35
  in ruler panegyric, 29 with n.57
Hippothous, 225
'Hirundo', 140ff.
Homer
  alluded to, 7 n.9, 10, 17, 103, 104ff.
  and Ch. 3 *passim*, 202f.
  characters' feelings in the style, 227 n.27, 231f.
  direct speech in, 222f.
  general action in, 222
  Iliad 22.25–33, 231f.
  interpositions in, 225
  interventions in, 233
  Muse in, 224, 225
  narrative style and technique of, 218ff.
  obituaries in, 224, 225
  'objectivity' in, 224–5
  plausibility of plot in, 218f.
  reported action in, 223–5
  'symmetry of treatment' in, 219f.
Homosexuality, 229, 235f.
Horace
  Juno in, 94f.
  on means and aims of war, 30
  Odes, 3.4.65ff., 30
  the plump propagandist, 30–1
'Huc tandem concede', 54f.
Humour, 36ff., 139
Hunting, 193ff., 202

Iarbas, 85, 221
'Ignem oculis haurire', 47f.
'Ignem/flammas uomere', 27ff.
'Iliadic' *Aeneid*, 107–13
Imagery, 8, 13ff. *and passim*
  linked, 19f., 193–200, 211
  romantic/frivolous used seriously, 14, 194
Images

blindness, 194 n.62
boiling cauldron, 69
bulls, 237f.
cooking, 13
doves, 53f.
fire, 118f., 120f., 194
flower cut by plough, 229
hunting, 192–200, 202
'militia amoris', 14f., 18, 19–23
plague, 125
poppy, 229
siege, 13f.
siege and sack, 18–21
snakes, 210f.
stained ivory, 119–21
storm, 5–8
sun (moon-) light reflected from water, 126
swallow, 140–4
top, 16
torches, 69
'two-flowers', 122
vomiting, 27ff.
wolves, 212f.
wound, 120f., 194
'Imperium sine fine dedi', expansive, bland, facile, 80–1
Implicit myth, 139f., 141–4
'Infelix', 230
Interpositions, 225
Intertextuality, designed, 103
Interventions, 5, 233–6
Invention, 'negative' (*see* Ch. 4, e.g. 150f. *also*), 55–6
Invention ('inuentio'), 2 *and passim*
Irony, dramatic (*see* Ch. 5 *also*), 32f., 37

Jason, and Aeneas, 123f., 132
Juno
  characterized by diction, 49–53
  concerned with status, 63, 95
  in Ennius, 94f. with n.52
  hatred of Troy explained, 63, 94–6
  in Horace, 94f.
  love of Carthage, 63
  nastiness of, 51–3, 94f., 144
  'reconciliation' of, 81–3, 94–8
  demands large 'quid pro quo', 96
  similarity to Hera, 64
  unconcerned on moral questions, 95
  Vergil's more chilling than the traditional Juno, 94f., 96

Index

'works with' Trojan women, 70
Jupiter
  acknowledges divine pride and status, 94–8
  comforts Venus, 80–1
  desires Troy's destruction, 76–8
  difference from Zeus, 74
  disingenuous, 89
  and Fate, 72–4, 86f., 89, 98
  Fury deployed by, 90–3
  incapacitates Turnus, 91–3
  indifference to human individuals, 86f.
  inscrutable, 75–8, 87ff.
  mendacious, 89f.
  'morality' of, 84ff.
  'omnipotens', 79, 85
  participates in war in Italy, 90–3
  prophecy of, 72–4
  reason for hostility to Troy, 77f.
  'reconciles' Juno, 81–3, 94–8
  and responsibility, 84–7
  similarity to Zeus, 75ff., 78ff., 84, 93
  speaks rhetorically, 'packages', 79–83
  'subridens', 86, 98
  and the war in Italy, 78ff.
  Will of, 73f., 75–8, 93
  'works with' Aeneas, 70
Juturna, 86f., 139–44, 220–2
  contributes to Turnus' death?, 143f.
  as Procne, 141–4
  a Thetis figure, 86

Laocoon, 211
Laomedon, 131f.
'Laomedontius heros', 131f.
'Laquearia', 129
Lavinia, 114–22
  loves Turnus, 115ff.
  and Menelaus, 114ff.
'Limen', 14
Love, in the epic tradition, 161
Love and Death, 235
'Loyal lieutenants', 157f.
Lucretius, alluded to, 40f.
'Luminibus tacitis', 162

Maecenas, 158
Marcellus, effect on Aeneas, 208 n.1
Medea, and Aeneas, 126ff.
Menelaus, and Lavinia, 114ff.
'Merces', 52, 59
'Militia amoris', 14f., 18, 19–23

'Misera', 230
'Moira', 73
'Moritura', 116f. with n.27
'Mos', 'mores', meaning of, 81–3
Motifs, linked, 27–32, 193–200, 211
Muse
  in *Aeneid*, 226
  in Homer, 224, 225

Narrative technique, *see* Aeneid
'Natus', ('Nata'), *see [G]natus ([G]nata)*
Neptune
  motives of, 63–4, 98f.
  reason for hostility to Troy, 76
'Nequiquam', 54
'Nescius', 196
Night, description of, 38
Nisus, 228–30, 234–6
  his thoughts on divine/human causation, 66f.
  loves Euryalus, 229, 235

Obituaries, 224–27
'Objectivity', 218ff.
  unsatisfactory term, 225
'Odyssean' *Aeneid*, 104–7
Odysseus, and Aeneas, 105–7
Odysseus and Telemachus, 151
Oratory, Cicero and Vergil on, 215
'Ore effata', 54f.

Pallas, *see* Aeneas
Passion, *see* Aeneas
Patroclus, 157
Peace, as aim of war, 4 n.2, 111f.
Penthesilea, 136 n.57
Pessimists, Harvard, 217 n.1
Philomela, 141–2
'Pietas', 107
  versus 'furor', 28 with n.55
Plot, plausibility of, 218f.
'Praegnas', 53, 59f.
Priam and Hecuba, characterized in their relationship, 53–5
Procne and Itys, 141–4
Propertius
  understands Vergil's Amata, 16
  4.4.68ff., 16
Publilius Syrus 690 Duff, 206 n.78
'Pulcherrima', 71
Pylades, 157
Pyrrhus, 211

'Quae . . . aut quo . . .?', 54f.

Index

'Quassans caput', 51, 57

Remulus Numanus, 200ff.
Reported action, 223–5, 226f.
Responsibility (divine), 84ff.
Responsibility (human), 68f., 70, 75, 84–7
Revelations of the future, 208

Sacrifice and heroism, 190f.
'Sanguineus', 120
Scipio Aemilianus, 152
Self-effacement of author, 1, 218ff.
Shield of Aeneas, 207–9
'Signal' to implicit myth, 143
'Signals' to other texts, 27 n.51, 103f., 104, 108, 119, 120, 126, 139, 197 with n.69
Similes
   and the epic voice, 224f., 227
   first three in *Aeneid*, 7 n.9
   'multi-correspondence' etc. in, 24, 119ff., 141, 213
   'transfusion of terms', 121 n.32
'Soluuntur frigore membra', 135
Sophocles
   allusion to, 9
   OT, 'blindness' motif in, 194 n.62
Spoils (*see* Dido *also*), 34f., 188
Stoicism and *Aeneid*, 9, 73, 75, 78, 166f., 176, 182
Style, devices of, 2 *and passim*
'Subjective style', 227ff.
'Subridens', 86, 98
'Superbus', 231
Swallow, song interpreted as lament, 142
'Symmetry of treatment', 219f.

Tiberinus, bends facts, 83
Tibullus, alluded to, 16
'Too late' phenomenon, 167–75, 177–9
'Transfusion of terms', 121 n.32
Troy
   contribution to Roman race, 82f.
   eclipse of name of, 96
   reason for destruction of, 76–8
Turnus
   appeals to Aeneas, 186f.
   at death recalls Camilla and Dido, 136
   beloved brother, 220–2
   as Diomedes, 132–5
   as Hector, 110, 136
   as Patroclus, 136
   responsibility of, 68f.
   'subiectus', 187
   viewed as Achilles, 108
Typology, 101 n.1

Vengeance, 111 with n.19, 188
Venus
   allusively compared to Dionysus, 197
   bad press in *Aen.*, 19, 20, 26, 35, 71, 197f.
   in Caesarian propaganda, 35
   and Dido, 18–27, 194, 196f.
   epiphany of, 207
   a Fury? 27 n.51
   gives arms to Aeneas, 207
   huntress, 194, 196f.
   irresponsibility of, 26
   overdoses Dido, 26
   'Pulcherrima', 71
   recalls Allecto, 18, 24–7
   and Vulcan, 35–44
   'works with' Aeneas, 70f.
   'works with' Dido, 18, 69f.
Vergil
   comments on Roman/Stoic dogma, 31f., 182f.
   definition of, 2f.
   differs from Anchises in view of Roman mission, 214–16
   disapproves of passionate love, 121
   humour of, 36, 40ff., 139
   interested in perversity, 17f.
   Neoteric and Callimachean origin, 17f.
   personal voice of, 2–3
'Victor', 204
'Violo', 120f.
'Virtus', 8, 205f. with n.78
'Vis temperata', 30f.
Voice(s)
   ambiguity in, 231–3
   epic, 2, 217ff., *and passim*
   further, 217ff., *and passim*
      discretion of, 2, 12, 27, 236f.
      in *Georgics*, 140 with n.63
      modes of, 2, 236
      persistence of, 2, 12
      point at which they impinge on epic voice, 221f., 227ff.
   'sliding scale', 236f.
'Vomo', 27–32

Index

Vulcan
  father of Cacus (according to Vergil), 31
  forges Aeneas' weapons, 31, 207
  piqued because of wife's bastard offspring, 39
  sexual role-reversal of, 42f.
  and Venus, 35–44

World of the *Aeneid*, 179–81

Zeus
  plan of, 75f.
  reason for hostility to Troy, 77

Index of Passages in the *Aeneid* discussed

1.1–8, 71
1.2, 78
1.8ff., 62–4
1.21f., 231
1.22, 74
1.26–8, 63
1.32, 78
1.39ff., 95f.
1.92, 135
1.92ff., 104f.
1.148–53, 7 n.9
1.184ff., 196
1.223–5, 78
1.254–64, 72–4
1.257f., 73
1.257ff., 75–8
1.262, 74
1.263f., 79–81
1.279, 80–1
1.314f., 194, 207
1.407f., 209
1.430–6, 7 n.9
1.456ff., 209f.
1.461f., 209f.
1.498–502, 7 n.9, 123 n.41, 194
1.615ff., 69
1.643ff., 153f.
1.657ff., 123, 195
1.660, 16
1.673, 18, 20
1.712, 125

2.201ff., 211
2.289, 107, 183ff.
2.314, 106, 183ff.
2.353, 107
2.355–9, 212–14
2.379–82, 210–12
2.471ff., 211, 213
2.515–25, 53–5
2.594ff., 184ff.
2.601–3, 77f.
2.608–18, 76–8
2.635ff., 184f.
2.673–80, 147f., 150, 170, 176, 180, 184f.
2.681, 150
2.682–91, 184f.
2.707, 185, 188f.
2.711, 150f., 169, 176, 185
2.723f., 153

2.745ff., 168f.
2.776ff., 169f.
2.790, 181

3.343, 206 n.78
3.345, 146, 180

4.1f., 69, 120f.
4.67, 120f.
4.69ff., 120f.
4.69–73, 194–6
4.90, 125
4.93f., 23
4.143–9, 123–5
4.198, 85
4.219ff., 70
4.219–21, 85
4.281, 231
4.301ff., 197 n.69
4.331–3, 163, 173
4.333–61, 164–7, 181
4.340–4, 165, 172
4.353f., 70
4.360, 166, 174
4.364, 162
4.369–70, 173
4.384, 121
4.390, 146f., 180f.
4.393–6, 163, 172, 173
4.402–7, 19
4.433f., 45
4.447–9, 163
4.465, 196f.
4.467–70, 197
4.469f., 197
4.471–3, 27 n.51
4.494–7, 21–3
4.507f., 21–3
4.522–31, 128–32
4.541f., 131f.
4.547, 173
4.607ff., 130f., 173
4.645ff., 21–3
4.651f., 48
4.651–62, 46–9
4.654, 131
4.661, 47f.
4.669–71, 19f.
4.689, 120f.
4.696, 231

Index

5.4–7, 232f.
5.575ff., 154
5.613ff., 70
5.662f., 70
5.700ff., 154
5.811, 99

6.5ff., 227f.
6.86–90, 108
6.455–68, 171–5
6.463f., 174
6.539, 146, 180
6.756–866, 208 with n.1
6.801f., 29
6.847–53, 214–16
6.851–3, 4, 31, 111, 187

7.116, 154
7.280–3, 138f.
7.291f., 51, 56f.
7.291–320, 49–53, 56–60
7.299, 52, 58f.
7.301, 57f.
7.306, 58
7.317, 52, 59
7.318, 51, 58
7.319f., 53, 59f.
7.319–21, 109
7.341ff., 13ff.
7.355f., 16
7.363f., 109
7.377–84, 16, 24, 69
7.385–405, 26 n.50
7.436–57, 68f.
7.456f., 69
7.462–6, 69
7.476ff., 198–200
7.536–9, 226f.
7.583f., 79

8.18–30, 125–32
8.40, 83
8.86ff., 228
8.185–9, 33
8.198f., 27
8.200f., 33
8.213–18, 34
8.252f., 27
8.259, 27
8.291, 84
8.362–5, 36f.
8.366, 38
8.367f., 38
8.369, 38
8.370ff., 36–44
8.372, 38
8.373–86, 39f.
8.387–9, 40
8.394, 40f.

8.395ff., 41f.
8.407–15, 42–4
8.415, 38
8.514–17, 156
8.520–3, 158, 178f., 180f.
8.537, 6, 31
8.611, 207
8.615, 207
8.620, 27, 31f.
8.626ff., 207–9
8.642, 84
8.680, 27, 31f.
8.729–31, 209
8.731, 189, 208f.

9.184f., 66f.
9.435–7, 229f.
9.446–9, 234–6
9.590–2, 202
9.621ff., 200–6
9.638–62, 201–6
9.742, 108
9.806–13, 113

10.8f., 78f.
10.104ff., 88–90
10.107, 90
10.159–62, 162
10.271, 27, 32
10.501ff., 234
10.613ff., 89
10.689, 88f.
10.791–3, 234f.

11.42ff., 159, 178f.
11.108ff., 31
11.152f., 160
11.831, 136

12.4f., 120
12.52f., 133f.
12.54–69, 114–22
12.103–6, 237f.
12.110f., 189f.
12.168f., 190
12.176ff., 4, 31, 112
12.430, 204, 206
12.432–4, 153, 191–3
12.435ff., 8–10, 152, 192f. with n.56, 205f.
12.450–7, 5ff.
12.473–7, 140–4
12.554–69, 66, 70f.
12.603, 17
12.715–22, 237f.
12.791ff., 94–8
12.804, 79
12.829ff., 96f.
12.833–7, 81–3

12.843ff., 90–3
12.872ff., 86f., 143, 220–2
12.896–907, 92f., 134
12.908–13, 6 with n.8
12.930, 187
12.931ff., 186–8
12.951, 135
12.952, 135f.